Computers and the Social Studies

Educating for the Future

Nancy Roberts

Susan Friel

Thomas Ladenburg

▲▼ Addison-Wesley Publishing Company

Menlo Park, California · Reading, Massachusetts · New York
Don Mills, Ontario · Wokingham, England · Amsterdam · Bonn
Sydney · Singapore · Tokyo · Madrid · Bogotá · Santiago · San Juan

To
Ed, Tom, and Muriel

Acknowledgments

Pages 15, 19, 22, 26, 28, 29, 31, 33, 35, 36, 43: Andrea Roberts; Page 73: Courtesy of Grolier Electronic Publishing, Inc.; page 137: Courtesy of IBM Corporation; page 138: Courtesy of IBM Corporation; page 141: Paul Donaldson, Cruft Laboratory, Harvard University; page 145: Courtesy of IBM Corporation; page 147: Iowa State University; page 148: Historical Pictures Service; page 149: Institute for Advanced Study, Princeton, NJ; page 153: Courtesy of Radio Shack, a Division of Tandy Corporation; page 158: T.J. Florian/Rainbow

This book is published by the Addison-Wesley Innovative Division.

Production Services: Miller/Scheier Associates
Design: Rogondino & Associates
Typesetting: Lauren Langford
Technical Illustrations: Lyn Smith
Editorial Illustrations: Jane McCreary
Cover Design: Rogondino & Associates

ISBN 0-201-06403-0

ABCDEFG-ML-8910987

Contents

Preface

This book is written for social studies educators, administrators, and post secondary school faculty and their students. This book is particularly appropriate, at the college level, for courses such as "Methods and Materials of Teaching Social Studies," where the instructor wishes to integrate the use of computers into a standard offering. In addition, this text provides a comprehensive resource for general courses, such as "Integrating Computers into the Classroom," that includes a section on computers in the social studies. It is also a valuable resource for all practicing teachers.

In this book the authors identify two distinct areas of importance for reflecting on the use of computers in the social studies. Part I focuses on the variety of software now available for use in social studies education. The authors present a comprehensive overview of software applications and computer tools. Included are database use, graphing, and model-building, in addition to more conventional drill-and-practice materials, tutorials, and simulations. Chapters 3, 4, and 5 give details for several classroom activities.

Part II gives a history of computer technology and the attending issues created by the increasing presence of that technology in our world. The authors present an overview of computing as well as an examination of related technologies and their impact on society. A variety of possible scenarios for the future are described to provide matter for discussion.

The book concludes with a review of the process of innovation in an educational setting in order to help teachers and administrators integrate computers into the curriculum.

No assumptions regarding the reader's experience with computers are made. If the reader wishes to begin with the basics of computer education the authors recommend *The Practical Guide to Computers in Education*. The *Practical Guide* presents an overview of all the topics and issues confronting teachers, curriculum supervisors, administrators, parents, or school board members interested in integrating computers into the curriculum. Computer jargon is explained thoroughly, and necessary background information, along with many vignettes, are included to fill in the reader's missing experiences in the area of educational computing. Other books with special focus on computers in education include; *Computers in Mathematics; Computers and Reading Instruction; Computers, Education and Special Needs; Administrator's Guide to Computers in Education; Computers in the Language Classroom;* and *Writing and Computers.*

The authors would like to thank Evelyn Woldman for doing an extraordinarily thorough job creating an updated resource section so finely tuned to the needs of social studies teachers. Evelyn's background as teacher, computer curriculum coordinator, active member of the Massachusetts Council for the Social Studies, software developer, and consultant in applications of technology to education made her an ideal editor for this section of the book. The authors also greatly appreciate the time and contributions of the three manuscript reviewers: Beverly Hunter, of Targeted Learning Company; Donald V. Salvucci, of Brockton High School; and Charles S. White, of Indiana University. Their careful and thoughtful comments and suggestions have considerably improved the quality and relevance of this text.

June 1987

Nancy Roberts
Susan Friel
Thomas Ladenburg

PART I

Computers and the Social Studies

Where We Are,
Where We're Going

Social studies teachers are well aware that technological change, fueled by the computer, is occurring at a dizzying pace — far faster than at any other time in history. People have hardly begun to understand one generation of computers and their unique capabilities before scientists have already created the next generation of more powerful and versatile machines. With the introduction of the mass-produced microchip, computers are available for thousands of everyday uses.

Parents are aware of the computer's ability to fascinate the young through video games. Business people are delighted with the ability of computers to do their payrolls, keep their inventories, and control production. Writers of all ages and professions are enamored with the computer's word-processing capabilities. Educators realize that computers offer increasing potential for use in the classroom. Social studies teachers in particular recognize that computers and related technologies are ushering in an entire new era, the Information Age.

Since the mid-1960s, gathering, transmitting, and analyzing information has been supplanting manufacturing as the major productive activity of our society. Social studies educators, using whenever possible the most up-to-date teaching techniques, have a responsibility to themselves and their students to prepare for this changing reality.

Overview of the Social Studies

After almost a century of thought and discussion there now seems to be general agreement among academics about what should be taught in the social studies. "Most social studies educators currently accept the concept of citizenship education as the primary purpose of the field, and most would even agree to the primary objectives that are requisite to the citizenship education goal: knowledge, skills, values, and performance" (Barr, Barth, and Shermis, p. 52). It is the belief of the authors of this book that the microcomputer can aid social studies educators in important and meaningful ways to attain this goal with their students.

There are computer programs currently available that support each of the following objectives identified as requisite to the development of good citizenship:

1.   Knowledge – Computer-based tutorial type programs provide the greatest choice of any software category today. Some of the programs are poor, some excellent — the same diversity of quality as is found in any other curriculum area. The discussion of currently available software in chapter 2 describes several such programs. The research literature suggests that students seem to "learn" facts faster when interacting with a computer. The software can also include immediate evaluation of a student's answer to a given problem so that students do not retain incorrect information for long. Using the computer as an aid for imparting knowledge might free the teacher to focus on higher level skills.

2.   Skills – Today students must acquire the skill of processing information, thus learning to live with the information explosion people are currently experiencing. While computers are largely "to blame" for this predicament, they are also the most effective tool for coping with the situation. Students must be taught to use the computer to find, understand, manipulate, and analyze the wealth of information now available. Chapters 3 and 4 deal with this subject in depth.

Critical thinking, another important skill area for the social studies teacher, is also enhanced by the use of the computer. *Historian*, a program reviewed in chapter 2, takes students through the steps of historical research — forming a hypothesis, collecting data, testing a hypothesis, and drawing a conclusion — in a manner close to that of working historians.

3.   Values – Students must develop values that support good citizenry in a democracy and understand the responsibility of publicly declaring such values. Simulation/games, used as pedagogic tools for this purpose for several decades now, seem to offer the most potential for aiding the teacher in accomplishing this. The use of computers often makes simulation/games easier to implement in the classroom. The

main contribution of the computer is its ability to do quickly whatever calculating is required between rounds of play. In addition, the computer can add the ability to research an issue regarding values, because a computerized simulation/game provides a consistent model that is replicable play after play. One simulation/game, recently released, does a superb job of creating an environment that forces players to demonstrate their values regarding cooperation, conflict, and trust. Chapter 2 describes this software, called *The Other Side*, at length.

4. Performance – Students must act in a manner supportive of a democratic society. This is probably the most complex and difficult objective for the teacher to attain, and no less so with the aid of a computer. However, there is some software that might help the teacher, even here. Particularly of note is a set of simulation games called *The Search Series*, also described in chapter 2. One of the primary goals of this software is to dramatize the importance of group cooperation by making such cooperation the first prerequisite for successfully completing the simulation, whether it be sailing across the ocean in search of gold, locating a new homeland because of famine, or searching for oil.

In addition to concluding that indeed there is general agreement on the goals of social studies, Barr, Barth, and Shermis in the course of their research have also identified three dominant teaching traditions. They label these: social studies as citizenship transmission (discussed above), social studies as social science, and social studies as reflective inquiry (p. 65). Whichever tradition the reader tends to follow in his or her teaching, the authors of this book believe the use of microcomputers provides opportunities for enhancing teaching.

A computer's contribution to social studies as reflective inquiry is presented at length in discussions of tool-type software in chapters 3 and 4. Chapter 5 continues to look at methods for increasing students' thinking skills by suggesting model-building and simulation design as activities that immerse students in reflective inquiry.

To discuss the possible role of computers in teaching social studies as social science, the reader should have some idea of how social scientists use computers. We next look at a brief sampling of the uses social scientists are finding for the computer. Some of the uses described are currently replicable in the classroom; some are not. Those applications, now impractical for a precollege setting, might become practical in the next several years as computers continue to increase in power and decrease in cost. Since this clearly has been the trend over the last thirty years, we can expect it to continue a while longer.

Computers and the Social Scientist

Perhaps surprisingly, some of the most innovative uses of computers among social scientists are to be found in historial research. Arthur Loeb, from Harvard University, found that tracing dynastic relationships in the Middle Ages using the traditional tool of family trees was unsatisfactory. With the large amount of intermarriage among ruling families of Europe during this period, important family relationships that explain the basis of power and succession are often hidden by family trees: this happens because, for the sake of clarity, descent is shown only through the male side, except when offspring are all female.

Loeb's solution was to develop a computer database of all known relationships among ruling families during the period. The user of the database may request to see the relations of any of the nobility of this period, either in terms of past or future relations, or at any time during his or her life. The problem of identifying family relationships is compounded by the fact that many persons, even siblings, had exactly the same name or used several different names throughout life as they acquired titles. The computer program is designed to keep track of all this information. On request from the researcher, the computer can list all spouses, siblings, cousins, children, or grandparents of the person under study. New relatives can be added to the database as they are discovered or become pertinent to the current research. According to Loeb, "The power structure of the late Middle Ages in Western Europe can be studied effectively by examining the dynastic structure of the ruling families in France, England, and the Low Countries" (p. 30).

At Rutgers University a database has been created of all medieval science documents written in Latin (Hahn). Called the Benjamin Data Bank (for the professor who initiated the work) it is available, for a search fee, to anyone with an interest in this area of study. Through Benjamin, scholars are now able to find all references made to a particular document and where the source document is currently located. To facilitate communication between scholars the database also records which scholars are working in what areas.

Imagine being able to write on a computer in hieroglyphics — or have your students do it. A computer-based word processing system that "speaks" in hieroglyphics has been developed at the University of Cambridge in England (Nancarrow). This system allows the study, in far greater depth and by far more people, of passages written in hieroglyphics as well as the study of the origins of these symbols. Furthermore, the procedure used to encode hieroglyphics can be applied to Chinese, Japanese, or any other language made up of unique symbols, providing a tool for studying a range of modern and ancient languages potentially available to many people. The additional historical information revealed by such study could dramatically change people's understanding of the past.

A second social science area where fascinating computer applications are occurring is geography. Creating accurate maps has been one quest of geographers almost since the beginning of civilization. Geoffrey Dutton, at Harvard University, has been working on the problem of creating more accurate terrain maps using the computer's ability to produce high quality graphics. The computer takes data about the terrain of an area and generates what geographers refer to as "hillshaded maps." These are maps that are colored to show the contours of land by including shadows produced by sunlight coming from a specified direction. The current method of producing contour maps ignores a great deal of information about the terrain, such as peaks, passes, ridges, and stream courses. Computer-generated terrain maps are able to provide all this information.

Another mapping application is the computer creation of land-use maps ("In Brief"). Given a database on land resources available in a particular area, a geographer can ask the computer "what if" questions involving the impact of changing the use of a portion of land in that area; the computer's answer is in the form of a newly configured land-use map. This application is being used to allow people in a town or city to understand the impact of various land-use policies. For example, in one town certain groups might support business development, others conservation, and still others residential development. A neutral tool, such as the computer, might facilitate rational decision-making by allowing people to explore the impact of one set of decisions versus another.

Economics, another area of social science generally taught in the schools, has a long history of computer applications. Computer-based economic models of cities, states, countries, and the world have been used for over twenty years. One of the more ambitious of these projects is called Project Link, begun at the University of Pennsylvania in 1968. The goal of this project is to link together individual national and regional models to "generate a consistent model system for studying the world economy" (Klein, Pauly, and Voisin, p. 5). Currently Project Link includes economic models of several of the countries belonging to the Organization for Economic Cooperation and Development and some of the centrally planned economies (including the Soviet Union and the People's Republic of China) as well as regional models for Africa, Asia, Latin America, the Middle East, and the Pacific Far East. The combined model is used both to examine the effects of individual national or various regional economic policies on the world economy and to evaluate the effect on the world economy of past decisions. Some of the topics studied using the model include: effects of protectionism, effects of oil changes and supply shocks, industrial policies, and commodity shocks (Klein, p. 13). With the increasing availability of worldwide computer links, the future goal of the project is to make the combined model available locally to all the cooperating partners. This would allow greatly increased research and timely updates of the economic database.

Another computer-based economic model of a very different character was done for the United States Federal Emergency Management Agency in an attempt to predict the time it would take the U. S. economy to recover from a nuclear attack (Pugh-Roberts). The research team that built this model included economists, psychologists, sociologists, and computer scientists.

An interesting problem the team confronted was where to get data on the effect of such a disaster on the survivors. Since there has never been a comparable disaster, the closest the researchers could come was the Black Plague that spread through Europe, Asia, and Africa during the fourteenth century. Studying the literature on the effects of this catastrophic event suggested the complete inability of governments to regain the confidence of their subjects following such a disaster. The problem of establishing order out of chaos is, indeed, potentially overwhelming.

The computer model developed by this group suggested that the United States would never recover economically to its present level. Moreover, recovery, to the extent that it occurs, would be very slow, taking at a minimum several generations.

In the early 1960s an economically motivated computer study was made by Battelle Memorial Institute to help decide whether a certain dam should be built on the Susquehanna River. The Army Corps of Engineers favored the dam. The utility companies serving the Susquehanna River basin area felt there would be no need for the additional power produced by such a dam in the near future and therefore the construction of the dam was unwarranted.

The study was essentially a demographic one. The focus was a simulation model that predicted and demonstrated the future power requirements of the basin area; the computer model convinced the Army not to build the dam (Hamilton et al.).

As we move into some of the newer social science disciplines, we find an interesting computer application being made in urban studies. A simulation game has been developed at the University of Southern California "in response to the need for training air pollution officers" (James and McGinty, p. 12). The game simulates a typical urban community. Players take various roles as they play the game cycles to understand better the political, social, and economic implications of different decisions on all aspects of a community. Such topics as public budgeting, taxation, mass transit, and energy can be explored. The game has been used in undergraduate and graduate courses across the United States as well as in other countries.

Anthropologists use computer model-building and simulation to study primitive societies. One such study investigated the Tsembaga tribe of New Guinea (Shantzis and Behrens III). This group maintains their population equilibrium through a rigid but delicately balanced set of signals and rituals. The tribe lives in a land area, limited by mountains, that can only support a certain population level. Pigs are a sign of wealth in this community and therefore are only killed for religious purposes; the agricultural system thus must feed both pigs and people. When population pressures begin to mount from both people and pig populations, the following happens:

1. The leaders declare a religious celebration leading to a feast that results in the killing of about 85 percent of the pig population.
2. This is followed by a declaration of war against one or more neighboring clans. The wars are limited, resulting in the loss of only about 10 percent of the population.

After this reduction of both pig and human populations, food pressures do not build again for about another fifteen years, the usual length of these cycles.

The question raised by the anthropologists was how a government policy to raise the health or nutritional levels of these people would affect these cycles. Or, if the government ended the warfare, what effect would this have on the traditional method of population control? Because of the delicate balance between land and population, any outside intervention must be understood in all its ramifications or swift disaster could result.

Models such as the one used by the anthropologists in the above study can be used in a precollege setting in the same way they are in a research environment, provided the classroom has the required computer and software. For the model of the Tsembaga, the class would need an Apple IIe microcomputer and the MicroDYNAMO software package (see resource section).

The concluding project described here was chosen because it truly represents the cutting edge of applied computer technology. The project is currently underway at the Center for Adaptive Systems at Boston University. This interdisciplinary center is composed of researchers from neurobiology, psychology, computer science and mathematics. The "center's main purpose is to develop mathematical models of the human brain and behavior" (Brodman, p. 39). The psychologist's contribution is in her understanding of human ability to adapt to new situations. The long term goal of the project is to develop more intelligent computers that can learn from experience by adapting, as people do.

The Computer in the Social Studies Class

With the previous sections as background, we can move to the focus of this book: the computer in the social studies classroom. The microcomputer is just reaching the point of being an exciting enhancement to the teaching of social studies. Until recently there has not been enough microcomputer software available to aid greatly the social studies teacher. Today computer use is still limited, but primarily by the scarcity of hardware in schools rather than by lack of software. Some extremely useful and exciting computer applications are now on the market, and many allow the teacher to emulate some of the applications just described.

The next two examples illustrate how teaching strategies might change based on expanding availability of hardware and software. Two scenarios are reported; the first describes a relatively common use of computers today and the second an expanded use of technology as resources become more abundant. Both happen to involve fourth grade students studying economics. With more sophisticated materials, the situation could take place as easily in a high school class.

Given one computer for a few weeks of the year, a local fourth grade teacher integrates the simulation *Lemonade* (see resource section) into a unit that includes economic objectives. The class is divided into teams each attempting to sell as much lemonade as possible. The elements within student control are the costs, including how many advertising signs and how many glasses of lemonade to make, and how much to charge per glass. Not under student control, but under computer control, is the weather each day as well as the "best price" — the price that results in the most sales. Lively class discussions occur as the class analyzes the computer world (the computer model) while simulating several days at their lemonade stand.

A contrasting example is presented by some fourth grade classes with more abundant technology. These students, in Hartford, Connecticut, Houston, Texas, and Fairbanks, Alaska, are also studying economics but are linked together via an electronic mail system as part of a funded government project. The classes do comparative shopping for the "best price" of a variety of items, enter the information they collect into their computers, and then access comparable product prices in these very different parts of the United States. The students attempt to understand why there is a great price discrepancy found in some items and not others. Part of the results of the fourth graders' study of these instances of "best price" is the students' ability to discuss their theories about current local economic situations with peers and teachers across the country as those situations are occurring. In addition to the microcomputer, each class has a modem allowing the class to connect, by telephone, its classroom computer to a larger computer at some distance; the class also has a subscription to an electronic information service, CompuServe (see resource section). With a minimal amount of hardware and cost (about $150 for the modem and $5 a month for the electronic information service), these students are dealing with the real world of economics rather than the simulated world of *Lemonade*.

Part I of this book focuses on a variety of tool applications as well as other kinds of social studies software. Chapter 2 reviews several pieces of software now available. Chapters 3 and 4 give an in-depth look at tool and applications packages. Chapter 5 introduces perhaps the most powerful tool application of microcomputers to the social studies: model-building and simulation.

In addition to using computers to enhance teaching, the social studies teacher has the new era of computers to include as part of the content of social studies. Called "the information age", this historical period follows the industrial revolution and brings new areas of study to the traditional social studies. A second goal of this book, covered in Part II, is to provide the reader with an overview of the topics and issues of this new era. Chapter 6 presents a synopsis of the critical historical events that might explain today's rapid emergence of the new information technologies. Chapter 7 assesses other current technologies and their impact on education. Chapter 8 looks into the future from several points of view. Chapter 9 reviews the process school systems generally go through in adopting innovation. This review provides a long-term perspective for the reader who might wish to become or already is involved in integrating computers into the social studies curriculum.

References

Barr, R. D.; Barth, J. L.; Shermis, S.S., *Defining the Social Studies.* Arlington, Va.: NCSS Bulletin 51 (1977).

Brodman, J., "Model Brains," *Bostonia*, vol. 59, no. 2 (1985) 36–40.

Dutton, G., "Land Alive," *Perspectives*, vol. 2, no. 1 (1982) 26–39.

Hahn, N. L., "From Medieval Scribe to Microcomputer," *Perspectives*, vol. 1, no. 3 (1981) 20–29.

Hamilton, H.; Goldstein, S.; Milliman, J.; Pugh III, A.; Roberts, E.; and Zellner, A., *System Simulation for Regional Analysis*, Boston: MIT Press, 1969.

"In Brief," *Perspectives*. vol. 2, no. 2 (1982) 49.

Klein, L. R.; Pauly, P.; Voisin, P., "The World Economy — A Global Model," *Perspectives*. vol. 2, no. 2 (1982) 4–17.

James, M., and McGinty, R. T., "A Gaming-Simulation System for Exploring Urban Issues," *Perspectives*. vol. 1, no. 4 (1981) 12–21.

Loeb, A.L., "Kinship Graphs — A New Representation of Dynastic Relations," *Perspectives*. vol. 3, no. 2 (1983) 28–45.

Nancarrow, P.H., "A Convention for the Unconventional — Hieroglyphics and the Computer," *Perspectives*, vol. 2, no. 1 (1982) 40–48.

Pugh-Roberts, Associates, *Development of a Dynamic Model to Evaluate Economic Recovery Following a Nuclear Attack: Final Report*, Washington, D.C.: Federal Emergency Management Agency, November, 1980.

Shantzis, S.B., and Behrens II, W. W., "Population Control Mechanisms in a Primitive Agricultural Society." In Meadows and Meadows (eds.), *Toward Global Equilibrium*. Cambridge, Mass: Wright-Allen Press, 1973.

Computer Software in the Social Studies

Because of their commitment to creating good citizens, social studies teachers concern themselves with imparting appropriate knowledge, skills, and values to their students. No other discipline is as committed to teaching critical thinking, because this skill is a prerequisite for citizenry in a democracy. Computers lend themselves well to the development of programs that allow practice in hypothesis formation, testing, and drawing conclusions. The social studies are also committed to maintaining participatory government. What better way for students to understand this concept than to be in a class environment requiring cooperative group-participation for success? Well-designed software can readily create such an environment. In addition, programs can teach the understanding of certain fundamentals by providing opportunities to apply such important concepts as the law of supply and demand. Finally, good software can help teachers reinforce the learning of facts essential to every social studies course.

If computers lend themselves so well to so many aspects of the social studies, there should be a wide selection of good software for social studies teachers to use. There is not as much computer-based material as there should be. However, there is much more today than there was a few years ago, with better and more exciting programs coming out all the time.

A word of caution, however, before everyone runs to the nearest computer store. Not every publisher is offering programs that will help the average student get into Harvard. In fact, there often may not be a good match between available programs and a particular teacher's needs based on discipline, grade, and student ability.

Because selecting good software is full of pitfalls, this chapter is intended to familiarize the reader with currently available computer software to help him or her become a more sophisticated software consumer. Teachers need to be able to distinguish the good and the promising from the mediocre and the useless. There is yet another benefit: By exercising discerning judgment, social studies teachers can influence the quality of software that is developed and marketed.

The Power of a Good Example

It is an old adage that nothing teaches better than a good example. This analysis of software therefore begins with a review of an exemplary program that other software companies should emulate. This program uses sound educational philosophy, contains solid factual content, is intellectually challenging, fosters active learning, and satisfies a whole host of other important functions.

This exemplary program, called *Historian*, was developed by a group of historians, high school teachers, and programmers led by Professor Willis Copeland and supported by the National Endowment for the Humanities. It consists of a series of simulations and uses thesis writing as its model. Its various exercises focus on such challenging historical questions as Spain's delay in colonizing southern California, Lincoln's use of the Fort Sumter crisis, the repeal of Prohibition, and the reasons for the Great Depression. Let us look at the first of these programs.

The flagship inquiry of the *Historian* program is a question that has long vexed historians: Why did Spain wait over 200 years after the conquest of Mexico to settle the California coast? For centuries favorable winds and currents enabled Spanish galleons to make the relatively easy voyage from western Mexico to the Philippines. In making the return trip, however, ships were required to follow a northern route almost as far as the Aleutians and then sail due south down the California coast in order to avoid this westerly current. It was a hazardous journey and could have been made considerably easier had there been friendly settlements in California.

Students are introduced to this problem and divided into a maximum of six different research teams to explore it. Following tentative clues, each team forms its own initial hypothesis and types it into the computer. Picking key words, the computer helps students clarify their theses. Each team is then given several choices on how to proceed. With some friendly advice from the computer, one group of students elects to

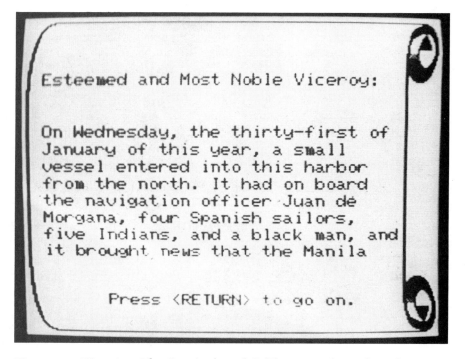

Figure 2.1 *Historian*: The Spaniards and California—A letter from the viceroy of New Spain to the royal officers of the Port of Acapulco, February 1, 1596.

search for manuscripts in the basement archives in Spain (stored on the computer) and comes up with documents that make the students change the thesis or pursue it further. After considerable research, each team has the opportunity to present its findings to the rest of the class.

Undoubtedly, *Historian* is an excellent simulation for academically talented high school students. The general breadth and power of the program is remarkable. It teaches important research skills and allows for students to sift and dispassionately weigh evidence. Moreover it has a quality that many successful computer programs have — the computer acts as a catalyst and advisor; it allows the students to remain in control so they may continue to explore the problem at hand.

Criteria for Selecting Social Studies Software

Certainly, *Historian* is not for all classes, not for all juniors taking U. S. history, and perhaps not even for all bright, inquisitive, competent juniors taking American history. Nevertheless, *Historian* has qualities that make it a remarkably good model for computer software developers, reviewers, and teachers because the software:

1. employs a sound educational philosophy;

2. is intellectually challenging for its intended audience;

3. teaches important facts, skills, and concepts;

4. allows for learning as an ongoing process even after the computer is turned off;

5. effectively uses the inherent capabilities of the computer;

6. contains no derogatory, sexist, racist remarks or assumptions regarding any group;

7. contains no factually incorrect statements, nor rests on antiquated scholarship;

8. gives no overly difficult directions.

(Note: One of the documents consulted in making the above list was the *NCSS Social Studies Microcomputer Courseware Evaluation Guidelines* by Stephen A. Rose, Allan R. Brandhorst, Allen D. Glenn, James O. Hodges, and Charles S. White, published in the November/December, 1984 issue of *Social Education*. This valuable compilation is reproduced on page 197 of this book.)

Let's consider these eight points, beginning with the first.

Educational Philosophy

Much of the literature on computers is replete with admonitions concerning philosophy and approaches to education in general. For instance, Susan Ohanian writing in the October, 1983, issue of *Classroom Computer Learning* leaves it clear on which side of the desk the good guys stand. She states, "When I recall my crystal moments in teaching . . . I am likely to think of something that had nothing to do with the CR blend, the eight-times table, or any of the other minutiae of the ostensible curriculum. . . (but) I like to think that children with me for ten months develop some sense of self-reliance, a love for the sound of our language, at least a beginning awareness that they can experience joy in words . . . I also throw in a bit about the power of numbers and the wonders of messing around in science. I try to help children get a feeling of the 'connectiveness' of things. . . ."

One of the best known software designers also subscribes to this philosophy. He is Tom Snyder, author of the *Search Series* and a number of other successful computer programs. In a talk Snyder gave at the Lesley College Computer Conference in May, 1984, he ridiculed the computer publicists who claim that computer programs teach spatial relations, creative thinking, logic, and social communication skills. "What is truly important," Snyder said, "is that students are provided with a stimulating environment, one where learning is fun, where students are encouraged to interact with one another and to learn to cooperate to accomplish a goal. If at the same time they learn some science or social studies — that's OK, too."

Despite some differences in projected outcomes and goals, both Ohanian and Snyder share a developmental orientation, one where, as Jean Piaget demonstrated, students in an engaging interactive learning environment shed their more concrete modes of operation to take on increasingly more abstract styles of thought. It is generally believed that such development is most likely to be fostered by an intellectually stimulating environment.

At the other end of the spectrum of educational philosophies lies the behaviorist school long associated with B.F. Skinner. Though much maligned because of his unsuccessful "teaching machines" of the late 1950s, Skinner is still a feisty advocate of behaviorism. Using pigeons as his experimental animals, Skinner reports he can modify behavior by eliciting the correct (desired) response, and then reinforce it with a positive reward. If the task is complex, he breaks it down into a series of simple steps and teaches each step in succession. In this way he teaches pigeons to turn figure eights, recognize patterns, and even guide a missile. Based on these findings Skinner recommends methods using similar principles to teach human beings:

> The main thing in programming is to break the subject matter up into small steps that are easily taken. The steps should progress so that after you have taken one, you're in a better position to take the next. And, of course, you need to learn immediately whether you are in a better position to take the next. . . . There should be no penalities attached to failure, no testing going on. Slowly you find yourself doing more and more things successfully. Present the material, give the student every help to be right, and then slowly remove that help so that the student is right because he knows the stuff. (Green, p. 28).

There is a more primitive behavioral theory — first associated with the famous Russian psychologist, Ivan Pavlov. It is most widely known as stimulus-response conditioning, using negative reinforcement. While excellent in teaching a child not to put its hand on a hot stove, this thinking is less effective in inducing positive connections to more abstract learning. Nevertheless, many educators hold the fear of failing, of ostracism, of calls home, of threats of detention, of the principal's wrath, as ways of eliciting the desired behavior from students.

Since these varied philosophies have shaped the strategies for designing computer assisted instruction (CAI), it stands to reason that the philosophy governs (or should) the teacher's selection of software. The developmentalist is most attracted to programs that stimulate the mind, enrich the student's experiences, and allow for a full range of responses not necessarily tied to specific subject matter. Those more inclined to the behaviorist view seek lessons that break subject matter into small, manageable pieces for students to master before moving on to the more complex. The stimulus-response school, on the other hand, prefers those programs designed to give immediate rewards, as well as some form of negative reinforcement for "incorrect answers."

Criteria Two Through Five

The second criterion, that the material be intellectually challenging, is so important that it almost sounds trite to make this statement. Actually, teachers and publishers all too frequently underestimate the intellectual challenge that motivated students can handle. Junior- and senior-high school students in their daily lives are constantly bombarded with traumatic questions of personal relationships and conflicting loyalties as well as the global threat of nuclear destruction. Rather than avoid these issues in the curriculum, teachers should provide students with the skills to think about them rationally. Students cannot be taught to think critically if they are not given critical issues about which to think. Good software, like a good curriculum, should challenge the mind.

Good software helps teach important facts, skills, and/or concepts, if not for life at least for the subject matter. In general, knowing complex concepts such as the balance of trade, which helps students explain the world around them, is more important than knowing isolated facts such as birth dates. Knowing current information, such as the names and philosophies of the Supreme Court justices today, is more important than knowing their names in 1822. Understanding *Brown v. School Committee*, 1954, is more important than knowing about the "midnight judges" in 1801. Learning skills necessary for independent learning is more important than learning test-taking skills. Teachers have their own opinion of what in their curriculum is important and should seek out software that most closely corresponds to their views.

In a strictly behaviorist sense, software need only teach students skills, facts, or concepts important to the curriculum. However, teachers really should seek software that does more than that. Truly successful software serves as a stimulus to students to interact with one another or to pursue a question long after the computer has been turned off. One of the more successful social studies computer programs is the *Search Series*, produced by McGraw-Hill, depicted in the panel below.

The success of this series is due less to what students see on the screen of the computer and much more to what students do to get ready to use the programs. Developer Tom Snyder deliberately organizes the presentation of data on the screen so that no single student can possibly

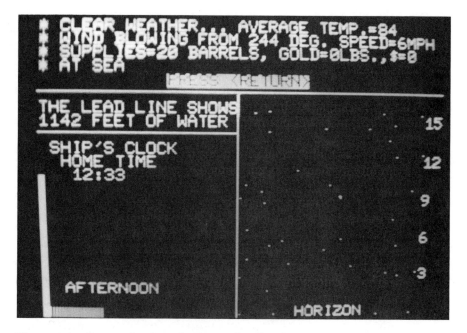

Figure 2.2   *Geography Search*: Report for the ship's crew.

read it all as it passes by. Each group in front of the computer must assign different members the responsibility of noting certain pieces of information as they cross the screen. Students are not told they need to cooperate, but are put in a position that enables them to discover on their own the need for group cooperation. Sharing occurs after the simulation as each group reports its findings, discovers that others have arrived at widely differing conclusions, and draws comparisons with its own methods. In *Historian* each group must analyze the evidence from the computer and decide whether to look for more evidence, consult with experts, or refine its thesis. At the end of the exercise, as in the *Search Series*, the groups report on their findings and the evidence that supports them. Often (at least for the developmentalists) it is in these sharing exercises that the really important learning takes place. This learning is about the intangibles — the tentativeness of hypotheses, the pleasures of working together, and the fun of discovery.

In regard to the quality of off-computer activities, teachers should take a careful look at the documentation (directions and explanations) provided with the software. Publishers who have addressed the issue of off-time activities include suggestions for making effective use of these times.

Well-designed software takes advantage of the technical potential of the computer. It neither puts the technological cart before the educational horse, nor avoids the chance to provide graphics, motivational materials, excitement, and a sense of fun and adventure. Ultimately, one test for the software is whether the teacher can just (or almost) as effectively use another aid such as a book, slide-tape, film, or lecture. Good software makes effective use of the computer's inherent asset — its ability to interact with the learner. While brilliant colors, rock music, three-dimensional graphs, and swiftly-paced action tend to increase interest in the program, they may also serve to distract by calling more attention to outside appearances than to essential concepts. This is, of course, the educators' point of view. Programmers may be more interested in winning awards for originality than in classroom dynamics and the nature of learning, but these qualities should not distract teachers.

The Don'ts

Criteria six through eight emphasize what not to do. A poor rating in any of the following is an automatic argument against using the program.

Software obviously should not contain such things as racial slurs, sexist language, or any negative references to national, racial, religious, or other groups. But omission itself is also a form of prejudice. One hopes that the software chosen includes multi-cultural and multi-ethnic materials, girls or women doing a wide variety of things that include those once stereotyped as strictly male, and males performing roles once characterized as female. In this respect it must be noted that all but one of the programs reviewed were deficient in that they presented neither the history nor the perspective of minority groups.

Good software, of course, is factually accurate and based on up-to-date scholarship. While in many cases it is easy to spot a factual error, it is more difficult to determine the unstated sexist assumptions or the incorrect historical analyses underlying the program. Serious errors in both categories are common because writing educational computer programs is a relatively new industry that has attracted a large number of independent developers. Many of these people do not have enough time, capital, and/or dedication to produce flawless programs based on the most recent scholarship.

For reasons discussed above, computer software is sometimes riddled with programming errors, difficult directions for use, and poor error-trapping. Such software could spoil a teacher's entire day. Fortunately, most software producers allow educators to hold materials for a thirty-day trial period before making a final decision. This should provide adequate time for educators to examine carefully the software that comes across their desks and enlist help from a colleague or a student knowledgeable in computers.

Software is often categorized as drill-and-practice, tutorial, simulation, or game (see *Practical Guide* for an in-depth discussion of software categories). The remainder of this chapter describes several pieces of social studies software that fall in each of these areas.

Drill-and-Practice Exercises

The simplest software category is the drill-and-practice program, though many of these now claim to teach a student new information as well as test what the student already knows. While typically using a quiz-game format to appeal to students, these programs often rely on a primitive stimulus-and-response psychology. All too frequently, these programs ask too few questions, or ask questions covering material and terms the teacher has not taught. Some software corrects for this shortcoming by allowing teachers to add their own questions. Many of these problems will be corrected as more and more book publishers write computer exercises for their own texts.

Teachers who consider buying drill-and-practice programs should first decide whether this is a wise expenditure of limited instructional funds. A printed multiple-choice test might be equally effective. Good drill-and-practice computer exercises, however, have advantages over paper-and-pencil tests if the student is given access to explanations of why a particular answer is incorrect. This technique makes the test interactive, putting students in charge of their own learning.

Focus Media's *Western Civilization* and *Non-Western Cultures* programs offer good examples of the problems associated with many drill-and-practice exercises. Both make extensive use of negative reinforcement. If, for instance, the student can locate the Aegean Sea, he or she may select one of four instruments to help climb Focus Mountain; an incorrect response causes a loss of some 200 meters down the slope. Furthermore, the program seems to spend more time on the reward or punishment phase than on the instruction. With all of the time spent on climbing up or sliding down Focus Mountain, there are only fifteen multiple-choice questions covering history from Ancient Greece to early Europe. The background information provided with each question is short and generally superficial.

Hartley's *Medalist* series illustrates other common failings of computer programs in general and drill-and-practice programs in particular. In Hartley's programs on the Presidents and on Black Americans, students can "buy" clues to the identity of a famous person, clues that cost from five to fifty points. The less expensive clues generally cover such information as the first name of the President's wife. This rewards students for knowing the comparatively trivial questions at the expense of more important things such as the leader's beliefs, values, and accomplishments. The program itself often conveys either misleading or incomplete information. Under President Nixon, for instance, the word "Watergate" and the phrase "worked hard to end the Vietnam War" appeared with no other reference; the first statement, without more information, could be meaningless to many of the upper-elementary-school students who were not born until after Nixon's resignation. The second statement, to say the least, is misleading. Another problem with

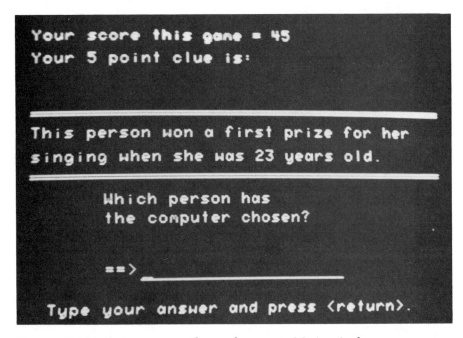

Figure 2.3 *Black Americans:* Clue and request—Marian Anderson.

the *Medalist* series is that students cannot access by computer a particular leader directly but must scroll through a long list until they get to the person they are studying. The redeeming features of these programs are their provision for teachers to add test questions to those already programmed and the fact that at least one program covers minority history.

Fortunately there are good drill-and-practice programs. For instance, Microlab, Inc. has produced an excellent one entitled *U. S. Constitution Tutor.* The subject is divided into three parts, and students can select for study the executive, legislative, and/or judicial branches of government. There are a great number of questions covering the important information in each of the three areas. Students who cannot answer particular questions can ask for further information, although students generally get much more information than they want or need. Indeed, too much information in a program seems to be far better than the more frequent case of too little.

Silwa Enterprises, Inc. has produced two interesting drill-and-practice programs. Their *American History* program consists of four disks, fifteen topics on each disk, each topic with twenty questions — an imposing total number of questions. Furthermore, students can elect, without losing credit, not to answer questions, and teachers can replace questions they do not want in the program. There are a few problems with this software. Some of the answers, for example the one that places Mt. Rainier in Oregon, are wrong. A feature called "in-depth analysis" actually only provides a piece of information that in some cases is interesting, in others irrelevant or obvious, but in no case is either "in-depth" or "analysis."

A second program by Silwa, entitled *Ancient Civilizations*, provides seventeen programs on thirteen different civilizations. It includes the standards — Egypt, Greece, Rome, and China — as well as civilizations in Asia and Central and South America (though none in sub-Saharan Africa). There are twenty multiple-choice questions on each civilization. Provisions are made that allow teachers to add their own questions. Unlike *American History*, there is no attempt here at "in-depth analyses." Both programs give the right answer after the first mistake and keep a running score of a student's successes and failures.

Versa Computing, Inc. has developed a new twist in computerized drill-and-practice programs in *Meet the Presidents*. While a computer portrait of a president forms before their eyes, students must try to answer questions about him; after each answer the students are given their scores as well as the correct answers. There is a good deal of space left in the program for teachers or students to add questions.

Perhaps because of perceptions that schools need to return to the basics (and nothing is more basic than geography), there seems to be no end of drill-and-practice geography programs. The ones examined are straightforward and suffer from no glaring errors. They are probably useful for students who need review in this area. Versa Computing has a program that provides geography tests on eight world areas along with questions in world history. Students must name certain states or countries and the capitals of each. A misspelled name results in a negative score. This is a tough program, good for ambitious students who are willing to work hard at mastering difficult facts. One problem with the program is that the maps are not clear and are extremely hard to read, though the student can, of course, always consult an atlas. Two easier, "viewer friendly" programs put out by the Minnesota Educational Computer Consortium (MECC) are appropriately titled *Capitals* and *Continents*. Although they lack interesting gimmicks or graphics they are quite serviceable.

Tutorials

Rather than emphasizing factual recall, tutorials usually teach concepts or general principles, which students are then asked to apply in different situations. Since this form lends itself particularly well to disciplines with a large, generally accepted body of concepts, there are more tutorials related to economics than to other social science disciplines. However, there has been a general increase in tutorial programs in recent years, and it is a welcome development.

One of the better tutorial programs is *Nationalism: Past and Present*, produced by Focus Media. It begins with a general introduction to the central concept of nationalism. The program continues by presenting the works of Herder, Hegel, and Rousseau in exploring the economic, political, social, and intellectual roots of nationalism. At each step along the way, students are asked to explain, identify, or classify information. This is followed by two case studies, one on the nationalist movement that succeeded in unifying Germany, and the other on the events that unified Italy. In one classifying exercise, students have to identify events as either political, economic, or attitudinal/intellectual. The students are then asked to assign point values to the events, indicating how close the nationalists were to achieving their goals. In the next stages, students do their own research on nationalism. The students then categorize and assign point values to the events leading to national unity and, with the help of the computer, use this information to make their own graphs of the nation-building process. The unit continues with an exercise on nationalism as a destructive force, using the breakup of the Austro-Hungarian Empire as a case study. The concluding unit is on the nationalistic forces at work today in the Soviet Union, posing the question, Could the Soviet Union, like the Hapsburg's empire, be destroyed by centrifugal forces?

This tutorial has a great deal to recommend it, particularly as models both of behaviorist learning theory and of effective use of computer capabilities. A complex topic, nationalism, is broken into smaller, easily comprehendable parts. Questions are posed in a non-threatening way that allow students to check whether they understand the concept and its ramifications. A simple but useful schema for analyzing nationalist movements is presented, and students are asked to apply what they learned by reviewing events leading to the unification of Germany and Italy. Students are then asked to do outside research and to apply this schema to analyzing the events they researched.

Three aspects of the *Nationalism* program could be improved. It never asks students to consider seriously if nationalism — which, after all, gave us a Nazi Germany as well as a unified Italy — is basically a negative or positive force. Secondly, it does not direct students' thinking to the significant national liberation movements that have been at least as important in the twentieth century as German unification was in the nineteenth. Third, it does not have students take the next and most important step after analysis — namely, evaluation by means of writing a comprehensive essay on the influence of the underlying economic, political, and ideological forces that have shaped the history of nationalism. These, of course, are problems that a talented teacher can easily overcome, and they certainly should not negate the imaginative and professional way the program was conceived and developed. Another program by Focus Media, *Revolutions: Past and Present*, uses the same techniques and, though it suffers from similar weaknesses, is equally interesting and recommendable.

An example of software with factual errors is *The U. S. Constitution: Nationalism and Federalism*, also from Focus Media. One disk covers the Articles of Confederation; the second the writing of the Constitution and such key concepts as the separation of powers. A third disk contains a quiz game based on information supplied by the first two. Despite some valuable features, glaring factual errors such as an assertion that, in Great Britain at the time of the American Revolution, Parliament exercised supreme power and the King was merely a "symbol of national authority" reduce the value of this software as an educational tool.

Another tutorial from Focus Media, *Time Travel*, uses the traditional quiz-game strategy in allowing students to select from eight different clues regarding the early childhood, political opponent, running mate, and major contribution of each of our forty presidents. Students can use this software to learn these facts about each president and then to check their knowledge.

For at least the past twenty years, the Joint Council of Economic Education has been a national voice for teaching fundamental economic reasoning and principles from the low elementary grades through high school and even college. The Council has become directly involved in computer education. One of its early programs, *Marketplace*, teaches students the concepts behind the supply-and-demand curve and how changes in demand and supply affect prices. An extension of the program into explanations of the differences between elastic and inelastic demand would have been useful.

If economic educators had assumed (as they well might have) that the Joint Council's comprehensive package of eight disks on economic concepts, supported with extensive guidelines and classware, all wrapped in a loose leaf notebook, would become the definitive software package for economics, they would probably be disappointed. Despite a parentage that includes a long list of foundations, and despite many excellent features, this software package entitled *Income/Outcome$* has some severe limitations. First, however, let us examine some of the brighter aspects of this comprehensive program.

Income/Outcome$ is based on the reasoning model on which the inquiry method in all the social sciences is based: state the problem, gather information, observe relationships, form a hypothesis, and test the hypothesis. The set of eight conceptually related programs begins by presenting students with the parts from which they can create their own model of circular flow in an enclosed economic system. Subsequent lessons examine such concepts as: economic growth; interest rates and their effects on investment decisions; loanable funds and market clearing rates of growth; public and private investments, and opportunity costs; macroeconomic decisions on money supply; changes in government spending; and, finally, comparative advantage and specialization in relation to foreign trade.

One of the problems with integrating this program into a standard economics course is that some of the concepts taught are not central to such courses. Another is that the computer graphics are mundane; loading time is too long, and much of what one waits to learn from the computer can be more easily obtained from a printout. Also lacking are considerations of real economic problems, such as in the U. S. the slow growth rate in the 1980s, the perpetual budget deficits, the farm problem, and the imbalance of trade.

Economics can be as complex as any of the social sciences. Therefore, it should not come as a surprise that the program, *Biznes*, an economic simulation developed for college use, is challenging to advanced high school seniors. Provided with wages, sales, and capital, students are asked to investigate such economic principles as the law of diminishing returns and marginal revenues as well as the concept of elasticity of demand. One could wish for economics software that covers these topics in an easier format such as that in the *Income/Outcome$* program.

An economics simulation called *South Dakota* focuses on a small farmer deciding which of several grains to plant, how many hands to hire, and how much money to borrow. It gives students a realistic introduction to the financial hardships of farmers who face the daily possibility of natural disaster as well as the long time between harvests.

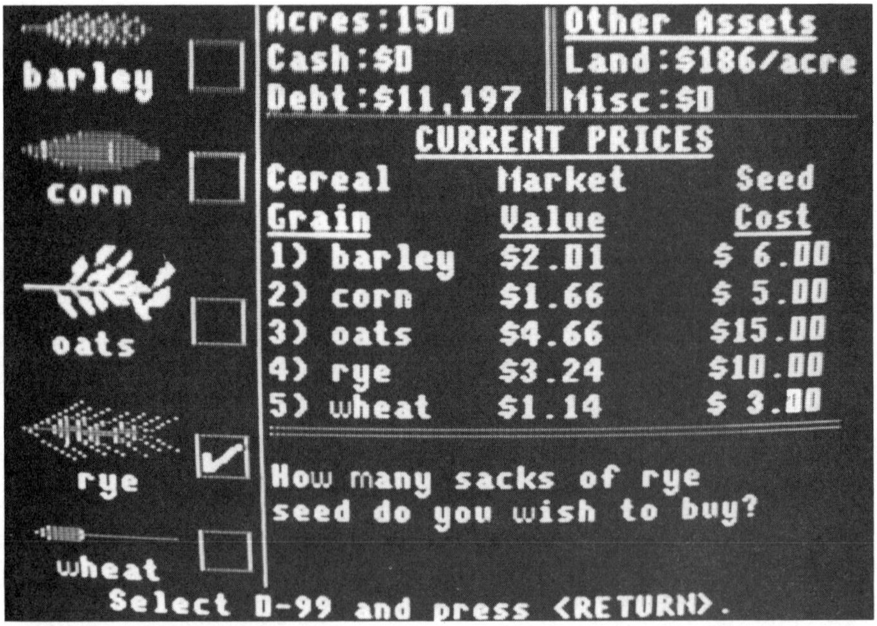

Figure 2.4   *South Dakota.*

Aside from real insight into the plight of farmers, this simulation helps students develop reasoning skills through a trial-and-error process of hiring too many farm hands one year and buying too little seed grain the next. Students must form hypotheses in answering the questions surrounding spring planting and have them proven right or wrong, like the small farmer who counts his receipts in the fall and tries to pay off his bills.

The *Economics Computer Package* is for teachers who are in the market for software that presents such basic economic terms as needs, wants, and resources and covers the factors of production, resources, capital, labor, and management. The software explains the three basic economic questions — what, how, and for whom, and illustrates their meaning in terms of production possibility and opportunity cost-curves — and then shows how societies operating on tradition, command, and in the free market, answer the economic problem. In addition to the foregoing, this Focus Media software explains the law of supply-and-demand and delves at some length into how capitalism, communism, and socialism evolved to answer the basic economic questions. Unfortunately, this program stops at this point — the remaining space on the six-disk package is filled by a "demonstration disk," a chart-making disk, and a quiz contest, all of which add little to what has already been presented.

Another tutorial program, *MECC's Bargain,* is designed to teach the specific concept of cooperative negotiation. Students are motivated with a reminder that they have been involved in negotiating their bedtime and other such issues most of their lives. The program involves students in simulating labor negotiations over wages, benefits, and vacations. Unlike most simulations, which are generally built on a competitive basis, the goal here is to arrive at a reasonable and fair settlement rather than the best solution for one side. Given the importance of resolving the conflicts in this manner, we could change the classification of this tutorial from "economics" to "life skills" or another similar topic that recognizes bargaining as a metaphor for successfully conducting human relations.

In *The Presidency Series* from Focus Media three separate programs examine the evolution of the presidency from debates during the Constitutional Convention to the expansion of powers reflected in the addition of cabinet positions and personnel serving the President. Using a tutorial approach, the programs proceed by occasionally putting the student in the position of the President, asking him/her which of the many official presidential functions come to play under various hypothetical situations. The final disk ends the series with a crossword puzzle on various cabinet functions.

Another program developed for the college student, *Demo-Graphics* by Conduit, can be used by high school classes for researching such questions as "What country has the highest life expectancy?" It can also be used to teach advanced demographic concepts, and, for example, to follow the age pyramid of America's baby-boom children. Students see how, over a number of years, as these children reach school age, there is a need for more teachers, and then later, as this generation approaches old age, a need for increased elderly care. *Demo-Graphics* also provides statistics to discuss the very serious problem of the effects of continued high birth rates on total world population.

Two easier tutorials by Rand McNally, *Unlocking the Map Code* and *Choice or Chance*, are designed for grades 4-6 and 5-8, respectively. *Unlocking* contains separate programs to teach various geographical concepts to youngsters, including symbols for elevation, rainfall, location, measurement, time, and distance. Students are given clear directions and an accompanying workbook. The final lesson is a simulated flight plan using the various concepts taught in the other units.

Choice or Chance is for somewhat older students. It raises the issue of geographical determination in settling the United States, using colonization, westward migration, and industrialization as examples. Students are asked to make decisions on where to settle — but they are given neither a clear idea why one place might be considered better than the other, nor a hint as to the implications of either choice. Unless carefully prepared by teachers, students are unlikely to learn much about the important concepts encountered in this tutorial.

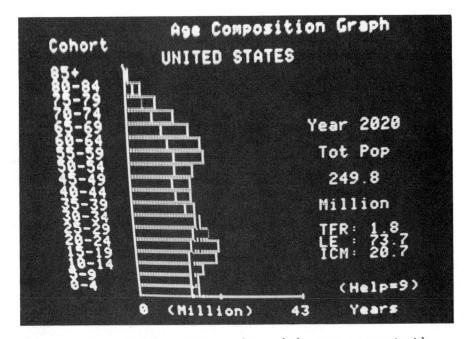

Figure 2.5 *Demo-Graphics*: 1980 population (bulge at 15–29 years) with 2020 projection (bulge at 50–69 years).

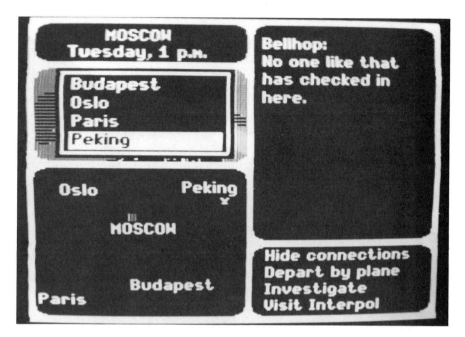

Figure 2.6   *Where in the World Is Carmen Sandiego?*

As a middle and junior high school grades tutorial, *Travels with Za-Zoom,* even at the easiest level, seemed to be too difficult. However, repeated attempts to use the program by younger people will undoubtedly result in their learning identifying facts about the cities and tourist attractions encountered in their "travels." If these are the facts teachers wish students to learn, *Za-Zoom* should provide a sufficiently interesting format for successfully achieving that end.

Finally, an engaging tutorial masquerading as a game, *Where in the World is Carmen Sandiego?* and its companion, *Where in the United States is Carmen Sandiego?,* both from Broderbund, employ a detective technique. Thieves steal jewels and leave just enough clues to get the student to the "next country" where most likely another clue requiring geographical knowledge allows the student to continue the chase.

Simulations

Simulations are uniquely suited to the style and content of most social studies classes. They contain elements that follow from the developmentalist and behaviorist philosophies. Properly used, they allow the fulfillment of such diverse goals as teaching facts, developing understanding, stimulating growth, reviewing content, fostering empathy, and heightening interest. Using a simulation successfully, however, is not always easy.

Most computer simulations require group process activities, which developers such as Tom Snyder believe are the main purpose of any educational software. Students learn more from the activities, not only if they are encouraged to work together, but also if they are made to reflect on the process in which they are engaged. For these reasons it is important for teachers to monitor the simulation carefully, to hold "debriefing" sessions afterward, and to require some kind of written work from each participant. Students also need help in making the connections between the simulation and the curriculum it elucidates. Finally, teachers should be aware that simulations often require a fairly substantial amount of class time.

There have been a number of captivating simulations done for middle elementary to junior high school by MECC and McGraw-Hill. These have worked well for many teachers throughout the country. The successful series of simulations from McGraw-Hill is the *Search Series*. The five programs in the series are *Geography Search, Geology Search, Energy Search, Archaeology Search,* and *Community Search* — the first and last being the most popular. The series is designed to encourage students to work together away from the computer. Students, typically, are faced with a problem — such as looking for a new place to live. This takes such forms as sailing to a new world or trekking cross-country to arable land. In order to find whatever they are seeking, students must learn to use tools such as the sextant for "shooting the sun" to find the ship's position. By design, the information students need to accomplish their assigned task is flashed across the screen too rapidly for any one individual to copy; groups must therefore divide responsibilities. Widespread participation in decision-making is assured because each student in the group has an important responsibility. Furthermore, required workbook exercises give teachers a chance to monitor students' progress, and class discussions provide an opportunity for debriefing after the simulation is completed.

Perhaps the best known of all social studies simulations is MECC's *Oregon Trail,* which several other publishers have altered slightly and published under their own names. The simulation itself is hardly impressive. The 2040-mile trek to Oregon is accomplished in nine two-week stages. Teams of students have to make decisions on spending their limited funds on clothing, food, ammunition, and medicine. To beat the odds, each student team has to research all aspects of the perilous trek. Since it was first developed, *Oregon Trail* has undergone a major overhaul in its computer graphics. Students now can aim their computer guns as they shoot deer, buffalo, or birds to augment their food supply; get glimpses of Independence, Missouri; meet "Matt the supplier" as they purchase merchandise needed for the trip; watch their wagon with oxen as it fords or floats across a river. Students are given a running account of food consumption en route, and they can choose to be a farmer, carpenter, or banker before beginning their journey.

Figure 2.7 *Oregon Trail*: An attempt to trade.

It is the combination of research with group decision-making that makes the game such an effective teaching tool. Two other games produced by MECC, *Furs* and *Voyagers*, try to capitalize on this formula. These simulations can succeed if the teacher has students research the fur trade of that period — then these have the same potential for classroom drama as found in the trek to Oregon.

A simulation that has the potential for even more excitement than *Oregon* is another MECC creation, *Fail Safe*. This program is structured around the chilling possibility of American bombers mistakenly heading for the Soviet Union under orders to bomb Russia. Headquarters in Washington realizes what is happening but cannot communicate with its bombers. One student, playing the president, is advised by eleven classmates, each assigned a role ranging from hawks to doves. As debate over strategy proceeds, various recommendations are made and fed into the computer. After less desperate measures fail, the president faces the dilemma of (1) bombing one of his own cities to convince the Soviets that the United States is sincere in its desire to prevent a nuclear war, or (2) risking a retaliatory attack. Though this scenario is highly unlikely in an age of intercontinental ballistic missiles, the life-and-death issues it raises are very real. Undoubtedly teachers can locate good current materials to follow up this engaging simulation.

Another of the early computer classics was the *Sell Series*, including *Sell Lemonade*. Students must sell their products and try to make a profit. Beginning with minimum capital (by today's standards), players decide how much to spend on advertising, how much lemonade to make, and how much to charge. Just what is actually "learned" depends on how skillfully the teacher organizes the debriefing, analyzes the computer model, and weaves economic concepts into subsequent lessons.

A fourth perennial favorite from MECC is *Sumer*. It is based on the hypothetical situation of a ruler who must decide how to divide the empire's resources both to cultivate food and seed for the next year and to buy more land (ostensibly to expand his empire).Though designed for middle-elementary to junior high school, this simulation still should have provided far more realistic figures, added roles for priests and noblemen, and included hand-outs to stimulate further discussion and to hold students responsible for the materials covered.

A simulation that balances gamesmanship and real learning, *Road Rally U.S.A.* ranks high on the plus side. Students can select from eight road maps, each covering a different region of the country, and from a variety of driving modes from Sunday driver to highway hotshot. They then switch on a computer roadmap that shows the highways but not their route numbers and the place locations (usually cities) without the accompanying name identifications. From this point on students are on their own, manipulating the keyboard to change direction and to stop — moving off a map on one scale to another on a much different scale. Further complications are introduced as students run out of gas or break down on the road. Meanwhile a clock is ticking away the minutes and hours on the road as individual students or small teams of drivers race against records set by others. As soon as one destination is reached, students are given their assignment to the next. With the clock still ticking they must chose the best route and move on.

In playing this game successfully, students must familiarize themselves with the names of, and some facts about, the major cities in various regions. This software should prove very useful to teachers who wish to teach these map reading skills and place geography.

And If Re-Elected by Focus Media is a clever simulation based on the principle that candidates who play the political game well get re-elected but not necessarily a favorable nod from historians. Students can select from nine different lists of twelve crises, with each crisis followed by a multiple-choice set of four different courses of action that might be followed. Depending on how well they guessed the programmer's preference for popular policy, the candidate either goes up or down in the opinion polls. Election day follows the twelfth crisis, and the screen registers a state-by-state counting of both popular and electoral votes. The game is captivating; the text is humorous; the election night heroics are exciting; and the philosophical questions on the nature of our political system are interesting. One complaint is that it is hard to discern what strategy to follow in order to go up in the polls and win the election — but maybe that is the point.

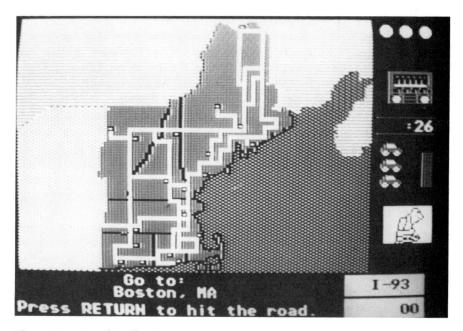

Figure 2.8   *Road Rally*: Review map.

Decisions, Decisions from Tom Snyder Productions is the newest product employing the very successful techniques originally used in the McGraw-Hill *Search Series.* The *Decisions* software is presented in two packets: the American History Pack on colonization, revolutionary wars, immigration, and urbanization; and the Critical Issues Pack on the budget process, foreign policy, and television. The American History Pack covers the generic term *revolution*, rather than the American Revolution in particular, by presenting a situation where the student team, acting the role of governor of the province of Catalan, must respond to an impending invasion from the mother country, Democ. The choices are: to maintain peace, to help the rebels, to keep a position of power, and/or to unite the people of the province. Students have to prioritize their goals and respond to each intermediate step as the crisis develops. An interactive process is guaranteed by the presence of four aides to the governor — each reading different suggestions from the text accompanying the software — while the governor attempts to make the best possible decision according to his goals. Divided into teams, preferably of five each, students take turns at the computer and spend the waiting time deciding on their next move. In the debriefing time after the simulation, teachers and students discuss how realistic their simulation was in comparison with the case they are studying — probably the American Revolution, although the French, Russian, and numerous other revolutions could be studied using the same format.

Versatility of format is claimed by series programmer and co-developer David Dockterman as one of the prime virtues of the seven simulations in his two packets *American History* and *Critical Issues.* In the case of the Revolution simulation, however, one should guard against the situation becoming so abstract that the relationships to the Revolution become tenuous. The same precaution should also guide teachers who are considering the software in the other packets.

Using a personal mode (students get their full names attached to the bill they introduce) *Congressional Bill Simulator* from Focus Media takes them through the legislative process from assignment to committee to an attempt to override a presidential veto. Students are asked to select a bill from a provided list or make their own. They proceed by making such decisions as: which committee will most likely take their bill; how much lobbying they need to do; how many witnesses, friendly or otherwise, will testify; and whether the House, Senate, and President are of their political party. Depending in large part on students' answers to these questions, the bill makes its way through the tedious steps of being reported out of committee, voted up or down in the House, getting through the Senate, being negotiated through its different versions from the two Houses of Congress, arriving on the President's desk, and facing possible veto and override. Few social studies teachers achieve great success in teaching this lesson in civics, and it is not unlikely that this software makes the job at least somewhat easier.

The Balance of Power by Mindscape is a complex simulation produced for the home-video rather than the classroom market. Designer Chris Crawford used the concept of "credibility" in programming a struggle in which two superpowers compete for a favorable balance of power by threats, political overthrows, destabilization, terrorism, and armed intervention. As the superpowers careen through the world, they approach the nuclear threshold and spark an Armageddon in which all sides lose. Players learn how to avoid military solutions to problems that can lead to nuclear holocausts and to use such indirect options as treaties and diplomatic pressure. Although this game was not designed for the school market, it certainly would be worth its price of slightly under $50.00 for an adventurous social studies teacher with a Macintosh and a classroom full of vibrant youngsters. The game, by the way, provides a world map and such vital statistics as GNP and the military capabilities of each of the sixty-two countries involved in the simulation.

Finally, there are two simulation games that may set the standard for judging other such software. These complex and multi-faceted programs are *The Other Side,* produced by Tom Snyder Productions, Inc. and *Simplicon,* produced by Cross Cultural Software. The former is a highly imaginative game in which two groups need to cooperate with one another to build a bridge. The world presented in *The Other Side* — of different colored fuels and a mad computer called C.A.D. (standing for Computer Assisted Defense) — is intentionally fanciful. *Simplicon,* on

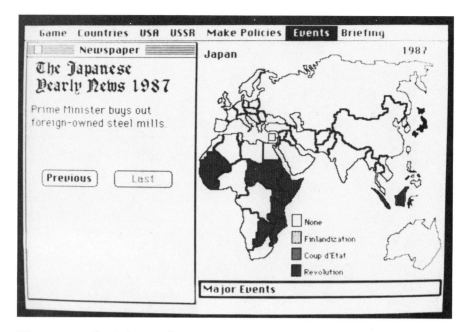

Figure 2.9 *The Balance of Power:* Events—Newspapers.

the other hand, attempts to present a replica of the real world in which undeveloped countries try to develop and sustain their economies in an often hostile environment. Both of these simulations deserve a more detailed examination.

The Other Side presents the challenge literally to bridge the gulf between the two teams. This task is achieved by buying increasingly expensive bricks for the bridge. In order to earn the money needed to buy bricks, each side must mix a fuel that requires a rare ingredient only found on the other side. Each side has drillers to find oil, a bomb that can be exploded to release the entrapped oil, and patrols to find out what is going on in other parts of the world. These items are maneuvered to secure the needed fuel, but must operate in a way not to arouse the other side's Computer Assisted Defense (a metaphor for the fear and suspicion that make cooperation impossible). The purpose of the game is, in the words of its producer, to "develop skills and give us practice at overcoming conflict on many levels." The game can be played with one or two computers and with as many as four students sharing the controls in each group. It requires several hours to complete, and the producer advises teachers to allow students to play it through to the end at least two or three times. A detailed student guide explains the many moves and rules of the game. A teacher's manual helps explain the purpose of the game and gives suggested analogies for discussion, but expects teachers to find the materials that provide the substance for these dialogues.

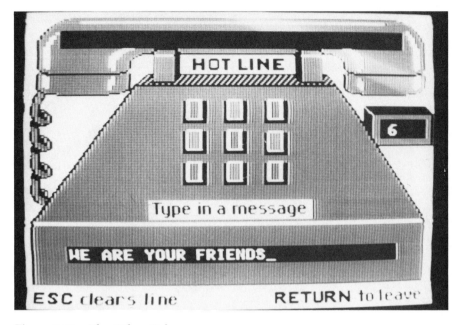

Figure 2.10   *The Other Side.*

Simplicon (Simulation of Political and Economic Development) is a complex simulation that has students make a series of practical decisions for helping an undeveloped country become an industrial nation. In the early stages of this game, students must be most concerned with producing food and obtaining medicine for survival. As they are able to accumulate surpluses for their countries, students can invest in education, resource development, and production of machines. In later stages, players focus on foreign trade, military preparedness, and pollution.

The game is played by investigating a series of 200 different production possibilities. Students decide the ends they hope to achieve in a series of "rounds" representing years of development. Students then reason backwards to figure out what they must first produce to achieve their goals and how to continue. The goals and plans must be revised as their own errors and natural as well as man-made disasters interfere with their development program.

The simulation's documentation provides teachers with many different developmental models for students and allows students to investigate real-life events based on situations modeled in the game. The developer claims *Simplicon* can serve any educational level from junior high school through the university, and it has been under consideration for use in training Peace Corps workers.

Perhaps the extreme complexity of *Simplicon* is both its greatest asset and its major weakness. It is not a program that a teacher can simply pick up during a free period and use an hour later in class. Teachers have to spend several hours working with the game to understand it well enough to use it with their classes. Students will need at least forty-five minutes just to familiarize themselves with the order of play. For instructors teaching Economics, Geography, World History, Problems of Democracy, and World Culture, however, this game could well be worth the four or more classroom hours needed.

Games and Interactive Video

Computer games have enjoyed a great deal of popularity for some time and have provided developers with a lucrative market. They can be divided into several categories, including arcade, fantasy, adventure, strategic, and learning games. Usually made for the home market, games compete against other forms of entertainment. To be competitive, developers use highly imaginative formats, state-of-the-art graphics, and captivating sound effects. The learning games are usually made for young children and are marketed to their parents. They are designed to teach youngsters the rudiments of writing, reading, math, and science, as well as practical skills such as telling time and counting money. Learning games for middle- and upper-elementary age groups claim to teach logic, thinking, and creative problem solving. *Rocky's Boots*, to cite a popular example, "builds a basic groundwork in logical skills that [children will] use for the rest of their lives" (Hammett, p. 51). Youngsters play games at home, and adults enjoy them too. Many games make their way into the schools. While they supposedly teach youngsters, the boundary lines between entertainment, stimulating growth or development, and actual teaching are not easily defined.

A new generation of games with vastly greater power than those just described is now reaching the market. Instead of providing players with a choice between two or three alternatives, they allow over one hundred possibilities. The games themselves are so involved and complex that even the programmers cannot always predict the outcome. These games take from ten to twelve hours to play and involve complicated mysteries. Suspects give conflicting testimony, get killed, or disappear. Employing "smart" vocabularies of 600 words, they respond to typed instructions, make corrections, and draw attention to mistakes. Imagine the possibilities when this technology is incorporated in the social studies curriculum. Historical characters could come to life and answer questions, reenact events, converse with famous people from other eras, debate issues of historic importance, or just raise interesting questions for students to research.

Interactive video is another exciting new technological innovation in computer-aided instruction (see chapter 7). This technology combines the interactive features of a computer with the visual imagery of film. The possibilities of this combination are breathtaking. Imagine having access to 54,000 different visuals that can be frozen, repeated, or rearranged in a half-hour of instruction. With a price tag of less than $800 for the hardware, the cost will not make this technology prohibitive. The Defense Department and private industry have produced (respectively) interactive video flight simulators and sales pitch training sessions that make full use of this technology. MECC has produced an interactive economics course. There is no doubt that sometime in the future the inherent possibilities of interactive video will be fully realized, even in the field of education.

We can imagine the impact of interactive video and the new educational games. These technologies will cause unprecedented changes in social studies classrooms — their impact will be felt in the curriculum as well as in the interactions of students and teachers. With these technologies the computer may play a dominating role in the classroom of the next decade. It is therefore of utmost importance that teachers position themselves so they may have a voice in the development of the courseware. It is our job to see that the social studies curriculum prepares students for the new world — the age of information — defined by the same computer technology that increasingly is found in social studies classes.

References

Green, John O., "B.F. Skinner's Technology of Teaching," *Classroom Computer Learning*, February, 1984, pp. 22-29.

Hammett Microcomputer Division Catalog, 1984.

Using General Purpose Computer Tools in the Social Studies

It is the ability to use and design successful tools that make humans distinctive. During the Industrial Revolution new tools extended human muscle power. Now, during the Information Revolution, tools for thought provide the potential for extending human mind power. The primary instrument of the current revolution is the computer, a general purpose machine that can be used for many different tasks. The computer's resource is information. More and more, people's ability to function effectively depends on their skills to acquire, organize, and use information and on their ability to use computer-based tools for working with information. Such tools include computer programs that can:

- write, edit, and print letters, reports, and compositions;
- store and retrieve data for business, government, and educational purposes;
- display data in a variety of ways such as graphs, tables, and charts;
- conduct and analyze the results of surveys;
- perform statistical analyses of data; and
- build and explore models that simulate real-world situations.

The application of information technology is particularly relevant to the social studies. However, using computer-based tools capably requires thinking differently about what is taught and how it is taught.

The Nature of Tool-Based Learning Environments

As these computer tools are used in the social studies, new roles emerge for both teacher and student. These roles reflect a new kind of learning environment — a "tool-based" learning environment focused on critical thinking and problem solving. In such an environment, emphasis shifts away from the traditional educational paradigm. Rather than an instructor imparting content, the teacher becomes a facilitator of learning. The student is directly involved in the creation of knowledge rather than acting primarily as a passive receptor. The process of learning is emphasized rather than the accumulation of information.

Hilda Taba, in her book *Curriculum Development*, drew distinctions between content and process. Any area of knowledge has two main characteristics: its own fund of acquired information and a specialized method of inquiry, or a strategy of acquiring knowledge (p. 172).

While education must serve a dual purpose in achieving both, educators have differing opinions concerning the value of content and the value of process. The problem of coverage is continually being confronted. Certain content *must* be covered to the sacrifice, if need be, of teaching students the process of independent knowledge acquisition. On the other hand, the underlying goal of many subjects is the development of critical thinking and problem-solving skills, thus involving the process of the discipline. In a world accelerated by change and inundated by the geometric growth of knowledge, social studies teachers need to address the content-versus-process debate directly.

In developing a tool-based learning environment, careful thought needs to be given to the nature of the questions that guide exploration. Effective questions and questioning strategies are related to the intellectual skills developed. The National Council for the Social Studies (NCSS), in a preliminary position paper on a Scope and Sequence for Social Studies, identified the intellectual skills related to organizing and using information:

1.   classification, including grouping, sequencing, and organizing data;
2.   interpretation, including stating relationships between categories of information, noting cause and effect, and drawing inferences;
3.   analysis, including examining relationships between and among elements of a topic and detecting bias in data presentation;
4.   summarization, including skills of extracting, combining, and restating information and of stating hypotheses;
5.   synthesis, including developing new plans, reinterpreting, and communicating;
6.   evaluation, including considering relevancy, adequacy, and validity of information (p. 261).

Hilda Taba's rank-ordering of the questions, "What?," "Why?," and "What does this mean?" as part of a process of inductive thinking, help bring these skills into focus. The first question, "What?," deals with concept formation and involves identifying data needed for problem solution, grouping the data, and developing categories and labels (skill 1 above). The second question, "Why?," deals with interpreting data and involves inferring and generalizing (skill 2). The final question, "What does this mean?," focuses on the application of principles and developing, explaining, and verifying predictions and hypotheses (skills 3–6).

The purpose of a tool-based learning environment is to help extend student potential in critical thinking and problem solving through the use of appropriate content. Students need to learn that certain kinds of questions yield specific kinds of information. Students also need to be encouraged to ask the higher level questions, those dealing with analysis, synthesis, and evaluation, and to determine how the tools and information available to them can help answer these questions.

The Kinds of Computer Tools That May Be Used

In this chapter and the next, a variety of computer programs that may be used as tools are presented. In this chapter, programs that help with writing and programs that help students organize, store, and search for information are discussed. Such programs can be considered general purpose tools.

Writing is a process that is integrated into the social studies. Using word processing software, students can create and edit any number of different writing assignments from journal entries to research papers. Students enjoy working with word processing and often experience increased success in writing.

Databases provide many opportunities for students to interact with and use information — the raw material of social studies. Commercial databases can be used to find historical facts or locate the latest information on some current events topic. Students can also create their own databases. This provides many opportunities for focusing on such skills as classifying and organizing information, looking for patterns in information, and evaluating the nature of the information.

Writing Aids

The Process of Writing

Writing is a process of thinking and problem solving in which ideas may go through many changes before becoming an acceptable reflection of a writer's intent. Writers develop sequences of composing, shaping, and editing that may vary significantly from one writer to another. While there is no single correct way to write, there are various stages and drafts through which any piece of writing goes. These stages can generally be categorized as pre-writing, composing, and revising.

Pre-writing prepares the way for writing by identifying the topic, audience, and general organization. During pre-writing, students are involved in thinking, listening, talking, making notes, outlining, and brainstorming. It is the time when ideas are generated.

During the second stage, composing, a written version is created. Ideas are developed into a composition as students change their first thoughts into prose.

Revising, the third stage, involves proofreading, editing, and, in some instances, major rethinking. At this point, language is changed, organization is adjusted, necessary information is added, irrelevant information is deleted, and spelling and punctuation are examined.

The separation into three stages offers a somewhat simplified view of the writing process, for the stages often do merge. Students may be revising during the composing phase. Planning as a pre-writing activity can occur after a draft is complete and before any revision is done.

Computer Assistance in the Writing Process

Software classified as a writing aid is designed to help in one or more of the three stages of the writing process. Programs are available that are particularly suited for use during the pre-writing stage. One such program is *ThinkTank*, an "idea processor." It can be used to produce an outline from information entered in any order. The information is kept in the order entered until a decision is made to reorganize it as ideas "take shape." The author may change the order in which ideas are listed and make one idea subordinate to another, hence developing an outline. Major headings can be entered at any time and subordinate ideas added as they are developed. Any part of the outline can be expanded. It is also possible to view only the major headings, hiding subordinate ideas in order to assess the overall impact of the subject.

For the composing stage, word processors allow great flexibility for creating and editing text. In the past few years, *Bank Street Writer*, a word processing program, has gained popularity in the schools. Developed specifically for young writers, it is a simple program that is easy to learn and use by people of all ages. There are three modes in *Bank Street Writer* (and in many other word processors): the write mode, the edit mode, and the transfer mode. In the write mode, text can be entered and mistakes corrected.

To enter the edit mode, a key is pressed and a new menu appears, indicating the major editing functions that are possible. These provide ways to move, delete, or replace text. It is from the edit menu that the transfer mode is entered. This is done by selecting the Transfer Menu. Transfer involves actions with the disk drive or with the printer. A previously saved text file may be retrieved from the disk. A text file currently in the computer memory may be saved to the disk. Files on the disk may be deleted or their names changed. In addition, a text file in the computer memory may be printed, in draft or final form, on a printer attached to the computer. See figure 3.1.

Most word processing programs function in a similar manner. However, the write, edit, and transfer modes may not all result in separate menus. In many, write and edit are combined, with single or combined key strokes used to initiate actions such as search, replace, and move. *Applewriter IIe* is one such program which is more sophisticated than *Bank Street Writer*.

Most word processors automatically "wrap" words as text is entered. Usually the carriage return needs to be used only between paragraphs. This permits a writer to engage in "sprint writing," entering text rapidly without concern for grammar and other errors and thus keeping up with his or her thoughts. Editing capabilities permit complete ease in rewriting and revision to make the text a polished work.

A variety of text analyzer programs are available for use with word processing programs. Spelling checkers, such as *Bank Street Speller*, are one example. Such programs are either in-context programs that can check the spelling of a word right after it is typed or post-editing programs that examine the entire text at once when entry or editing is finished. In addition to spelling checkers, there are a few programs

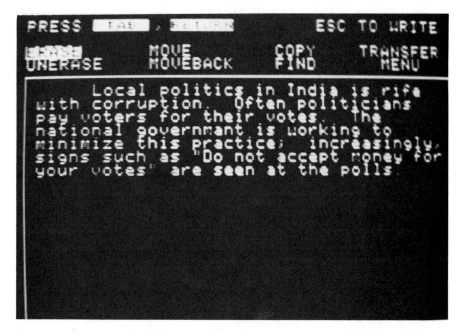

Figure 3.1 *Bank Street Writer.*

capable of analyzing writing style and identifying common punctuation errors.

Recently software developers have begun to create programs that include more than word processing and can assist the teacher in teaching the entire writing process. One such program is *Quill*, designed for use in grades 3–9. This package offers word processing as well as pre- and post-writing programs, a program for storing a class's information in a database, and an electronic mail system for sharing information.

The pre-writing program part of *Quill*, called *Planner*, provides a series of ideas or questions designed to stimulate the writer's thoughts prior to composing. The writer enters his or her responses to the ideas or questions and later uses these notes to help organize and compose a text. Teachers and students can create their own *Planners* that can then be used to help organize their ideas.

The *Writer's Assistant* is part of both the *Library* and *Mailbag* in *Quill*. It is a word processing program that allows entry and revision of written text. Once entered, the piece of writing is stored in *Library* or *Mailbag*.

The *Library* is used by students and teachers to store text. Once stored, the writing is available to others who use the computer. The texts are organized by author(s), title, and topic (which is identified by one or more key words). More than a word processor, the *Library* is designed to create a communication environment in which students write for each other as well as for the teacher.

Mailbag is used for direct communication between students and teachers in the classroom. Combining features of the post office, telephone, and bulletin board, *Mailbag* permits students to send and receive messages and information from other people. The writing experience thus becomes more personalized.

Computer aids to writing do not necessarily make a student a better writer but rather help remove some of the mechanical barriers to success. Messy papers, smeared writing, and illegible penmanship discourage even the most creative of writers. By using word processing, students can concentrate more on ideas than on a manuscript's appearance. Furthermore, since revision does not mean recopying, students are encouraged to think creatively about alternate ways of expressing themselves.

What Purpose Does Writing Serve?

The central purpose of writing in the schools is to record what a student has already learned. In such forms as term papers, book reports, and essays, written work is treated as an end-product that is used for evaluation, judgment, and grading. Little is done in the category of expressive writing in which students are encouraged to use writing to explore new information and to try out new ideas. As a result, students' have a narrow sense of both the intended audience (most often the teacher) and purpose of writing (most often for evaluation) in school (Healy, 1981).

A very different view is one in which the purpose of writing is to help students discover connections within a subject. The act of putting thoughts into words encourages discovery of ideas, helps students sharpen their thoughts, and begins to provide order to their thinking. Students view the act of writing as an aid to learning. Writing helps them acquire mastery of new information and reveals their current understanding of a given subject. Writing is treated as something that is directly and immediately useful and not as a product at the end of some segment of learning. This view incorporates writing as a part of every step in the learning process. Both teachers and students work together to respond to, rather than evaluate, writing (Healy, 1981).

Writing Activities for Social Studies

In designing writing activities that relate to social studies, the issue of writing for the purpose of recording and evaluation as well as writing for discovery and response must be considered. Clearly the computer tools available can be used effectively by students for either purpose. However, if writing as a means for understanding content is to be encouraged, then ways must be developed to include it as a comprehensive component throughout the social studies curriculum.

Journal writing is useful for a variety of purposes in social studies classes. Instead of paper journals, students can have electronic journals made available through the use of word processing. Such journals can provide students opportunities to react to lessons in progress and to keep recollections of information given in lectures, demonstrations, and films. This information is then immediately available to the student for longer papers. Having their thoughts ready for editing, students can rely on their own reconstructions of ideas rather than on what has been recorded on teacher-made worksheets. Writing in such an expressive mode encourages students to make connections between new information and their previous body of knowledge.

Word processing may be used as a record of student brainstorming and discussion sessions. Rather than writing notes on the chalkboard, ideas in the form of notes can be entered in a word processor and later printed out for everyone's records. This can also be done with small groups of students gathered around a computer, one student serving as recorder and entering text. Such small groups, using word processing or some other specific pre-writing tool, may also meet to plan research projects. The ideas generated guide the direction of the research and can be included in a written report.

A more formal activity, still focusing on the response to writing by peers, is a class newspaper. The sections of the newspaper are designated and editors identified. Reporters enter their articles using word processing and save them on the class's disks. The editors read and react, making those revisions about which the reporter and editor agree. Each article is submitted to the managing editor for final approval. The newspaper is then printed and distibuted to students on a regular basis and in a minimum of time.

Peer editing, as a method of response to student writing, can be initiated at any time for any writing project. Using such a procedure, students work in pairs to react to and help improve each other's writing. After a piece of writing is completed, student pairs may work together in a variety of ways. They may sit together at the computer and jointly edit the piece, or the partner can edit the piece, making changes that may or may not be implemented. Alternatively, the partner can enter a paragraph or two of comments at the end of the piece of writing with suggestions for change. Peer-editing can be extended to include the teacher as a "peer" who responds to a current draft. It is much easier to evaluate suggested changes on a fresh printout of an essay than on one covered with red pencil.

The work of social studies is writing. Computer programs that serve as writing aids help students deal with the mechanical aspects of writing. The overall result is a less restrictive writing environment.

Databases

Background

The terms *data* and *information* are often used interchangeably. However, there is a distinction: data are the facts, the raw material from which people create information; information is the meaning assigned to facts. Data become information when organized to solve problems.

While there are a variety of ways to store and retrieve information, computers are recognized as the primary tool for this task, particularly when large amounts of data are involved. At the simplest level, computers can be used to store facts such as dates, names of people and places, and population figures. This data can be retrieved for a variety of purposes such as comparing and contrasting facts. At a more sophisticated level, data can be used to provide information about voting patterns, attitudes or opinions, and economic trends.

A database is a collection of data that are related in some way and may be used for multiple purposes. An address book or a recipe file are examples of databases that may or may not be computerized. Generally, databases refer to computer databases. In most cases, computers allow people to use, update, and maintain data more effectively and easily than if done manually. To create and use a database, a computer needs a computer program known as a *database management system*. This software permits the entry, storage, retrieval, editing, and manipulation of data in order to provide information.

There are commercial and non-commercial databases. With commercial databases, the user is not directly involved in the design and development of the database but rather is interested in using the data provided. In a sense, such databases are analogous to libraries. People seek information from the books but generally have little impact on the development and maintenance of the library collection as a whole. To use a database, a person must learn to query the database with the aid of special indexing and language conventions in a fashion similar to learning to use the Dewey Decimal System to locate books. Essentially, such databases are "on-line," that is, people can use the data by connecting their microcomputers to the database computer via their telephones.

In non-commercial databases, a person not only uses the data but designs and maintains the database as well. Specific software known as a database manager is available for creating databases on microcomputers. These are "micro-sized" versions of the software used to run the commercial databases.

Since microcomputer databases are similar to the larger often commercial versions, they provide exciting educational opportunities that parallel real-world activities.

> *Creating a database involves students in many of the important decisions for managing information.

> *Using a class-created database brings quickly to light the impact of earlier decisions — such as unforeseen information biases, restrictions on retrieving data in useful forms, and constraints in adding unexpected kinds of data.

> *Using a computerized database allows the class to get to the hypothesis-generation and testing phases far more quickly than using traditional means of collecting and organizing data. Therefore, the likelihood of students being involved in the analysis, synthesis, and evaluation levels of thinking is greatly increased.

Creating and Using Microcomputer Databases in School

Another analogy can be drawn between using a database and using a set of index cards to keep a file of information on some topic. Suppose a group of students studying South America decides to set up an index card file to record information about the different countries in South America. As each student gathers data about a particular country, she or he records the facts on a large index card. Each card is one record in a database. The set of thirteen index cards, each representing a country in South America, is considered a file on South America. The complete database might eventually contain files for all countries and continents.

To create a database using a microcomputer, the class needs applications software known as a database management system (*DBMS*). Microcomputer DBMSs are generally divided into two groups: file managers and relational database systems. The distinction comes in the ease of use and in the number of files that can be used at one time. In the easier-to-use file managers, while many files can be supported, only one file may be used, or opened, at a time. Relational database systems make it possible to get data from two or more files at once using relationships established between files so that merging of data can be done. Such programs generally require a great deal more effort to master than the simpler file managers.

An extensive number of DBMSs are available for microcomputers, but the concepts and operation of each are similar. *PFS-File* is a text-entry file manager that is flexible and easy to use. The examples given in this chapter all use *PFS-File*. (See the resource section for descriptions of other DBMSs, some appropriate for elementary school.)

Unlike a manual index-card filing system, which allows recording information in any order, a computer database is not quite as flexible. When designing a computer database, decisions must be made in advance about what information to include in each record and how this information is organized. This is done by setting up a form for entering data — a template — which is then used for each record. The template is designed by deciding what fields to include in each record. Each field contains one piece of information, such as the name of a country, the population, or the land area. The maximum number of characters in each field usually can be specified. For example, the field for a country's name might be at least fifteen characters long because at least one of the countries in South America (French Guiana) has a long name. Figure 3.2 shows a possible form (using *PFS-File*) for entering data about countries in South America.

In this example, the form is forty characters wide (forms may also be eighty characters wide). The beginning of a field is noted by a colon (":"); the end of the field is marked by the beginning of the name of the next field. For example, the field COUNTRY: is for the name of a country in South America. It can extend to the space before the "C" in the field name CAPITAL:. This is actually much more space than is needed but, in the case of *PFS-File*, there is plenty of room for storing records. Using the form arranged in this fashion makes it easier to see and search. Notice that the fields for industries, crops, and minerals are quite long. Quite a bit of information might be recorded in those fields for some of the countries in South America.

Once the form is designed, it can be used for entering data. For each record, the computer displays a blank copy of the form just created (Figure 3.2). It is possible to move back and forth making changes and corrections and to return at a later time to change, delete, or add information. Figures 3.3 and 3.4 on pages 50 and 51 show completed records for Venezuela and Brazil (1984 *World Almanac*).

```
COUNTRY:

CAPITAL:

POPULATION (1982 EST):

AREA IN SQUARE MILES:

POPULATION DENSITY (PER SQ.MI):

LATITUDES:

LOW (30S - 30N):
MIDDLE (31S - 60S):
HIGH (> 60S):


INDUSTRIES:


CROPS:


MINERALS:
```

Figure 3.2. *PFS:FILE:* Sample record form, page 1 and 2.

Knowing the size of each database is important. Most DBMSs provide some mechanism for letting you know how much information can be stored. In *PFS-File*, as data are entered, the program reports the percentage of the file that is filled. For example, after thirteen records are entered in the database on South America, the file is 4 percent full. The number of records possible in a file generally depends on both the software and the hardware being used.

Information can be stored as both numbers and letters. Some databases require you to identify which kind of information is to be used in each field. In this way the computer can treat each type of data differently. Some software allows sorting by either numbers (numeric sort) or letters (alphabetic sort). This gives more flexible control in handling data. *PFS-File*, one of the simpler databases, treats data in all fields as alphanumeric data and only performs alphabetic sorts. This can cause strange results when trying to sort numbers. For example, *PFS-File* evaluates 2.07 as "greater" than 13.20 because the 2 in 2.07 (read "two-point-zero-seven") when treated alphabetically comes later than the 1 in 13.20 (read "one-three-point-two-zero"). Consequently, in *PFS-File*,

```
COUNTRY: VENEZUELA

CAPITAL: CARACAS

POPULATION (1982 EST): 018700000

AREA IN SQUARE MILES: 0352143

POPULATION DENSITY (PER SQ.MI): 53.10

LATITUDES:

LOW (30S - 30N): X
MIDDLE (31S - 60S):
HIGH (> 60S):
```

```
INDUSTRIES: STEEL, OIL PRODUCTS,
TEXTILES, CONTAINERS, PAPER, SHOES


CROPS: COFFEE, RICE, FRUITS, SUGAR


MINERALS: OIL, IRON, GOLD
```

Figure 3.3.   Record for Venezuela.

fixed-length data must be used for all numeric fields. In the South America database, the population field has a fixed-length of nine characters. For Brazil's population, 127700000 (127,700,000) is entered; for Ecuador's population, 008500000 (8,500,000). This also needs to be done for the field that identifies the area of the country. A fixed-length of seven characters is needed to insure that *PFS-File* will sort the data as anticipated.

Some DBMSs also allow computed fields. These are numeric fields whose data are determined by computations using data found in other fields. For example, in the South America database the field for population density could clearly benefit by being a computed field. Density is computed by dividing the population of the country by its land area.

```
COUNTRY: BRAZIL

CAPITAL: BRASILIA

POPULATION (1982 EST): 127700000

AREA IN SQUARE MILES: 3286470

POPULATION DENSITY (PER SQ.MI): 38.86

LATITUDES:

LOW (30S - 30N): X
MIDDLE (31S - 60S):
HIGH (> 60S):
```

```
INDUSTRIES: STEEL, AUTOS, CHEMICALS,
SHIPS, APPLIANCES, SHOES, PAPER,
PETROCHEMICALS, MACHINERY


CROPS: COFFEE, COTTON, SOYBEANS, SUGAR,
COCOA, RICE, CORN, FRUITS


MINERALS: CHROMIUM, IRON, MANGANESE,
TIN, QUARTZ, CRYSTALS, BERYL, SHEET
MICA, COLUMBIUM, TITANIUM, DIAMONDS,
THORIUM, GOLD, NICKEL, GEM STONES, COAL,
TIN, TUNGSTEN, BAUXITE, OIL
```

Figure 3.4.   Record for Brazil.

Most versions of *PFS-File* do not provide an option for computed fields (to do so, the software needs to distinguish numeric and alphanumeric fields). For this database, students can use a calculator to determine population densities and then enter the data to two decimal places. This field is then a fixed-length of five characters (four integers and a decimal point).

Once the database is created, it is ready for use. Now the real power in manipulating data becomes obvious. The two functions of search and sort provide opportunities for looking at data in order to identify patterns, make observations, and test hypotheses. Let us consider some questions we might ask using the database on South American countries.

What country has the largest population and what country has the smallest? The answer can be provided by sorting and displaying the data based on population:

```
COUNTRY: FRENCH GUIANA
POPULATION (1982 EST): 000066800

COUNTRY: SURINAM
POPULATION (1982 EST): 000420000

COUNTRY: GUYANA
POPULATION (1982 EST): 000900000

COUNTRY: URUGUAY
POPULATION (1982 EST): 002934942

COUNTRY: PARAGUAY
POPULATION (1982 EST): 003300000

COUNTRY: BOLIVIA
POPULATION (1982 EST): 005600000

COUNTRY: ECUADOR
POPULATION (1982 EST): 008500000

COUNTRY: CHILE
POPULATION (1982 EST): 011500000

COUNTRY: PERU
POPULATION (1982 EST): 018600000

COUNTRY: VENEZUELA
POPULATION (1982 EST): 018700000

COUNTRY: COLOMBIA
POPULATION (1982 EST): 025600000

COUNTRY: ARGENTINA
POPULATION (1982 EST): 028438000

COUNTRY: BRAZIL
POPULATION (1982 EST): 127700000
```

Figure 3.5. Data sorted by population size.

Figure 3.5 indicates that French Guiana has the smallest population and Brazil the largest.

Does population relate to land size? Sorting the data by area yields:

```
COUNTRY: FRENCH GUIANA
AREA IN SQUARE MILES: 0032252

COUNTRY: SURINAM
AREA IN SQUARE MILES: 0063037

COUNTRY: URUGUAY
AREA IN SQUARE MILES: 0068037

COUNTRY: GUYANA
AREA IN SQUARE MILES: 0083000

COUNTRY: ECUADOR
AREA IN SQUARE MILES: 0108624

COUNTRY: PARAGUAY
AREA IN SQUARE MILES: 0157047

COUNTRY: CHILE
AREA IN SQUARE MILES: 0292135

COUNTRY: VENEZUELA
AREA IN SQUARE MILES: 0352143

COUNTRY: BOLIVIA
AREA IN SQUARE MILES: 0424165

COUNTRY: COLOMBIA
AREA IN SQUARE MILES: 0440831

COUNTRY: PERU
AREA IN SQUARE MILES: 0496222

COUNTRY: ARGENTINA
AREA IN SQUARE MILES: 1065189

COUNTRY: BRAZIL
AREA IN SQUARE MILES: 3286470
```

Figure 3.6. Data sorted by area.

French Guiana has the smallest area and Brazil has the largest. However, there is not a "one-to-one" pairing between the other countries when the two printouts are compared.

This may bring us to consider population density — what countries really have the most people in relation to their area? This time we sort the data by population density:

```
COUNTRY: FRENCH GUIANA
POPULATION DENSITY (PER SQ.MI): 02.07

COUNTRY: SURINAM
POPULATION DENSITY (PER SQ.MI): 06.66

COUNTRY: GUYANA
POPULATION DENSITY (PER SQ.MI): 10.84

COUNTRY: BOLIVIA
POPULATION DENSITY (PER SQ.MI): 13.20

COUNTRY: PARAGUAY
POPULATION DENSITY (PER SQ.MI): 21.00

COUNTRY: ARGENTINA
POPULATION DENSITY (PER SQ.MI): 26.70

COUNTRY: PERU
POPULATION DENSITY (PER SQ.MI): 37.48

COUNTRY: BRAZIL
POPULATION DENSITY (PER SQ.MI): 38.86

COUNTRY: CHILE
POPULATION DENSITY (PER SQ.MI): 39.37

COUNTRY: URUGUAY
POPULATION DENSITY (PER SQ.MI): 43.14

COUNTRY: VENEZUELA
POPULATION DENSITY (PER SQ.MI): 53.10

COUNTRY: COLOMBIA
POPULATION DENSITY (PER SQ.MI): 58.07

COUNTRY: ECUADOR
POPULATION DENSITY (PER SQ.MI): 78.25
```

Figure 3.7. Data sorted by population density.

Now we can make some observations. Ecuador, Colombia, Venezuela, and Uruguay have the highest population densities. Next, let's look at a map of South America. Where are these countries located? What are their climates like? Can we form any hypotheses about why these countries' population densities are so high? Why are the populations of French Guiana, Surinam, and Guyana so low when they are located in low — and more desirable — latitudes and on the coast?

PFS-File has a companion software package, *PFS-Report*, that permits showing data in table form. Using the *Report* software, up to nine columns can be created using fields from a record. The data is sorted either alphabetically or numerically by the first column. Figure 3.8 shows the data sorted numerically by population.

POPULATION/AREA/DENSITY

POPULATION	AREA/SQ MI	POP DEN	COUNTRY
127,700,000	3,286,470	38.86	BRAZIL
28,438,000	1,065,189	26.70	ARGENTINA
25,600,000	440,831	58.07	COLOMBIA
18,700,000	352,143	53.10	VENEZUELA
18,600,000	496,222	37.48	PERU
11,500,000	292,135	39.37	CHILE
8,500,000	108,624	78.25	ECUADOR
5,600,000	424,165	13.20	BOLIVIA
3,300,000	157,047	21.00	PARAGUAY
2,934,942	68,037	43.14	URUGUAY
900,000	83,000	10.84	GUYANA
420,000	63,037	6.66	SURINAM
66,800	32,252	2.07	FRENCH GUIANA

Figure 3.8   Data sorted numerically by population.

PFS-Report allows the user to designate numeric data. When this is done, the data is printed lined up along the decimal points and with commas inserted. Using *Report*, computed columns based on numeric data in other columns are also possible. The user can shorten field names in order to make column headings of proper length.

In addition to sorting the data, the class may want to search through it. For example, what are the most common major crops? Students might hypothesize that coffee is quite common. To test this hypothesis, search the field named CROPS for the occurrence of coffee. *PFS-File* lets us do this, showing each record that includes "coffee," and finishes by reporting how many records were found. In this database, six countries have coffee as a major crop. Figure 3.9 (page 56) summarizes this in a table created using *PFS-Report*.

Using this table, students can make observations about other crops common to this group of countries. In addition, they can perform other searches. What can be said about other crops, industries, or minerals?

More comprehensive searches may be done depending on how the data are arranged. For example: Is coffee a crop in any of those countries located entirely in the middle latitudes or partially in middle and low

COFFEE PRODUCING COUNTRIES

COUNTRY	CROPS
BOLIVIA	POTATOES, SUGAR, COFFEE, BARLEY, COCOA, RICE, CORN, BANANAS, FRUITS
BRAZIL	COFFEE, COTTON, SOYBEANS, SUGAR, COCOA, RICE, CORN, FRUITS
COLOMBIA	COFFEE, RICE, TOBACCO, COTTON, SUGAR, BANANAS
ECUADOR	BANANAS, COFFEE, RICE, GRAINS, FRUITS, COCOA, KAPOK
PERU	COTTON, SUGAR, COFFEE, RICE, POTATOES, BEANS, CORN, BARLEY, TOBACCO
VENEZUELA	COFFEE, RICE, FRUITS, SUGAR

Figure 3.9. Data search for "coffee."

latitudes? One way to answer this question is to search all three latitudes for those countries having coffee as a crop. Figure 3.10 shows that only countries in low latitudes grow coffee beans.

LATITUDE/COFFEE COUNTRIES

COUNTRY	LOW	MIDDLE	HIGH
BOLIVIA	X		
BRAZIL	X		
COLOMBIA	X		
ECUADOR	X		
PERU	X		
VENEZUELA	X		

Figure 3.10. Data search for "coffee" by latitude.

A database of thirteen countries is small, and it can be argued that many of the questions can be answered with the information on index cards. What would happen, however, if we wanted to add many other countries in the world to this database? Should the form be redesigned? Do continents need to be identified as well? A computer database makes data manipulation easy and timely as the database grows.

Setting up a database requires research and thought. What kind of data are you gathering, how do you want the data organized, and what do you hope to do with the data? These questions are not easily answered, but using the design of a database to aid in answering them helps clarify many aspects of the project. Do not be surprised if you create and re-create your database form. Since redesigning a form probably means re-entering all the data, it is a good idea to create a database and try using it with just a few records. If it is the South America database, start with only three or four countries. By using it — by exploring what questions you want to ask — you can determine if it is arranged in a way that makes finding the information possible.

What Skills Do Students Use?

Let's create another database. Suppose students' social studies work focuses on explorers and discoverers. The students create a database of

```
   LNAME:
   FNAME:

   YEAR BORN:
        TOWN:
     COUNTRY:

   YEAR DIED:
        TOWN:
     COUNTRY:

   HOME-BASE COUNTRY:

   EXPLORED BY:

     LAND:      SEA:      AIR:      SPACE:


   WHY EXPLORED:


   ACCOMPLISHMENTS:


   WHAT WAS LEARNED:


   DESCRIPTORS:
```

Figure 3.11.   Record form for explorers database.

explorers to be added to over the weeks of involvement in this unit. To decide what should be in the database and how to design the form, students first need to do some research. They might start with Christopher Columbus, Ferdinand Magellan, Vasco Balboa, and Henry Hudson. These were all explorers who traveled by water. The class needs to discuss what information should be included in the database and how it

```
EXPLORER:

LNAME: COLUMBUS
FNAME: CHRISTOPHER

YEAR BORN: 1451
      TOWN: GENOA
   COUNTRY: ITALY

YEAR DIED: 1506
      TOWN: VALLADOLID
   COUNTRY: SPAIN

HOME-BASE COUNTRY: SPAIN

EXPLORED BY:

   LAND:     SEA: X   AIR:       SPACE:
```
```
WHY EXPLORED: WANTED TO FIND A WESTWARD
WATER ROUTE TO INDIA


ACCOMPLISHMENTS: IN 1492, DISCOVERED THE
NEW WORLD - COMPLETED FOUR VOYAGES TO
THE NEW WORLD


WHAT WAS LEARNED: NEW WORLD DISCOVERED
- INDIA LOCATED TO WEST OF NEW WORLD -
EARTH WAS ROUND (NOT PROVEN)


DESCRIPTORS: NEW WORLD, INDIA, AMERICA,
WESTWARD PASSAGE
```

Figure 3.12.   Record for Columbus (data from *Explorers and Discoverers*).

should be classified — classification skills, indeed, are used extensively in database work.

If this database is being used for older students, a form similar to the one shown in figure 3.11 (page 57) might be developed. Notice that the design of the form requires more advanced thinking as the students do their research. The record for Christopher Columbus is shown in figure 3.12. The first part of the record is factual data. However, to enter information in the fields WHY EXPLORED, ACCOMPLISHMENTS, and WHAT WAS LEARNED requires students' analysis, synthesis, and evaluation skills. Gathering data can go beyond merely finding the facts.

This database has one final field: a DESCRIPTORS field. Assuming that this will be a large database, it is helpful to develop a set of descriptors (terms) useful for describing the work of each explorer. Depending on the thoughtfulness given to this task, the descriptor field becomes helpful in researching and making observations about the history of exploration.

Once the database is created, the questions you and your students ask influence the level of thinking that is achieved. Consider the database for explorers with the following data entered:

EXPLORERS DATABASE

LNAME	FNAME	BORN
BALBOA	VASCO	1475
BERING	VITUS	1681
BYRD	RICHARD	1888
CARTIER	JACQUES	1491
COLUMBUS	CHRISTOPHER	1451
DE SOTO	HERNANDO	1496
GLENN	JOHN	1921
HUDSON	HENRY	1563
MAGELLAN	FERDINAND	1480
PERRY	ROBERT	1856
POLO	MARCO	1254

Figure 3.13. Explorers database.

Suppose we wanted students to make some observations about the search for a westward passage to India. Using the descriptor field in which westward passage is listed for any explorer who sought such a passage and sorting by year of birth, the following information is produced:

```
               EXPLORERS/WESTWARD PASSAGE
  BORN     LNAME       FNAME              LEARNED
  ──────────────────────────────────────────────────
  1451   COLUMBUS   CHRISTOPHER   NEW WORLD DISCOVERED -
                                  INDIA LOCATED TO WEST OF
                                  NEW WORLD - EARTH WAS ROUND
                                  (NOT PROVEN)

  1480   MAGELLAN   FERDINAND     VOYAGE PROVED EARTH WAS
                                  ROUND

  1491   CARTIER    JACQUES       GEOGRAPHY OF CANADA, NEW-
                                  FOUNDLAND AREA

  1563   HUDSON     HENRY         PROVIDED BASIS FOR DUTCH
                                  COLONIZATION - DISPROVED
                                  MYTH THAT THERE WAS AN
                                  ISTHMUS LOCATED AT 40
                                  DEGREE N. LATITUDE
```

Figure 3.14. Searching for "westward passage."

Looking at this data, students can discuss how such a search progressed. Columbus was the first to sail; he did not know what would be discovered; his information influenced later explorers. Magellan traveled south along the coast of South America and did find a passage westward. Cartier went north, hoping to find a passage around the area we know as Canada. Hudson looked for a route that was thought to exist; his explorations disproved the existence of a route in the area we know as New York State.

```
               EXPLORERS/PACIFIC OCEAN
  BORN     LNAME       FNAME              LEARNED
  ──────────────────────────────────────────────────
  1475   BALBOA     VASCO         DISCOVERY SUPPORTED BELIEF
                                  THAT EARTH WAS ROUND - CON-
                                  FIRMED THAT EARTH LARGER THAN
                                  BEEN ASSUMED

  1480   MAGELLAN   FERDINAND     VOYAGE PROVED EARTH WAS ROUND

  1681   BERING     VITUS         NEW MATERIAL ON THE GEOGRAPHY
                                  OF THE NORTHERN PACIFIC AREA
```

Figure 3.15. Searching for "Pacific Ocean."

Using the descriptor field again, we can look for all the explorers whose explorations involved the Pacific Ocean (see figure 3.15). Again, student observations can extend well beyond mere facts.

Databases for Teachers and Students

A natural use of databases is to help teachers organize and manage the administrative aspects of their jobs. Probably one of the first uses for a database is to help design some type of record-keeping file. It might be as simple as one in which each record contains the student's name, homeroom number, and a list of assignments for a social studies unit. As a student completes assignments, he or she can access the database and place an "x" by that assignment. Teachers can quickly search the database to determine which students have completed (or not completed) assignments.

Another type of database is a bibliographical resource. Continuing with the explorers example, envision setting up a database that contains information on books that students use in their research. Each record might include the book title, author, publication date, a brief summary, and a descriptor field for key terms related to the research on explorers. Students add to this database by entering new books or by adding to the descriptor field of a book already entered. They can also use it as a resource to help locate reference sources.

Databases to be used with such software as *PFS-File* are now being commercially produced. For example, Scholastic has available curriculum databases on U. S. History that cover the twentieth century, inventions, and the American frontier. Also available are data files on the American Government: elections and voting patterns, the size of and spending in the Federal government, and the Constitutional Convention (see resource section).

To emphasize the value of databases in a variety of fields, students can design databases for a variety of "clients." Clients might be parents who need some type of business application completed, such as a mailing list or a product inventory, or other teachers who want help organizing their record-keeping systems. Students can be encouraged to seek relevant career applications of databases as part of a unit on careers.

Commercial Databases

The use of computerized databases is ubiquitous. Airline reservation systems involve databases of flight and passenger information. Lawyers make use of a variety of databases that, among other things, provide full texts of court decisions, statutes, and regulations. High school students use the Academic American Encyclopedia (an electronic encyclopedia) provided on some information utilities. Fast food restaurants use databases for inventory control and product-purchasing decisions. Baseball coaches use databases to provide data showing players' hitting and pitching performances against other teams in order to plan lineup and playing decisions during a game.

Many more databases are being created. *Bionet* will provide information on genetics and permit scientists to formulate and share theories and methods with other scientists throughout the country instantaneously. The Oxford University Press is in the process of computerizing their unabridged version of the *Oxford English Dictionary* because it is no longer practical or economical to update it using traditional typesetting methods. The computerized version will open up new areas of research not possible before.

Databases can be classified by the kind of information they contain or by their purpose (Edlehart and Davies, 1983). Information may be in the form of numbers or words. Numeric databases generally contain raw data in the form of strings of numbers or equations. Alphanumeric databases contain both numbers and text — the majority of databases are alphanumeric. Databases may be used as references. Such databases contain bibliographical information that provides some information and directs the user to other sources for additional information. Source databases contain complete information all in one place. For example, the full text of the *Wall Street Journal* is available through the Dow Jones News/Retrieval Information Service. Problem-oriented databases help the user learn about a particular problem such as pollution. Discipline-oriented databases focus on gathering information in a particular field. LEXIS is a law database. Finally, inter- and multidisciplinary databases cover more than one field. Social SciSearch, one such example, is described below.

What Do You Need To Do To Get On-Line?

In order to use a commercial or public database, you must "link" yourself to it via a telecommunications network, a network of telephone lines and computers. Networks usually provide local telephone numbers for connecting to the network. Once "on-line," you can potentially access any of the databases available through that network.

To turn a computer into a telecommunications tool, both hardware and software are needed. The computer has to connect to a telephone line and transmit and receive data in a certain way. This requires an RS-232 communications board and a port, which may come built into the computer and which makes it possible to transmit and receive data. The port provides a plug for the other piece of hardware needed — a modem. This device plugs into a telephone or telephone jack and permits data to be transmitted over the telephone lines to the computer. A communications software package that lets you dial up a network and use a database might also be needed.

In a variety of instances, producers of databases do not market the computerized versions themselves. Arrangements are made with vendors to provide the computers, enter the data, develop the search languages, and handle the finances. A single vendor therefore may provide access to several different databases. Two of the largest vendors are DIALOG Information Services and Bibliographic Retrieval Services (BRS). Telecommunications networks provide the communication links to suscribers of such services by means of telephone lines, computers, and microwave transmitting stations. Three of the major networks in America are Telenet, Tymshare, and Uninet. When using a database accessed through an on-line vendor, you actually "talk" only to the telecommunications network; this network, in turn, "talks" to the computer where the database is located.

What Information Can You Find On-Line?

Databases are historical in nature and may be used to provide historical or current information about almost any topic. In particular, there are a variety of databases relevant for use in the social studies. Some examples with descriptions follow.

> *CENDATA* provides data from current surveys and periodic censuses. Household data, population data, and demographic data is available.

> *ERIC* is a general educational database. It includes abstracts of instructional materials and abstracts of research materials and is a major resource for educators.

> *American: History and Life (AHL)* covers U.S. and Canadian history from prehistoric times to the present, area studies, and current affairs.

> *LEXIS* is a legal database which provides the full texts of court decisions, statutes, regulations, and other legal matters.

> *Biography Master Index* is a bibliographical database. It provides basic information about historical and current prominent figures and gives directions to locating printed biographies.

> *Historical Abstracts* holds citations and abstracts of worldwide historical literature appearing in journals, books, and dissertations for the past three years.

> *NEWSEARCH* is a general-interest database designed to provide easy access to current references.

> *NEXIS* provides general news and business information, giving access to full texts of articles from newspapers, magazines, newsletters, newswires, and related special-interest services.

Social SciSearch is one of the largest and most generally useful databases in the social sciences. It is multidisciplinary and covers many social-service journals and journals in the natural, physical, and biomedical sciences as well as monographs, conference reports, and reviews.

The above are only a small sampling of the databases available. Edlehart and Davies (1983, 1985), in the *OMNI Online Database Directory*, describe a number of the available databases, major on-line vendors, and information utilities (The Source and CompuServe), and provide a telecommunications directory. Their book is an invaluable resource.

Though not databases in the traditional sense, information utilities maintain an extensive number of information files in order to make a variety of data available to the general on-line user. Included are data on finance and business, shop-at-home services, entertainment, gardening, the industrial outlook, ski conditions, and much more. Two of the major information utilities providing such extensive services are The Source from Source Telecomputing Corporation and CompuServe from H. & R. Block. Such utilities generally require a one-time registration or subscription fee plus the costs for the "connect" time and telephone charges while using the service. CompuServe's connect charges are in the range of $5–$25 per hour depending on time of day and other factors.

CompuServe is menu-driven, which means that you proceed through a variety of program menus in order to find the services you want. Its main menu offers choices such as: Home Services, Business and Financial, Personal Computing, Services for Professionals, User Information, and Index.

```
Enter choice or <CR> for more !T

CompuServe

    1 Tour of the Service
    2 Sample Menus of the Service
    3 What's New
    4 Subscriber Information
    5 Find a Topic

Last menu page, enter choice !2

CompuServe

    1 Subscriber Assistance
    2 Find a Topic
    3 Communications/Bulletin Bds.
    4 News/Weather/Sports
```

(continued)

```
 5 Travel
 6 The Electronic MALL/Shopping
 7 Money Matters/Markets
 8 Entertainment/Games
 9 Home/Health/Family
10 Reference/Education
11 Computers/Technology
12 Business/Other Interests

Enter choice !10

CompuServe
```

REFERENCE/EDUCATION leads you to electronic reference
materials such as encyclopedias and government
publications. It also takes you to educational services
for teachers, parents and students, as well as special
features relating to special education and handicapped
issues. Grolier's Academic American, U.S. Government
publications, demographic information, and Information
U.S.A., a service that details the volumes of free
information offered by the U.S. Government, are just a few
of the services available.
The following page shows the various sections of this
area.

Press <CR> for more !

CompuServe

```
REFERENCE
  * IQuest
  * Academic Am. Encyclopedia ($)
  * Government Information
  * Demographics (W)
  * Other Reference Sources
EDUCATION
  * Services for Educators
  * Services for the Handicapped
  * Services for Students/Parents
  * Educational Games
  * Educational Forums
```

Figure 3.16. *CompuServe.*

In hierarchical fashion, these choices lead to several branching
menus. Selecting Reference/Education sends you to a menu from which
you then can choose (for example) the Academic American Encyclopedia, published by Grolier, and to other services such as news and sports
articles.

Such utilities also provide a few services that are interactive, letting users communicate directly with one another. In CompuServe three such services are the CB Simulator, the National Bulletin Board Service, and E Mail. These services provide opportunities for electronic mail, computer conferencing, and electronic bulletin-boarding. A variety of other on-line networks, in addition to information utilities, focus directly on such interactive services. All are variations in the use of computer-based message systems. These services involve the delivery of messages and data via telecommunication networks from one computer to another. Interchanges between people using computer message systems may involve real-time interactions — people currently on-line and communicating with one another from their respective computers or terminals — or messages may be "delivered" to electronic mailboxes to be read at a later time. Either way, such systems bypass the normal delays of the postal service and the frustration sometimes experienced in trying to reach someone by phone. Electronic mail reduces the "information float" — the time when information is in transit and, therefore, not being used.

Information utilities provide real opportunities for "linking" students from many different parts of the country — or of the world — together in interactive networks. As an example, students living in La Jolla, California, and students living in a remote Eskimo village near the Arctic Circle became pen pals. These third- and fourth-grade students were participating in a writing program in which the idea was to improve children's writing by providing a ready audience of other American children who lived quite different lifestyles. Using a computer in the classroom, children typed messages that were later entered into an electronic mail account maintained on The Source. Through The Source, the messages were sent to Fairbanks, Alaska, and, from there via satellite, to Wainwright, the Eskimo village. Unlike traditional pen-pal communications, correspondence occurred quickly and back-and-forth queries encouraged thoughtful exploration of lifestyles to motivate the students to write further (*Boston Sunday Globe,* 5/22/83).

How Do You Use an On-Line Database?

On-line searching costs money. One of the key skills involved in using a database is knowing how to conduct a computer on-line search. This requires a general understanding of search languages and the ability to use enough symbolic logic to perform an *economical* search. Prior to initiating a search, a user should determine as specifically as possible the information required. This helps keep costs down once on-line.

Suppose students are involved in a unit on immigrant labor. One aspect of their study involves the current status of immigration in the United States. A place to search for the most recent articles is *NEW-SEARCH*. After signing onto this database, such a search might proceed as follows:

Note: Three column headings are printed. The first, SET, refers to the number of the current set of information. The second column, ITEMS, tells how many articles are in this set. The final column, DESCRIPTION, notes the word or words that were used to find these articles. The information after the "?" is typed by the user. It directs the search for all articles. The first search (shown below) is a full-text search (title, abstract, and descriptor fields). This is set 1, and four articles have been found that contain the word *immigrant* somewhere in the text.

```
                      SET       ITEMS      DESCRIPTION
?SS IMMIGRANT
                       1          4        IMMIGRANT
```

In the second search (below), only the descriptor field of all articles is searched. When completed, set 2 contains no articles. This indicates that *immigrant* is not a descriptor in this database. A database thesaurus would have helped.

```
                      SET       ITEMS      DESCRIPTION
?SS IMMIGRANT/DE
                       2          0        IMMIGRANT/DE
```

Next, a search of the descriptor fields for *immigration* yields ninety articles in set 3. A full-text search for *immigration* yields ninety-four articles in set 4. This means that there are four articles that have the term *immigration* in a text that is not part of the descriptor field.

```
                      SET       ITEMS      DESCRIPTION
?SS IMMIGRATION/DE
                       3         90        IMMIGRATION/DE
?SS IMMIGRATION
                       4         94        IMMIGRATION
```

Finally, both a full-text and a descriptor field search for *labor* are done. Then, the number of articles that have both *immigration* (set 4) and *labor* (set 5) somewhere in the text is determined (set 6). The last search narrows the search significantly. There are six articles.

```
                      SET       ITEMS      DESCRIPTION
?SS LABOR
                       5         440       LABOR
?SS LABOR/DE
                       6         290       LABOR/DE
?SS S4 AND S5
                       7          6        4 AND 5
```

Figure 3.17 shows printouts of descriptions of these articles provided on the database.

```
DIALNET: call cleared by request

Enter Service:


VER 1.4.00
CDI MINITERM SERIES 2000   2K CMOS RAM

Dialog Information Services' DIALNET
-2055:01-004-
Enter Service: dialog2

DIALNET: call connected

DIALOG INFORMATION SERVICES
PLEASE LOGON:
?********
ENTER PASSWORD:
?********

Welcome to DIALOG
Dialog version 2, level 10.14.12 B

        Set   Items   Description
        ---   -----   -----------
?ss immigration/de
        S1     109   IMMIGRATION/DE
?t 1/5/1-7

1419627    DATABASE: NNI File 111
 Litigation, deep debt and birth. (religious lawsuits,
racism, and immigration in the Northwest) (column)
Turner, Wallace
New York Times   v136   p8(N) pA16(L) Nov 24 1986
CODEN: NYTIA
col 1    018col in.
EDITION: Mon
ARTICLE TYPE: column
GEOGRAPHIC LOCATION: Northwestern States; Soviet Union
GEOGRAPHIC CODE: NNUSO; EEUR
NAMED PEOPLE: Ellis, Henry Day--cases; Miles, Robert
E.--public opinion; Finkel, Matvei--emigration and immi-
gration; Graham, Susan--public opinion
 DESCRIPTORS: Northwestern States--social conditions;
Racism--public opinion; Endowments--cases; Nuns--cases;
Jews in Soviet Union--emigration and immigration

 1/5/2
1417315    DATABASE: NNI File 111
 Immigration law sets off dispute over job rights for
legal aliens.
 Pear, Robert                                  (continued)
```

Figure 3.17. *continued*

New York Times   v136   Section 1   p1(N) p1(L)   Nov
23 1986
 CODEN: NYTIA
 col 1   019 col in.
 EDITION: Sun
 DESCRIPTORS: Aliens--legal status, laws, etc.; Emigration and immigration law--interpretation and
construction; Discrimination in employment--Law and legislation; Civil rights--law and legislation

 1/5/3
1417253   DATABASE: NNI File 111
 To overhaul the rules on lookout procedures for for-
eigners. (letter to the editor)
 Meissner, Doris M.
 New York Times   v136   Section 4   pE24(N) pE24(L)   Nov
23 1986
 CODEN: NYTIA
 col 4   007 col in.
 ARTICLE TYPE: letter to the editor
 DESCRIPTORS: Aliens--legal status, laws, etc.; Emigration and immigration law--interpretation and
construction; United States. Immigration and Naturalization Service--rules and regulations

 1/5/4
1417223   DATABASE: NNI File 111
 Immigration problems are perplexing Canada.
 Martin, Douglas
 New York Times   v136   Section 1   p18(N) p34(L)   Nov
23   1986
 CODEN: NYTIA
 col 1   014 col in.
 EDITION: Sun
 GEOGRAPHIC LOCATION: Canada
 GEOGRAPHIC CODE: NNCN
 DESCRIPTORS: Canada--emigration and immigration;
Aliens, Illegal--Canada Emigration and immigration law--
Canada; Refugees--Canada

 1/5/6
1417222   DATABASE: NNI File 111
 Some deportations suspended. (U.S. illegal aliens)
 New York Times   v136   Section 1   p18(N)   Nov 23   1986
 CODEN: NYTIA
 col 5   004 col in.
 EDITION: Sun
 DESCRIPTORS: Aliens, Illegal--legal status, laws, etc.;
Deportation--rules and regulations; United States.
Immigration and Naturalization Service--rules and reg-
ulations

(continued)

Figure 3.17. *continued*

```
1/5/6
1411284   DATABASE: NNI File 111
Mozambique reports 200,000 fled to Malawi,
New York Times    v136   P2(N)   PA10(L)   Nov 20   1986
CODEN: NYTIA
col 2    009 col in,
EDITION: Thu
GEOGRAPHIC LOCATION: Mozambique; Malawi
GEOGRAPHIC CODE: FSMZ; FSMW
DESCRIPTORS: Mozambique--emigration and immigration;
Malawi--emigration and immigration; Mozambique National
Resistance--military policy; Government, Resistance to--
Mozambique

    1/5/7
1407646   DATABASE: NNI File 111
INS exempts aliens caught near border from rights policy,
(Immigration and Naturalization Service)
McDonnell, Patrick
Los Angeles Times    v105    Section I   P3   Nov 18   1986
col 5    020 col in,
EDITION: Tue
Immigration Reform and Control Act of 1986 interpreta-
tion and construction
DESCRIPTORS: United States, Immigration and Naturaliza-
tion Service--rules and regulations; Aliens, Illegal--
legal status, laws, etc,; Emigration and immigration
law--interpretation and construction
?logoff
        25nov86 13:15:19 User 026486
    $2,16    0,018 Hrs File211
            $0,70   7 Types in format   5
    $0,70  7 Types
    $0,14  Dialnet
    $3,00  Estimated cost this file
    $3,11  Estimated total session cost   0,21 Hrs,
Logoff: level 10,14,12 B 13:15:19
```

Figure 3.17. *Newsearch.*

Using such a search, students can quickly determine what the current issues are with regard to immigration. These can then be compared and contrasted with other perspectives. Students can also use, as another component of such a unit, a software-based curriculum package called *Immigrant*, which involves students in a simulation dealing with the Irish immigration to Boston, 1840-1870.

How Should You and Your Students Evaluate a Database?

When you use databases, you generally use information that has been indexed, classified, and selected based on criteria determined by the vendor. This puts limits on your options to determine classifications and indexing techniques. It is not the same as going to a library and establishing your own search strategy using original text material. The extent to which this may narrow or bias the data needs to be considered. Consequently, you need to be concerned with:

1. The completeness and accuracy of the information:

    Is the data full-text, summarized, or bibliographical information?

    Is it interpreted data or raw data?

    Does it cover all major sources in a field?

    How current is the information?

    For example, information in *NEWSEARCH* is updated daily and retained for one month. It is not an archival database. It references a broad range of magazines, law and trade journals, business and management publications, and five major newspapers. Because of the extent of its sources, it is a good first database to search.

2. How you can search and use the information:

    Are you limited to the subject headings, descriptors, or other indexing conventions associated with the database?

    Can you "create" your own descriptors by doing your own word or phrase searches?

    Are only indexed terms searched or can the entire text be searched for keywords?

    Does the system of indexing preclude certain kinds of searches, certain ways of exploring the information?

    Can you limit a search in different ways, e.g. by dates, number of years, word combinations?

    Are abstracts provided or just bibliographical references?

    The *ERIC* database has an extensive indexing system. In preparation for a search, a thesaurus is used. Major descriptors, together with explanations, are identified. In addition, broader and narrower terms are provided. The descriptors are located in the descriptor field of each entry. Searching the descriptor field for words taken from the thesaurus is faster and more precise than other types of searches. In addition, free-text search in which the entire contents are searched is possible. This permits the user to search for material that may not be included as a descriptor in the indexing systems.

3. The characteristics of the database:

    How large is the database? Size relates both to amount of data and to searching strategies and time. It may not be better to use a large database if a smaller one provides the data needed.

    How does the database compare with hard copy references? Abstracts are someone else's summaries of original sources. It is wise to compare abstracts with the printed sources.

    What are the print, display, and storage options? For example, when using *ERIC*, any of the fields of a record can be displayed. To avoid the time and cost of obtaining a printout of the desired abstracts during a search, a printed copy can be ordered at the end of a search, with delivery in approximately one week.

    To involve students in thinking about such questions, pose the following problem:

    > The student must be prepared to make a presentation in class the next day on a previously assigned topic. For this report, the student is expected to make use of a single database to gather the information needed. (Ideally, databases would be only one resource.) The student has access to a number of databases through the school library. Several of the databases might provide the information needed, and the student is not limited by cost of use. What questions should this student ask about available databases in order to help select the right one?

    Because databases have their own informational concerns, students' understanding of the need to evaluate such sources is important.

New Advances in Providing Access to Databases

A new medium for providing access to databases is the CD-ROM (Compact Disk–Read Only Memory). Information may only be read from the disk; it cannot be recorded on the disk. The CD-ROM looks exactly like an audio compact-disk. Grolier Electronic Publishing has stored the entire contents of the *Academic American Encyclopedia* — over 30,000 articles — on such a disk. This information takes up less than half a disk that has the capacity to store 550 million bits of information. An equivalent amount of information would fill 1,500 floppy disks.

The encyclopedia can be searched by any word or combination of words using extremely easy-to-use search software (a database management system) provided on a floppy disk (see figure 3.18). To access information on the CD-ROM, a special disk drive that attaches to a personal computer is required. The whole package, including the special disk drive, interface card and cable for the computer, disk containing the

Figure 3.18 Grolier's Electronic Encyclopedia.

encyclopedia, and search software can be purchased for approximately $1100. Once the hardware is purchased, the cost of adding another disk of information is around $200.

Imagine the implications of this technology for the classroom. From a shelf-storage perspective, every classroom could theoretically contain all the written knowledge possibly needed by the student or teacher for any course or year's work. The cost might prevent such a collection, but the ease of accessing informaton should make the budgeting for such purchases very enticing. In addition to locating information within fractions of a second, selected information can be stored on floppy disks and then, using an ordinary word processor, incorporated into a document. Both the commercial and educational applications have yet to be explored.

Summary

Students need to be skilled in the use of databases and information utilities as well as in development of their own databases. Teaching that encompasses these skills looks at learning from a different perspective. How is information located? What understanding is needed about data classification and data organization? What evaluative judgments should be applied to selecting and using information? These questions, as well as others, focus on the methods of inquiry, rather than the specific content, of the social studies curriculum. In chapter 4 we look at additional, more specialized tools that also encourage inquiry.

References

Brevdy, J. "Think Tank." *InfoWorld*, 6, 34 (1984) 59-60.

Edelhart, M. and Davies, O. *OMNI Online Database Directory.* New York: Collier Books, 1983, 1985.

Educational Research Council Social Science Program. *Explorers and Discoverers.* Boston: Allyn & Bacon, 1977.

Healy, M.K. "Purpose in Learning to Write: An Approach to Writing in Three Curriculum Areas." In Frederiksen, C.H. and Dominic, J.F. (eds) *Writing: The Nature, Development, and Teaching of Written Communication,* vol. 2. Hillsdale, N.J.: Lawrence Earlbaum Associates, 1981. 223–233.

Lye, K. *Explorers.* Morristown, N.J.: Silver Burdett, 1981.

National Council for the Social Studies. "In Search of a Scope and Sequence for the Social Studies." *Social Education,* April, 1984, 249–273.

Taba, H. *Curriculum Development.* New York: Harcourt, Brace & World, 1962.

The World Almanac and Book of Facts 1984. New York: Newspaper Enterprise Association, Inc., 1983.

Xenakis, J.J. "You Have a Friend in a Database Manager." *Computer Update,* 7 (1984) 38–42.

Using Specialized Computer Tools in the Social Studies

Programs that help display and analyze data are discussed in this chapter. These programs can be considered specific-purpose tools. Such tools may be used for social science research activities — activities that often are not employed in the social studies curriculum. With the availability of such tools, students can become more involved in the inquiry-related applications of social studies.

Visually representing data is important in social studies. There are a variety of programs that can help students create graphs to display data. Bar, circle, and line graphs are used extensively in magazines, newspapers, textbooks, and many other daily reading sources. To understand and respond to information presented in this format, students not only need skills in reading graphs, they must also become adept at interpreting and evaluating the information that graphs provide.

One of the more common means of gathering information is through the use of some type of survey. Once the information is gathered, graphing software can be used to display data. Often use of elementary statistics is helpful in describing the data. There is a growing number of programs that can provide assistance in computing measures that describe data in interesting ways.

Another tool that has potential applications in the social studies is the spreadsheet program. Such programs can be used not only to store information but also to explore various options through "what if" thinking. Depending on their use, these programs are applicable at many different grade levels.

Data Display — Using Graphs

An important component in data analysis is communicating information through the use of tables and graphs. Tables help students arrange data in rows and columns so they can look at large amounts of information at one time. Graphs — picture, bar, pie, and line graphs — let students picture information in selected ways that not only communicate "a thousand words" but also influence the interpretation of the information shown.

A growing number of computer programs are available that can help students perform various data analysis activities, such as preparing and printing tables and graphs. However, in the enthusiasm to use such software, the teacher should not overlook why concrete representation of graphing concepts is needed. Avoid having the computer perform as a "magic box." Provide students with the appropriate experiences that help them understand the graphing concepts and grasp why a computer is suitable for use in creating graphs.

For any data analysis activity, students must decide:

1. what data is needed,

2. how to collect the data,

3. how to organize the data,

4. what graphs are appropriate for displaying the data, and

5. what scales are appropriate for the graph(s).

Then students must be able to construct the graphs (by hand or through the use of graphics software) and, more importantly, to interpret the data in some meaningful way. For beginning graphing activities, data can be gathered from students' experiences and background or can be provided by the teacher. Later, students may be encouraged to explore activities that require the use of sources such as almanacs, encyclopedias, or newspapers.

Bar graphs are very useful for making comparisons of two or more sets of data. To introduce the concept of a vertical bar graph in the elementary grades, start by determining how many boys and how many girls are in the class. After the data have been gathered, create a table that summarizes this information. Important parts of the table are the title, the column and row labels, and the numbers that represent the occurrences of the data (see figure 4.1).

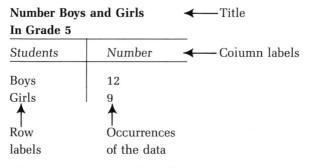

Figure 4.1 Structure of a table.

To construct a bar graph using this data (figure 4.2), the vertical axis (labeled "Number") is scaled by whole numbers and is used to show "how many." The horizontal axis is labeled "Students." Using the row labels from the table (Boys, Girls), the bars are also labeled. The height of each bar, when compared with the scale on the vertical axis, shows "how many" were counted. Note that the width of each bar is the same. The title is also shown on the graph.

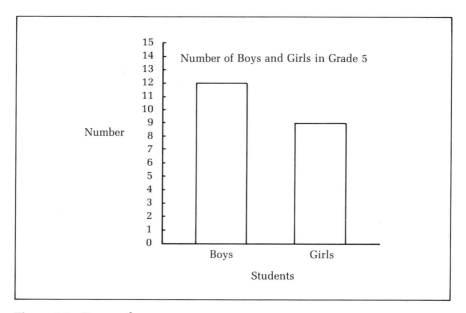

Figure 4.2 Bar graph.

Extending this introduction so that students' experience using data involves more than a two-bar graph, students can gather data on how students in the class usually travel to school. They need to determine the modes of transportation classmates use, such as school bus, car, bike, and walking, and then construct a table and, from that, a bar graph (see figures 4.3 and 4.4).

How Students Come to School — Grade 5 & 6

Mode	Number
Bus	27
Car	5
Walk	10
Bike	2

Figure 4.3   Student transportation table.

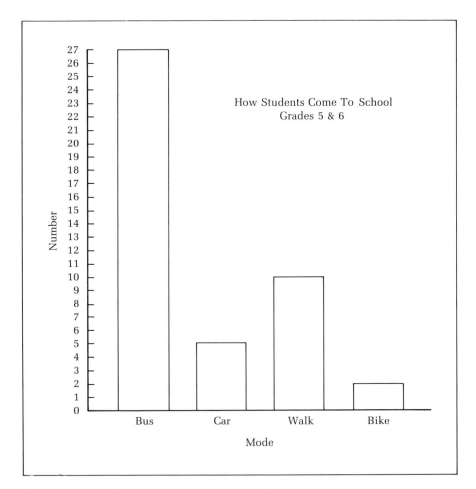

Figure 4.4   Student transportation bar graph.

After students are introduced to bar graphs, the teacher can develop a variety of data-collection activities to use when introducing computer-generated bar graphs. Some activities involve the use of data from a database. For example, students might use the South America database and create a bar graph showing the populations of each of the countries. Using *PFS-Graph*, a companion software package to *PFS-File*, it is possible to create bar, line, and pie graphs. *PFS-Graph* uses the database to create a table that displays nation names and populations (see figure 4.5).

	POPULATION
FRENCH GUIANA	66800
VENEZUELA	1.87000E7
URUGUAY	2.93494E6
SURINAM	4.20000E5
PERU	1.86000E7
PARAGUAY	3.30000E6
GUYANA	9E5
ECUADOR	8.50000E6
COLOMBIA	2.56000E7
CHILE	1.15000E7
BRAZIL	1.27700E8
BOLIVIA	5.60000E6
ARGENTINA	2.84380E7

Figure 4.5.   South American data in tabular form.

In this table, most of the populations, because they are large numbers, are written in scientific notation. To read such a number, shift the decimal point to the right the number of places shown after the "E." For example, 4.20000E5 means multiply 4.20000 by 10 raised to the fifth power (10^5 or 100,000), which shifts the decimal point five places to the right to give 420,000. For the population of Colombia, 2.56000E7 is 25,600,000.

Using *PFS-Graph*, students can label the horizontal and vertical axes, add a title to the graph, and set the range (minimum and maximum values) and scale of the vertical axis (*PFS-Graph* does this last part automatically if students do not). Figure 4.6 on page 80 shows the graph of the population data.

Figure 4.6 highlights some of the difficulties that can be encountered when there is a large range in the data. In this case the range of the populations is 66,800 (French Guiana) to 127,700,000 (Brazil). Because of the specifications for graphs in the software, it is not possible to have a graph that shows a bar for the populations of French Guiana, Surinam and Guyana. Could the students design such a graph by hand? What would be changed? (The vertical axis would need to be expanded to accommodate a more detailed scale.) Another solution is to graph the population data excluding Brazil, changing the maximum value for the range to 30 million instead of 130 million (see figure 4.7 on page 80).

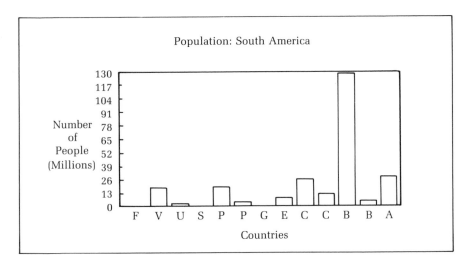

Figure 4.6   South American data in graphic form.

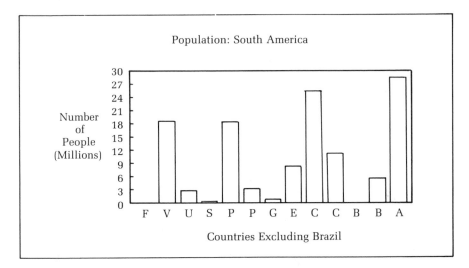

Figure 4.7   South American data excluding Brazil.

Students can think of this as "zooming in" on a portion of the original graph much like a zoom lens might do in photography. While noted as a country on the graph, Brazil's population is not shown. If it were shown, it would appear as a bar that extends to (and beyond) the top of the chart. Bars for the populations of Surinam and Guyana now appear, but French Guiana is still not shown. What other countries might be excluded in order to "zoom in" on a still smaller portion of the graph? How would the maximum value for the range be changed?

Students should compare and contrast the usefulness of information presented in a table and that of information presented in a graph. When is one method better than the other for clarifying or interpreting information?

Students can also use data for making graphs that have been stored in a database. Students in the middle grades, for example, might focus on the impact of immigration on America's growth as part of a larger unit of study. In one activity, students compare the immigration history of their families (and consequently also of the town in which they live) with that of the United States. To do this, students determine the country of origin of different family members. Using *The World Almanac*, the same data is gathered for the United States. Figure 4.8 shows a table with tallies of this information. Student data (headed "Families") was gathered from a group of middle school students in a New England town near Boston.

The data in figure 4.8 need to be redefined. It is quickly apparent that the U. S. data is in thousands while the family data is not. Comparing the

IMMIGRATION BY COUNTRY OF ORIGIN
(EUROPEAN COUNTRIES ONLY) 1820-1980

THOUSANDS

COUNTRY:	FAMILIES	% TOTAL	U.S.A.	% TOTAL
AUSTRIA/HUNGARY	7	4.4	4317	11.9
BELGIUM	2	1.3	204	.6
CZECHOSLOVAKIA	2	1.3	139	.4
DENMARK	0	0	365	1
FINLAND	0	0	33	.1
FRANCE	5	3.1	755	2.1
GERMANY	11	6.9	6990	19.2
GREAT BRITAIN	6	3.8	4927	13.6
GREECE	7	4.4	664	1.8
IRELAND	44	27.7	4732	13
ITALY	41	25.8	5304	14.6
NETHERLANDS	4	2.5	361	1
NORWAY	0	0	856	2.4
POLAND	6	3.8	524	1.4
PORTUGAL	0	0	458	1.3
SPAIN	0	0	263	.7
SWEDEN	5	3.1	1274	3.5
SWITZERLAND	5	3.1	351	1
USSR	5	3.1	3385	9.3
YUGOSLAVIA	3	1.9	117	.3
OTHER EUROPE	6	3.8	311	.9
	159	100	36330	100

*DATA FROM 1984 WORLD ALMANAC P. 204

Figure 4.8.   Student data compared to U.S. data.

data in its present form creates an inconveniently large range and, like the South American populations, presents problems of scale in graphing it. One way to redefine the data is to express it as percentages. For students' family data, the total number of immigrants must be determined, with each data item expressed as a percentage of the total. The total is 159 immigrants. The percentage of immigrants from Austria/Hungary is 4.4 (7 divided by 159). Similar categorization and division to find percentages are done for the U. S. data. Using a spreadsheet (see "Spreadsheets," on page 100, for an explanation), the table in figure 4.8 shows both the original data and the data expressed as percentages.

	FAMILIES	UNITED STATES
AUSTRIA/HUNGARY	4.40	11.90
FRANCE	3.10	2.10
GERMANY	6.90	19.20
GREAT BRITAIN	3.80	13.60
GREECE	4.40	1.80
IRELAND	27.70	13
ITALY	25.80	14.60
NETHERLANDS	2.50	1
POLAND	3.80	1.40
SWEDEN	3.10	3.50
SWITZERLAND	3.10	1
OTHER EUROPE	3.80	0.90
USSR	3.10	9.30

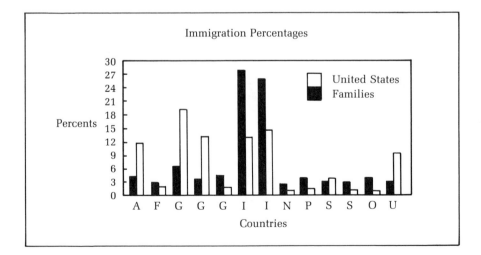

Figure 4.9. Table and graph comparing country-of-origin for students' families and U.S. in total.

Using *PFS-Graph*, students create two tables, entering names and percentages for each country. Excluded from the tables are countries with 0 in the students' family data and countries in which the percentage both in students' family data and in U. S. data is less than 2 percent. A bar graph is created, showing the data from these two tables (see figure 4.9).

What observations can students make about the immigration of their families (and town) as it compares to that of the United States? From the graph, it can be seen that a greater number of the students' families emigrated from Ireland and Italy than is true for the United States as a whole. Also, fewer numbers of immigrants were from Austria/Hungary, Germany, Great Britain, and the U. S. S. R. Are there other regions in the United States that were more heavily settled by immigrants from just a few countries? Why might this happen?

After students have had experiences creating bar graphs by hand, they are delighted to find software that makes the task easier. An "ah-ha" experience occurs the first time data is entered and displayed by a computer. Students quickly want to try using other kinds of graphs.

It is important to build similar understanding of the other kinds of graphs. Making graphs by hand and then having students discuss what they think a computer must do to their data to make similar graphs is important.

Finally, students must recognize that not all graphs can be used to communicate all kinds of information. Bar and picture graphs are appropriate for showing comparisons of most kinds of data. A pie or area graph requires knowing a "whole" and the "parts," such as the population of the world and individual country populations, or a "whole set" of team scores plus individual players' scores. A line graph connects points of data and displays trends such as in the stock market, in weather temperature, or in population changes over several years. Graphs are useful devices for stimulating speculation about the future based on past behavior. This encourages estimating and predicting — skills important in higher-level thinking.

Conducting Surveys

Surveys provide a method for gathering information about people and their activities. The surveys may concern demographics, the social environment, or the activities, opinions, or attitudes of people. Generally, surveys are given to a "sample" of individuals in order to learn something about a larger population of which the sample group is a part. Gallup polls, Harris surveys, market and opinion research, political polling, and town-planning surveys are all familar examples.

Surveys can serve a variety of purposes. A descriptive survey is used to provide facts. Data from such a survey may be used to describe a wide range of conditions, relationships, and behaviors. Explanatory surveys gather data that can be used to explain different relationships and develop observations of cause and effect. Surveys may be conducted to gather data that lead to the development of a hypothesis which, in turn, may be tested through the use of surveys.

Surveys can be classified in a number of ways:

1. By the size and type of sample used. How many people are involved in a survey? Are the people part of a special population such as doctors, teachers, the elderly, or high school juniors?
2. By the method of data collection. There are mail surveys, telephone surveys, personal interview surveys, and newer methods that record responses directly into computers.
3. By the content. The focus may be on what people think (attitudes and opinions), on what they do (behavior and activities), on how they live (social environment), or on certain facts about them (demographic characteristics) (Ferber, 1980).

Sampling may involve the whole population. The U. S. Census is an example of a demographic survey that involves the entire U. S. population. However, most samples do not include the entire population. Before selecting a sample, the target population must be defined. It might be people, such as all the people in the U. S., all the people in a given city, or all the teenagers in a specific location; or it might be organizations, such as businesses or government agencies. The reliability of survey results used as description or explanation of a target population depends directly on the care given in the selection of the sample.

Surveys are one of the common ways for conducting social science research. Because they find it relatively easy, students naturally gravitate to this method of research for gathering certain data. Using database, graphing, and specialized survey software to aid in the analysis of the results concentrates students' time on the meaning rather than the counting of the data.

The U. S. Census is an interesting model for students to explore. It provides an official count of the total number of people in the nation every ten years. Also included is information on such characteristics as age, sex, and marital status. While everyone completes a census questionnaire, some people's questionnaires are more extensive than others. The government actually uses both the whole population and a selected sample of the population in gathering data. The Census is required by the U. S. Constitution, and data concerning the count of the population is used to determine the number of seats each state has in the House of Representatives in Congress. The other data provide an opportunity to describe some of the characteristics of the U. S. population.

One activity that provides a variety of data analysis experiences is the conducting by students of their own census survey of their school or school district. To do this, it is ideal to start with a copy of the actual U. S. Census form, having students determine what data are collected and why and for whom this data might be valuable. The task is to design a school census form to collect data about questions of interest. With these facts, a variety of explorations are possible. Many may involve the use of computer software. Figure 4.10 shows a (completed) sample census form that was used by some intermediate school students. Such a form could easily be adapted for older students.

```
MALE:                 FEMALE: X

WHERE YOU LIVE:

CITY: HOMETOWN            STATE:  MA

WHERE YOU WERE BORN:

CITY: MYTOWN              STATE:  MA

MONTH YOU WERE BORN:

JAN-MARCH:            APRIL-JUNE: X
JULY-SEPT:              OCT-DEC:

YEAR BORN:  1973        GRADE:  6

1.  WHAT KIND OF LIVING QUARTERS?

    HOUSE: X
    APARTMENT:
    CONDOMINIUM:
    2-4 FAMILY HOUSE:
    MOBILE HOME OR TRAILER:
    OTHER-SPECIFY:

2.  DO YOU:

    HAVE YOUR OWN BEDROOM:  X
    SHARE A BEDROOM:

3.  HOW MANY TV'S IN HOUSEHOLD?:

    0:      1:      2:      3 OR MORE:  X

4.  HOW MANY COMPUTERS IN HOUSEHOLD?:

    0:      1:      2:      3 OR MORE:  X

5.  WHAT IS YOUR WEEKLY ALLOWANCE?:

    ENTER AMOUNT:  03.00

6.  HOW LONG DOES IT TAKE YOU TO GET TO SCHOOL?:

    0 -10 MIN:          10-20 MIN:  X
    20-30 MIN:          30-40 MIN:
    40-50 MIN:          50-60 MIN:
    1 HOUR OR MORE:
```
(continued)

```
7.  HOW DO YOU USUALLY GET TO SCHOOL?:

    CAR, TRUCK, OR VAN:
    SCHOOL BUS: X
    TAXICAB:
    BICYCLE:
    WALK:
    OTHER-SPECIFY:

8.  WHAT KIND(S) OF PET(S) DO YOU HAVE?:

    DOG:
    CAT:
    BIRD:
    WATER ANIMAL:
    RABBIT:
    GERBIL:
    HORSE:
    OTHER-SPECIFY:

    NONE: X
```

Figure 4.10.   Sample student census form.

Using *PFS-File*, the database consists of completed responses from twenty-one students in fifth grade and twenty students in sixth grade. Graphs are helpful in analyzing and interpreting this data. However, the data is not stored as numbers (like the populations of countries in South America). To use the data, counting or tallying it is necessary. The more flexible the software is in doing this task, the more quickly useful data can be obtained. While *PFS-File* can be used to count, *PFS-Report* offers more flexibility by providing tallies reported in tables. These counts can be entered by students using *PFS-Graph* to create the needed graphs.

For example, suppose students want to look at pet ownership. Using *PFS-Report*, two tables can be created (see figures 4.11 and 4.12). Using information from these tables, students enter data to create a table for pet ownership for grade five and one for grade six with *PFS-Graph*. Note that for the last category (horse) there was no entry on the table, so this category is not included in the graph. Also the category of "other" was not graphed. Figure 4.13 on page 88 shows the completed tables as paired data and the graph.

Several observations are possible. What is the most popular pet in the fifth grade? In the sixth grade? While the graph shows how many students own pets, it cannot be used to determine how many students do not own pets. Why? This is because some students indicated more than one kind of pet. Of course, the number of students responding "None" could also have been counted and graphed.

PETS – FIFTH GRADE

	D	C	B	WA	R	G	H	OHR
		X						
		X		X				
			X	X				
			X					
					X			
	X							
		X				X		
		X	X	X				
		X		X	X			
		X						
				X				
				X	X			
COUNT:	1	6	3	6	3	1	0	0

Figure 4.11. Pet ownership, grade five.

PETS – SIXTH GRADE

	D	C	B	WA	R	G	H	OHR
		X						
		X			X			
					X			
				X				
		X						
		X						
	X		X					
		X						
		X		X				
		X						
		X	X					
			X					MOUSE
		X						
COUNT:	1	9	3	2	2	0	0	1

Figure 4.12. Pet ownership, grade six.

	FIFTH GRADE	SIXTH GRADE
DOG	7	7
CAT	6	9
BIRD	3	3
WATER ANINAL	6	2
RABBIT	3	2
GERBIL	1	0

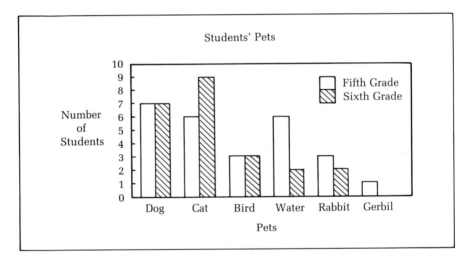

Figure 4.13. Comparison of pets, grades five and six.

Students must be careful how questions are posed. Consider these two questions:

How many students in the fifth grade own dogs?

How many dogs do students in the fifth grade own?

The second question cannot be answered using the charts, the graph, or the database. Why? This is because students did not indicate, as part of the survey, how many of each pet they owned. This provides an opportunity to discuss the necessity of pre-planning and considering what questions should be asked before a survey is designed.

Figure 4.14 shows a table that provides information on birth months for each of grades five and six and for the two grades combined. This data is shown graphed in figure 4.15.

	FIFTH GRADE	SIXTH GRADE	FIFTH/SIXTH GRADES
JAN-MARCH	1	4	5
APRIL-JUNE	6	4	10
JULY-SEPT	10	5	15
OCT-DEC	4	7	11

Figure 4.14. Table of birth months.

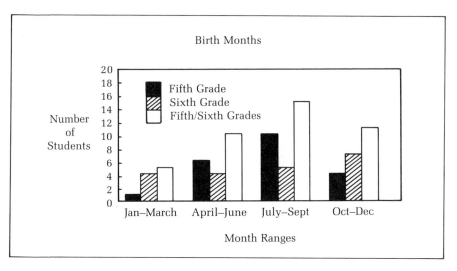

Figure 4.15 Graph of birth months.

In this case, three bars are shown for each month range: one shows just the fifth grade, one just the sixth grade, and one the combination of fifth and sixth grades. Again, it is the follow-up analysis and interpretation of the graph that makes this activity valuable. When were most students born? The graph indicates that July–September was the month range in which most students were born (in the combined fifth and sixth grades). Is this an accurate description of each of the separate grades? The sixth grade data is more evenly distributed, having less variability than that of the fifth grade, and actually shows the most births during the month range October–December.

An interesting survey for high school students to design might be a "computer match." Below are some questions from one such survey:

1. Are you:
   a. male
   b. female

2. Are you in the:
    a. ninth grade
    b. tenth grade
    c. eleventh grade
    d. twelfth grade
7. Which traits do you consider the most important in yourself?
    a. Creativity
    b. Sense of humor
    c. Intelligence
    d. Generosity
8. Your dream vacation would be:
    a. soaking up the sun on a Hawaiian beach.
    b. rubbing shoulders with the jet-set in Paris, New York, or Rome.
    c. a stay in a mountain cabin with close friends.
    d. a cross-country trip.
    e. a week-long visit to Disney World.
12. How do you feel about cigarette smoking?
    a. I don't approve of it.
    b. I don't care one way or the other.
    c. It's the individual's choice.
    d. I approve of it.

(These questions were taken from a Computer Match survey conducted by students in a Massachusetts high school.)

A computer can be used in a variety of ways to analyze this survey. *PFS-File* can be used to create a file of students' responses, giving students code names. Students can then search the database for names that have the exact matches desired. Using some method for decoding the code names the student can then make "contact" with these individuals. As a computer-literacy activity, this motivates students to use the databases and also helps students focus on the issues of personal privacy and of accuracy of data. In addition it provides the basis for discussion of how "facts" about an individual are not the "essence" of that person.

Using Statistics

Understanding elementary statistics is important not only for analyzing data but also simply for reading and interpreting information reported daily in such sources as magazines and newspapers. Data-gathering activities provide opportunities to introduce some statistics.

On the simplest level *PFS-Report*, in addition to counting data occurrences, can compute arithmetic averages (or means). Figure 4.16 shows the allowances of all students in grades five and six. The allowances are sorted by grade level, and average allowances for each grade and for both grades are determined. From this table it is seen that

ALLOWANCES - FIFTH, SIXTH GRADES

GR	AMOUNT
5	$20.00
	15.00
	5.00
	5.00
	5.00
	5.00
	5.00
	4.25
	4.00
	3.75
	2.50
	1.50
	1.50
	1.50
	1.25
	1.25
	1.00
	0.50
	0.50
	0.50
	0.50
AVERAGE:	$ 4.02
6	$15.00
	15.00
	10.00
	10.00
	10.00
	10.00
	4.75
	4.75
	4.50
	3.00
	3.00
	3.00
	2.75
	2.75
	1.75
	1.50
	1.00
	1.00
	0.75
	0.00
AVERAGE:	$ 5.22
AVERAGE:	$ 4.60

Figure 4.16.   Student allowances.

the average allowance for students in the fifth grade ($4.02) is less than that for the sixth grade ($5.22). The average allowance for both grades is $4.60, which is not an average of the two averages. That is, it is not determined by adding $4.02 and $5.22, then dividing by 2 ($4.62). Rather it is determined by adding all allowances and dividing by 41, the number of allowances reported.

    The allowances as reported are raw data that are not particularly meaningful without some organization. Data organization usually involves arranging the data in a frequency distribution. To create a frequency distribution groups must be identified. The number of groups should be between six and twenty. The following groups can be used for allowances:

0–$0.99	or 0–
$1.00–$1.99	or 1–
$2.00–$2.99	or 2–
$3.00–$3.99	or 3–
$4.00–$4.99	or 4–
$5.00–$5.99	or 5–
$6.00–or more	or 6–more

Having the number of groups between six and twenty makes it possible to see the true nature of the distribution. In this frequency distribution, the lengths of the intervals in the groups, with the exception of the last group, are the same. Generally, the interval length of each group should be the same and be an odd number. In this example, the interval length is .99.

    Using these groups, a table of frequencies can be created.

Class	Frequency	
	Fifth	*Sixth*
0–	4	2
1–	6	4
2–	1	2
3–	1	3
4–	2	3
5–	5	0
6–more	2	6

From this, a bar graph can be created using *PFS-Graph*, which will permit comparison of the data. Figure 4.17 shows such a graph.

	FIFTH GRADE	SIXTH GRADE
0 –	4	2
1 –	6	4
2 –	1	2
3 –	1	3
4 –	2	3
5 –	5	0
6 – MORE	2	6

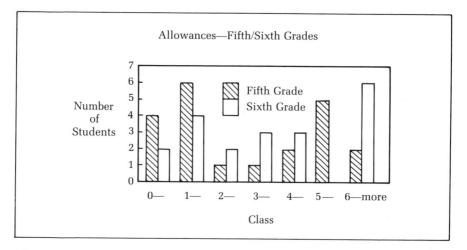

Figure 4.17. Table and bar graph of student allowances.

Using this data, three measures of central tendency can be determined. These are numerical calculations that provide some central value that describes the data. The arithmetic average or mean has already been determined for each of the two grades and for the two grades combined. This average is merely the sum of all the values of all the observations divided by the total number of observations.

The median is the value that falls in the middle of a group of sorted observations. When the number of observations is odd, the middle value is the median. For the fifth grade there are twenty-one observations. The eleventh observation is the median: $2.50. When the number of observations is even, the average of the two middle values is usually considered the median. For the sixth grade there are twenty observations. The middle two values happen to be $3.00 each, so the median is $3.00. For the two classes combined the allowances must be sorted again (see figure 4.18 on page 94). Because there are forty-one observations, the median is the twenty-first observation or $3.00.

The mode, the value that occurs most frequently in a set of observations, is used only occasionally. For the fifth grade, this is $5.00. For the

```
ALLOWANCES

AMOUNT
────────

$20.00
 15.00
 15.00
 15.00
 10.00
 10.00
 10.00
 10.00
  5.00
  5.00
  5.00
  5.00
  5.00
  4.75
  4.75
  4.50
  4.25
  4.00
  3.75
  3.00
  3.00
  3.00
  2.75
  2.75
  2.50
  1.75
  1.50
  1.50
  1.50
  1.50
  1.25
  1.25
  1.00
  1.00
  1.00
  0.75
  0.50
  0.50
  0.50
  0.50
  0.00


────────
AVERAGE:     $  4.60
```

Figure 4.18. Fifth and sixth grade allowances combined.

sixth grade, it is $10.00. For the combined classes, the mode is $5.00. It is possible to have more than one mode.

The three measures of central tendency are summarized:

Measure	Fifth grade	Sixth grade	Combined
Mean	4.02	5.22	4.60
Median	2.50	3.00	3.00
Mode	5.00	10.00	5.00

When choosing to use these measures, the range and variability in the data must be considered. For example, if the sixth grade mode were used to describe the central value for all students in that group, it would be a misleading statistic. It would suggest that many more students have an allowance near that amount than is actually the case. For these data, the arithmetic mean provides a better measure of central value.

There is specific software designed to help analyze, and in some cases administer, a survey. One such example is *Telofacts*, which is appropriate for high school students. Other software is being developed that can be used with elementary and middle school students (see resource section).

Telofacts is useful in the analysis of attitude surveys. Attitudes must be approached from several different angles. They cannot be accurately determined from the answer to a single question. Thus, such surveys are designed to gather a sample of an individual's beliefs, covering a range of the aspects of the attitude being assessed. The outcome is some form of average that provides a measure of the individual's position on an attitude continuum.

There are a variety of attitudinal measures. One such measure is the Likert scale, which assesses attitude by having the individual rate his or her belief as "strongly agree," "agree," "undecided," "disagree," or "strongly disagree" on each of several related items. Figure 4.19 on page 96 shows a Likert attitude scale, the General Attitudes Toward Computers Scale (Reece & Gable, 1982), developed to measure attitudes of students in elementary and middle school grades.

The ten statements assess cognitive, behavioral, and affective components of attitudes toward computers. Each person receives an attitude score based on his or her answers. This is done by weighting responses. In any one question, the response that indicates the most positive attitude is assigned five points, the response indicating the most negative attitude, one point. Thus, in question 1, SA is weighted five points and SD, one point. In questions 3 and 8, SD is weighted five points and SA, one point. Thus, on this attitude survey, high-scoring students are ones who exhibit positive attitudes towards computers, are eager to use them, and select courses that use computers.

1.	I will use a computer as soon as possible.	SA A U D SD
2.	I will take computer courses.	SA A U D SD
3.	Learning about computers is boring to me.	SA A U D SD
4.	Computers can be used to save lives.	SA A U D SD
5.	Computers make my life enjoyable.	SA A U D SD
6.	I enjoy computer work.	SA A U D SD
7.	Having computers in the classroom would be fun for me.	SA A U D SD
8.	I would never take a job where I had to work with computers.	SA A U D SD
9.	If I had the money, I would buy a computer.	SA A U D SD
10.	I like learning on a computer.	SA A U D SD

Figure 4.19   General attitudes toward computers.

Telofacts is useful for a variety of different surveys. In this case, it is used to analyze responses to the attitude survey shown in figure 4.19. Version one of *Telofacts* was used for examples in this book. There is a second, enhanced version, *Telofacts 2*, which provides additional options (see resource section).

Telofacts 1 allows you to make or change a questionnaire, to enter data, and to display or print results of single-question or total-survey analysis. Up to 100 questions are possible in a survey. Each question can have up to five different responses. Numerical values may be assigned to give preference or weight to different answers. This is how attitude scores are determined.

In designing an attitude survey using *Telofacts*, each statement is entered, one at a time. As each statement is entered, the possible responses are also entered and, optionally, the numerical values for the answers. For example:

```
1.  I will use a computer as soon as possible.

    A.  Strongly agree

    B.  Agree

    C.  Undecided

    D.  Disagree

    E.  Strongly disagree

Numerical value(s) of answers:

A [5]   B [4]   C [3]   D [2]   E [1]
```

In completing the survey, respondents do not use the computer. The computer is for the researcher, who must enter the data from hand-completed questionnaires. Data entry involves merely typing in the letter response to each question. The real computer power appears when *Telofacts* is used to display the results of analysis of the survey. *Telofacts* does not provide an attitude score for an individual. However, single questions or the whole questionnaire can be analyzed. Analyses involve specifying the criteria to be used in selecting the subgroup of respondents to be considered. This selection process is powerful yet takes time to master. Two summary analyses are shown here to provide examples of the types of reports possible with *Telofacts*. In figure 4.20 (page 98), the results of analysis of question six are shown.

The total number of respondents is ten. Also, ten respondents are selected for analysis because no criteria for exclusion are specified. In all cases, the term *selected* refers to the respondents who are chosen for the report, based on criteria specified by the researcher. The responses given are summarized, a bar-like graph is displayed, and summary statistics are provided. Measures of central tendency — median and average — are given, and a common measure of variability, the standard deviation, is also provided.

Two measures of dispersion or variability of data are the range and the standard deviation. The range is determined by finding the difference between the lowest and highest observations. Ranges were discussed earlier when considering populations of countries in South America. The standard deviation measures the variability of the distribution of observations as they differ from the mean of the observations. If this number is large, the data have greater variability than a set of data in which the standard deviation is small.

A second analysis that is possible with *Telofacts* is an analysis of the total survey. Figure 4.21 (page 99) provides this information. This summarizes how all respondents answered each of the ten items. The average, the standard deviation, and the median are provided for each question. Thus, for question one, the median response is 4, the average response is 3.3 (determined by using the weighting for responses), and the standard deviation is 1.268.

Telofacts is particularly useful software for working with attitude and marketing surveys, political polling, and educational and social science applications. As a tool for high school social science research applications it is invaluable.

In addition to database software and specialized software for survey analysis, there are a variety of statistical software packages available that can be used to provide measures of central tendency and of variability as well as other statistics. One such program is *Key Stat*. This program is used to provide summary statistics of the data from the student allowances discussed earlier. Figure 4.22 (page 100) summarizes this information first for the fifth grade (twenty-one values) and then for the sixth grade (twenty values). The mean, median, sum, and standard deviation are shown. The standard deviation is large, which indicates that

```
                                TeloFacts 1                                     v1.1
GENERAL ATTITUDES               SUSAN:GATC                       SUSAN:TRIAL1
                                Respondent No.     10
                                                                 !100              !
                            All Respondents                      !                 !
                        Question Number Analyzed:    6           !                 !
                                                                 ! 75              !
                    Number Of Respondents Checked:     10        !                 !
                    Number Of Respondents Selected:    10        !                 !
                                                                 !                 !
Number             1      1      3      3      2     10      0   ! 50              !
% Selected      10.0   10.0   30.0   30.0   20.0  100.0    0.0   !                 !
% Answering     10.0   10.0   30.0   30.0   20.0  100.0          !                 !
                --A--  --B--  --C--  --D--  --E--  Total No Ansr !       C D       !
                                                                 ! 25    C D E     !
                                                                 !       C D E     !
The Median Value for Respondents Answering Is:      4.000        !   A B C D E     !
The Average Value For Respondents Answering Is:     3.400        !   A B C D E     !
The Standard Deviation Of This Average Value Is:    1.200        ! 0 = = = = = =!
```

Figure 4.20. Analysis of question six.

TeloFacts 1
GENERAL ATTITUDES
All Respondents

Q #	# A's	% A's	# B's	% B's	# C's	% C's	# D's	% D's	# E's	% E's	Base 100.0%	No Ansr	Average Std Dev	Median
1.	1	10.0	2	20.0	2	20.0	3	30.0	2	20.0	10 100.0	0	3.300 1.268	4.000
2.	1	10.0	2	20.0	2	20.0	4	40.0	1	10.0	10 100.0	0	3.200 1.166	4.000
3.	2	20.0	3	30.0	3	30.0	1	10.0	1	10.0	10 100.0	0	3.400 1.200	3.000
4.	1	10.0	1	10.0	7	70.0	0	0.0	1	10.0	10 100.0	0	2.900 0.943	3.000
5.	1	10.0	2	20.0	3	30.0	3	30.0	1	10.0	10 100.0	0	3.100 1.135	3.000
6.	1	10.0	1	10.0	3	30.0	3	30.0	2	20.0	10 100.0	0	3.400 1.200	4.000
7.	1	10.0	0	0.0	3	30.0	3	30.0	3	30.0	10 100.0	0	3.700 1.187	4.000
8.	3	30.0	3	30.0	2	20.0	1	10.0	1	10.0	10 100.0	0	3.600 1.280	4.000
9.	3	30.0	0	0.0	5	50.0	0	0.0	2	20.0	10 100.0	0	2.800 1.400	3.000
10.	2	20.0	2	20.0	1	10.0	2	20.0	3	30.0	10 100.0	0	3.200 1.536	4.000

Figure 4.21. Total survey analysis.

there is great variability in this data. This is because of a few allowances of $10, $15, and $20, while the remaining are in the range of $0–$5. The other two reported measures are variance and standard error, which are discussed in texts dealing with elementary statistical concepts.

```
            SUMMARY FOR 21 VALUES

   MEAN = 4.02380952      VAR = 23.8119048

   MEDIAN = 2.5           S.D. = 4.87974434

   SUM = 84.5             S.E. = 1.06484751



            SUMMARY FOR 20 VALUES

   MEAN = 5.216           VAR = 22.0823305

   MEDIAN = 3             S.D. = 4.69918403

   SUM = 104.32           S.E. = 1.05076949
```

Figure 4.22. *Key Stat* summary.

With the growth in the amount of data in the social sciences and the need to interpret such data, statistics have become important tools for social studies. Increasingly, students are given statistical information, and they are expected to understand its meaning. Simple statistics such as mean, median, and mode as measures of central tendency, and elementary concepts related to variance, provide students with opportunities to analyze data they collect, to make comparisons, and to create hypotheses.

Spreadsheets

Spreadsheet programs are versatile tools for processing numbers. A spreadsheet can be used to store information, make calculations and predictions, and aid in a variety of "what if" planning tasks. There are many spreadsheet programs available. *Practicalc* and *Appleworks* (including an integrated database, a spreadsheet, and a word processor) are choices for use with students.

A spreadsheet is set up in a grid of columns and rows. In most spreadsheets, the rows are labeled with numbers and the columns are labeled with letters. The point at which a row and a column intersect is called a cell. The cell is labeled by its column and row referents. For example, in figure 4.23, note the locations of the cells A10, B1, B11, C4 and D5.

	A	B	C	D
1		B1		
2				
3				
4			C4	
5				D5
6				
7				
8				
9				
10	A10			
11		B11		
12				
13				
14				
15				
16				
17				
18				
19				
20				

Figure 4.23.   Spreadsheet, columns A–D.

The cursor can be moved from cell to cell, horizontally or vertically, on the spreadsheet. The spreadsheet is actually much larger than just the portion shown on the screen. As the cursor is moved, the column and row labels change to show what portion of the spreadsheet is being used. See figures 4.24, 4.25, and 4.26 on pages 102–103 for examples.

Two kinds of information can be entered on spreadsheets: labels (words) and values (numbers and variables). For example, a middle school student decided to use a spreadsheet to keep track of her paper route. She has five customers. Figure 4.27 (page 103) shows information regarding this route for one week.

Labels have been entered in the cells in columns A and B. This is also true for the cells in row 3 in columns C, D, and E. Cells C5 through C9 and D5 through D9 show numerical values that represent the amount of money paid for one week by both the customers and the paper carrier. The remaining cells are formulas that involve cells C5 through C9 and D5 through D9. For example, the formula for cell E5 is C5 − D5. What appears in the cell is the result of this computation. The formula for C11 is C5 + C6 + C7 + C8 + C9.

It is this capability to use formulas to show relationships that gives a spreadsheet its power. In this case, *what if* the Sunday paper had a price

	C	D	E	F
1				
2				
3				
4	C4			
5		D5		
6				
7				
8				
9				
10				
11				
12				
13				
14				
15				F15
16				F16
17				
18				
19				
20				

Figure 4.24. Spreadsheet, columns C–F.

	A	B	C	D
6				
7				
8				
9				
10	A10			
11		B11		
12				
13				
14				
15				
16				
17				
18				
19				
20				
21				
22				
23				
24				
25	A25			

Figure 4.25. Spreadsheet, rows 6–25.

	C	D	E	F
6				
7				
8				
9				
10				
11				
12				
13				
14				
15				F15
16				F16
17				
18				
19				
20				
21				
22				
23				
24				
25				

Figure 4.26. Spreadsheet, columns C–F and rows 6–25.

	A	B	C	D	E
1	NEWSPAPER ROUTE:				
2					
3	CUSTOMERS		PAYMENT	MY COST	NET
4					
5	JONES, B.		2.25	1.80	0.45
6	KELLEY, H.		1.95	1.65	0.30
7	MURPHY, T.		2.25	1.80	0.45
8	NEWSOME, W.		2.25	1.80	0.45
9	POWERS, J.		1.75	1.45	0.30
10					
11	TOTALS		10.45	8.50	1.95
12					

Figure 4.27. Paper route information.

increase such that now Mr. Jones, Mrs. Murphy, and Ms. Newsome each needed to pay $2.45 per week in order to cover the additional charges, and the paper carrier's costs increased to $1.90 for each of these customers? As the values are changed, all formulas that use these values are recomputed so that the effect of these changes can be immediately assessed. Figure 4.28 shows the sheet when only one value has been changed, and figure 4.29 shows the completed sheet.

	A	B	C	D	E
1	NEWSPAPER ROUTE:				
2					
3	CUSTOMERS		PAYMENT	MY COST	NET
4					
5	JONES, B,		2,45	1,80	0,65
6	KELLEY, H,		1,95	1,65	0,30
7	MURPHY, T,		2,25	1,80	0,45
8	NEWSOME, W,		2,25	1,80	0,45
9	POWERS, J,		1,75	1,45	0,30
10					
11	TOTALS		10,65	8,50	2,15
12					

Figure 4.28.   One value change.

	A	B	C	D	E
1	NEWSPAPER ROUTE:				
2					
3	CUSTOMERS		PAYMENT	MY COST	NET
4					
5	JONES, B,		2,45	1,90	0,55
6	KELLEY, H,		1,95	1,65	0,30
7	MURPHY, T,		2,45	1,90	0,55
8	NEWSOME, W,		2,45	1,90	0,55
9	POWERS, J,		1,75	1,45	0,30
10					
11	TOTALS		11,05	8,80	2,25
12					

Figure 4.29.   Completed spreadsheet with updated figures.

Note that this change has been in the paper carrier's favor. Her net income has increased.

As another example, consider the table shown earlier (figure 4.9) which provides data on immigration by country of origin. The same data is shown in figure 4.30.

	A	B	C	D	E	F
1	IMMIGRATION BY COUNTRY OF ORIGIN					
2	EUROPEAN COUNTRIES ONLY - 1820-1980					
3						THOUSANDS
4	COUNTRY:		FAMILIES	% TOTAL	U.S.A.	% TOTAL
5						
6	AUSTRIA/HUNGARY		7	4.4	4317	11.9
7	BELGIUM		2	1.3	204	.6
8	CZECHOSLOVAKIA		2	1.3	139	.4
9	DENMARK		0	0	365	1
10	FINLAND		0	0	33	.1
11	FRANCE		5	3.1	755	2.1
12	GERMANY		11	6.9	6990	19.2
13	GREAT BRITAIN		6	3.8	4927	13.6
14	GREECE		7	4.4	664	1.8
15	IRELAND		44	27.7	4732	13
16	ITALY		41	25.8	5304	14.6
17	NETHERLANDS		4	2.5	361	1
18	NORWAY		0	0	856	2.4
19	POLAND		6	3.8	524	1.4
20	PORTUGAL		0	0	458	1.3
21	SPAIN		0	0	263	.7
22	SWEDEN		5	3.1	1274	3.5
23	SWITZERLAND		5	3.1	351	1
24	USSR		5	3.1	3385	9.3
25	YUGOSLAVIA		3	1.9	117	.3
26	OTHER EUROPE		6	3.8	311	.9
27						
28			159	100	36330	100
29						
30						
31	*DATA FROM 1984 WORLD ALMANAC, P. 204					

Figure 4.30. Immigrant data entered into a spreadsheet.

This table was used in order to make comparisions between immigration history data for a set of families surveyed by middle school students and the same data for the United States as a whole. Both sets of data were converted to percentages to make comparison easier.

Examining the table, we see both labels and values present. In columns C and E, the values are numbers. In columns D and F, the values are the result of computations. Specifically, D8 is determined by dividing C8 by C29. C8 indicates that two people in the families surveyed emigrated from Belgium. C29 indicates the total number (159) of immigrants in the families surveyed. Dividing 2 by 159 yields the percent of this total. The actual formula is created so each percentage is computed to one decimal place. Other entries in columns D and F use similar formulas. Fortunately, with a few simple commands, this formula can be "copied" in several cells at one time, with the cell referents renamed. Finally, row 27 consists of summations of each of the columns.

In this case, a spreadsheet is useful because of the number of computations involved and because having a completed table is desirable. Changing entries under the column labeled "Families" permits other sets of data to be entered and percentages computed.

Spreadsheets are particularly helpful in working with simulations. In many instances, a simulation may require several numerical calculations. Based on the numbers entered, the results of the calculations provide information for decision making. A spreadsheet provides a way for students to explore the effects of different numerical entries without becoming bogged down in the actual computing. In this way, students are more likely to engage in "what if" thinking.

For example, consider the *Oil Monopoly Game* (see resource section) designed for a high school unit on the development of big business. The purpose of this simulation is to help students understand how John D. Rockefeller started the Standard Oil Corporation. It attempts to recreate the conditions that allowed Rockefeller to gain control of the oil industry.

Students can choose to play one of three parts:

    a refiner — Standard, Hewitt, Hanna, Archbold, or Stanley

    a railroad — Pennsylvania, Erie, or New York Central

    an exporter — Acme, Tidewater, Atlantic, or Mobil

The refineries are located in Cleveland, Ohio. They make use of the three railroads to transport oil to the exporters on the East Coast, specifically New York. See figure 4.31 for additional information about the game.

When this game is played without a computer, students maintain accounting sheets that show the numerical records of their deals: computations, profits and losses. The accounting sheets can be translated to a spreadsheet template (see figure 4.32 on page 108) that permits the students greater flexibility in experimenting with the "what if" decisions about prices to charge. Spreadsheets also remove computation as a major part of the process. Since the focus is problem solving and experimentation with decision making, the removal of the computation requirements helps eliminate unnecessary distractions in the game.

Chapters 3 and 4 have illustrated how the presentation of social studies materials can be enhanced by the use of computer-based tools.

Railroads	Refiners	Exporters
Erie	Standard	Acme
New York Central	Hewitt	Tidewater
Pennsylvania	Hanna	Mobil
	Archbold	Atlantic
	Stanley	

Railroads: 1. Get the refineries to give you their business.
2. Bargain for highest rate per barrel that you can get.
3. Cover your break-even point if you can, but it is better to sell at your variable cost than not to sell at all.

Refineries: 1. Make a deal with a railroad to take your oil.
2. Get as low a rate as you can.
3. Make a deal with an exporter to take your oil.
4. Get as high a price as you can.
5. Remember: You must pay the railroad.

Exporters: 1. Find a refiner to sell your oil, but first make sure he has a railroad to ship your oil to you.
2. Pay as little for the oil as possible.
3. Remember: You can sell all the oil you buy for $7.00 per barrel, but you must pay your own fixed and variable costs.

The object of the game is to make as much money as quickly as possible. Refiners, exporters, and railroads will compete against each other to get the best price for as much oil as they can take. Refiners will try to line up railroads and find exporters to buy their oil.

Figure 4.31. The *Oil Monopoly Game.*

More time and effort given to in-depth investigations of social science issues allow precollege social studies to be a more involving discipline. Students can assume the role of the social scientist and have access to many of the social scientist's tools for research.

The initial investment of time needed by teachers to develop a level of comfort using these tools is far from trivial. However, more and more students are coming to classes experienced in computer skills and thus can be of aid to teachers. The authors hope the examples presented here are enticing enough to encourage teachers to explore a more applications-oriented approach using such tools in their teaching of social studies.

```
OIL MONOPOLY GAME

KIND OF COMPANY: REFINERY    ROUND #1    ROUND #1    ROUND #1

                             STANDARD    HEWITT      ARCHBOLD

DAILY CAPACITY
        SCH A:                   2000        1000         500
        SCH B:                   2000        2000        1000

DAILY FIXED COSTS                 500         500         200

DAILY VAR COSTS/BBL               1.5           2        1.25

NUMBER OF BBL REFINED            2000        1000         750
DAILY VAR COSTS PD               3000        2000       937.5

AMOUNT PD RAILROAD/BBL            1.5         1.8           2
NUMBER BBL TRANS                 2000        1000         750
TRANS COSTS                      3000        1800        1500

NUMBER OF BBL SOLD               2000        1000         750
PRICE/BBL                           5           4         4.2
TOTAL DAILY REVEN               10000        4000        3150

TOTAL DAILY COSTS                6500        4300      2637.5

NET PROFIT/DAY                   3500        -300       512.5
NUMBER OF DAYS                    100         100         100
CUM PROFIT/LOSS                350000      -30000       51250

CASH ON HAND BEG               100000       50000       20000

CASH ON HAND END               450000       20000       71250
```

Figure 4.32.   Spreadsheet for the *Oil Monopoly Game.*

References

Ferber, R., et al. *What is A Survey?* Washington, D.C.: American Statistical Association, 1980.

Moser, C.A., and Kalton, G. *Survey Methods in Social Investigation.* New York: Basic Books, 1972.

Reece, M.J., and Gable R.K. "The Development and Validation of a Measure of General Attitudes Toward Computers." *Educational and Psychological Measurement,* 1982 (42) 913–916.

Model-Building and Simulation: An Advanced Tool

One of the most powerful and common uses of computers as tools in the social and natural sciences is model-building and simulation. For many years, the natural sciences have used the controlled environments of laboratories to investigate real-world phenomena. Biologists study genetics by breeding animals and flowers, and physicists study the effects of gravity by creating laboratory environments with differing amounts of gravity. Social scientists generally have had little means for creating hands-on experiments to understand areas of concern such as the implications of different forms of government or societal changes. Computers give social scientists the means to create a laboratory for controlled experimentation — an environment for developing both general and special-purpose tools.

People build various kinds of models for a variety of reasons: as toys; to display clothes in a store window; to help in planning large projects such as an architect's model. In each case, the model is built to simplify the real environment. Simplification is one strategy to aid in understanding a complex situation. This strategy is used in computer modelling and simulation.

History of Model-building and Simulation

Early uses of simulation were often for military purposes. Chess was reportedly used to simulate military battles during the Middle Ages. Visitors to Stockholm can still view the remains of a fortress built in the fifteenth century to aid the king in practicing defense maneuvers. The navigation tables created by the Portuguese were a simulation of the night skies. Simulation was used extensively during World War II for such tasks as measuring ballistic trajectories. In fact, the need for large amounts of "number crunching" for simulation during that war provided funds for the development of the digital computer.

Today simulation is used, with the aid of wind tunnels and wave tanks to test new designs for aircraft and ships, or, through river basin models, to study better ways to control flooding. These simulations often involve physical models that can be expensive, cumbersome, and therefore impractical. With the advent of computers, people have turned to building mathematical models rather than physical models. Mathematics is a language useful for describing real-world phenomena. Since mathematics is more readily usable for communicating with computers than other languages such as English, computers and mathematics have been combined to create the field of computer simulation. Mathematical models are simulated (or "run") over time on the computer. This process provides the problem-solver with an easy way to carry out experiments.

Computer models are used to study such things as the behavior of nuclear reactors during accidents, urban problems, weather patterns, economic behavior, and the management of large corporations. One of the more remarkable aspects of these models is their ability to be quite accurate while leaving out so much of the real world. Given the height and inclination of a hill and the weight of an elephant, a computer model can predict, to within a few seconds, the time it takes the elephant to slide down the hill. Left out of the model are such things as the muddiness of the hill, the colors of the scenery, and the feelings of the elephant.

Pedagogical Values of Model-building

The social sciences involve studying complex systems operative in the world. Models provide people with a means for better understanding complex interdependent situations. Why teach students model-building? Model-building integrates several skills important in the precollege years. A model is a theory statement about a problem. To create a model the student must simplify the problem. Having a tool requiring these skills helps students to develop clear, consistent, and logical thinking about how the world works. Simulating their model over time allows students to ask all their "what if" questions in the safe and inexpensive environment of the microcomputer.

In the absence of a means for developing concrete models, how do students construct theories about the world? Students use their minds, as best as possible, to create images of reality. Everyone has ideas from his or her experiences. Those people whose ideas, or mental models, come closest to how the world actually operates ought to function better. Mental models, however, are very limiting. Only a few elements can be mentally manipulated at the same time, while in reality the number of variables interacting in any one situation are endless. In addition, mental notions quickly become rigid — people develop strong loyalties to their ways of thinking. Education tries to teach children mental flexibility and adaptability, so that mental models can continuously change as new learning takes place. But resistance to change often creeps in. Finally, people generally have difficulty communicating what is on their minds. Ideas are expressed ambiguously and are therefore often misunderstood.

Good teachers have always understood the need to go beyond words in order to correct mental models. In the very early years of school, corners of the classroom are devoted to models of a house, a grocery store, or perhaps a workshop. In later years, days are often devoted to modelling United Nation activities or events leading to war. The modelling process becomes a mechanism for clearing up ambiguities. The concrete model becomes a mechanism for communicating one's thoughts to classmates and teachers. Students refine their models through study.

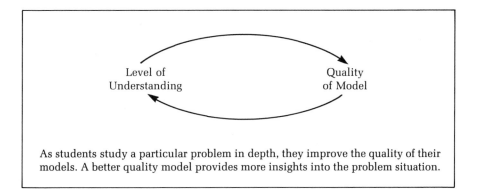

As students study a particular problem in depth, they improve the quality of their models. A better quality model provides more insights into the problem situation.

Figure 5.1   A reinforcing situation.

Because models are so often used for projections in areas crucial to everyone, such as policy decisions about the national economy, it is important that students have a sense of what it means to build and use a simulation model. The best way for students to get this sense is to build and use models themselves.

System Dynamics

Many approaches exist for model-building and simulation. The field falls into two distinct categories referred to as "discrete simulation" and "continuous simulation." Each approach is appropriate for different kinds of problems. Discrete simulation is applied generally to situations where individual events are critical, such as understanding the implications of the number of check-out lines available at a supermarket or determining how fast a new computer design will process information.

Continuous simulation is the approach presented here because it more readily lends itself to social science problems. Continuous simulation focuses on how a problem situation is affected over time by changes in strategy, policy, or the environment. Most of the problems considered by social scientists fall into this category: war and peace, urban development, social change, group interaction. The particular kind of continuous simulation that is often found in precollege settings is called "system dynamics" (Roberts, 1983). This field was developed at M.I.T. over thirty years ago. Its founder, Jay W. Forrester, was involved with the development of the digital computer during World War II. After the war Forrester went to the M.I.T. Sloan School of Management to put his background in electrical engineering and computers to work solving management problems.

The approach Forrester's group developed was first called "industrial dynamics." Because of its applicability to any complex interdependent problem, the name was changed to system dynamics to reflect its broader applications. Over the past three decades system dynamics has been applied to such diverse subjects as the allocation of natural resources, the management of health maintenance organizations (HMOs), the national economy, and the study of the spread of disease.

Since this field was originally designed for use with businessmen, the founders kept it as non-mathematical as possible. The computer language developed along with the field, called DYNAMO (see resource section), allows the model-builder to express his or her ideas in equations of abbreviated English words. In addition, a powerful pre-computer tool was developed for expressing simply a model or theory about a complex situation. Figure 5.1 is an illustration of this tool called causal-loop diagramming.

The theory about how the world works, integral to system dynamics, involves three main concepts: dynamic, feedback, and system. *Dynamic* suggests that since time never stops, considering the changing nature of problems is important. For example, in studying the weapons build-up in the world, the continuously changing dimensions of the problem are critical to include in any analysis. The concept of feedback comes from the field of cybernetics, the study of information flow. Feedback embodies the idea that every time a person or group takes an action, that action affects future options of that person or group.

Taking a systems approach to a problem means taking a top-down view first: defining the whole, then breaking the problem into its smaller parts, but always returning to the system perspective by studying the relationships between the parts.

This chapter suggests how the system dynamics approach to model-building and simulation can be incorporated into the K–12 social studies curriculum. This is then another example of how the social studies curriculum might begin to change in response to the computer's becoming a readily available resource.

Including system dynamics gives the social studies teacher leverage to accomplish better such things as helping children:

1. cope with complexity;

2. communicate their mental models, or theories about the world, more easily;

3. compare their mental models with data, often in the form of graphs, and change their models based on new information;

4. define problems in terms of manageable units;

5. carry on a class discussion focusing on the issues, using causal-loop diagrams as illustrated in chapter 1;

6. analyze problems both qualitatively and quantitatively;

7. be exposed to the use of computers for research and problem-solving in the same manner as used by social scientists.

Integrating Model-Building Concepts in the Primary Grade Curriculum

Using as a guide the Report of the National Council for the Social Studies Task Force on Scope and Sequence (*Social Education* 1984), the subject matter recommended for the primary grades focuses on the home, family, and local community. Three key system dynamics concepts may be introduced at the primary grade level in conjunction with these topics:

1. *Causation and Feedback* — a change in one element in a system will *cause* a change in another, eventually affecting the original element again (see figure 5.1).

2. *Change* — focusing on behavior as it changes over time;

3. *System* — encouraging the student to understand how all the parts of a system fit together (synthesis-level thinking). This way of thinking is quite natural for younger students but seems to disappear from the curriculum in the upper grades.

Figure 5.2 is an example of a situation incorporating these three concepts and understandable even by kindergarten students.

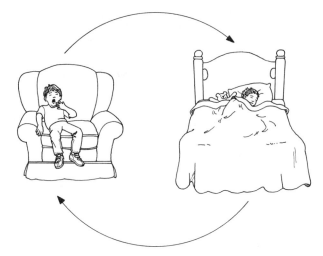

Figure 5.2   Tired-sleep circle story.

Using these two pictures, a teacher can begin generating a "circle" story such as:

Being tired *causes* you to sleep. When you've had a good night's sleep, and you go to bed the next night, you probably feel less tired, *causing* you to stay up late and play. Staying up late playing will probably *cause* you to be tired again.

Figure 5.3   Tired-sleep circle story II.

In causal-loop diagram notation, these ideas could be expressed as shown in figure 5.4. The amount of tiredness affects how much sleep you get, and the amount of sleep you get affects how tired you feel.

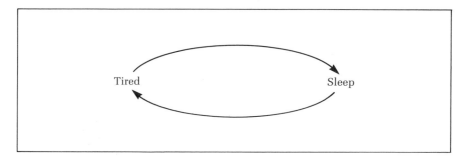

Figure 5.4   Tired-sleep causal-loop.

This is an example of a self-adjusting system. Over time, the body sends out a variety of signals that *causes* the person to go to sleep. Once this concept of a self-adjusting system is introduced, children can look for such behavior in a variety of other situations. Another example is given in figure 5.5. The causal-loop representing these pictures could be expressed as shown in figure 5.6. Another causal example, readily understood by primary grade children, and often found in the curriculum is illustrated in figure 5.7. Counting the number of seeds produced by one zinnia is a concrete example of this phenomenon, which is called a reinforcing system. Children might ask, then, "If this is a system that continues to produce more and more plants, how come our world is not completely overrun by zinnias?" If students have ever grown radish seeds in milk cartons, they might have learned to pull out the weaker seedlings to allow more room for the stronger plants. This second piece of the system is diagrammed in figure 5.8. Putting both diagrams together (figure 5.9), even primary-aged children can begin to understand the complexity of systems.

The ability to think mathematically, to assign numbers to events for clarity, is critical for many careers today. Rather than say, "I can no longer live on my income," it is far more precise to say, "I need a 15 percent raise because the costs of my children's music lessons have doubled, my car insurance has increased by 5 percent, and I'd like to save 50 percent more money each year." This kind of thinking can be nurtured from an early age by quantifying behavior even as simply as using terms such as "more" and "less" (see figures 5.7, 5.8, and 5.9). This problem-solving approach also encourages qualitative skills, two approaches that should be developed hand-in-hand.

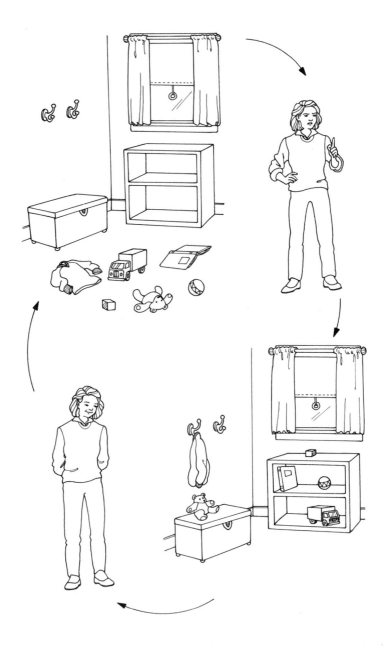

This series of pictures suggests that when a child leaves a room messy, it might *cause* the child's mother to be angry. An angry mother might *cause* the child to straighten up his or her room. When the mother notices the clean room, it might cause her to be happy and relaxed, perhaps causing the child, the next time at play, to forget and leave the room somewhat messy again.

Figure 5.5   Family system.

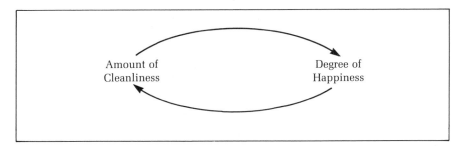

Figure 5.6 Family system causal-loop.

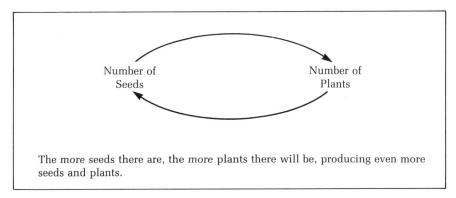

The *more* seeds there are, the *more* plants there will be, producing even more seeds and plants.

Figure 5.7 Seed-plant cycle.

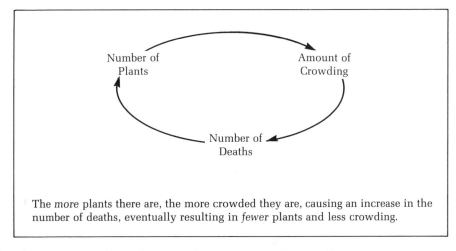

The *more* plants there are, the more crowded they are, causing an increase in the number of deaths, eventually resulting in *fewer* plants and less crowding.

Figure 5.8 A self-regulating cycle.

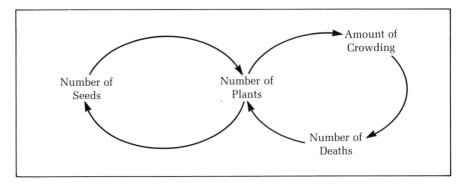

Figure 5.9   A plant system.

Studies of the characteristics of populations can begin by looking at plants in the primary grades, animal populations in the middle grades, and finally, human populations using a computer model at the secondary level. This is an example of how fundamental concepts in one area can be continuously developed in sophistication as children mature.

The Intermediate Grades

According to the Scope and Sequence Report (*Social Education* 1984), the foci for the fourth, fifth, and sixth grades include the adaptability of human beings to different environments, economic development, and the interdependence of nations. Continuing with the population theme begun in the primary grades, it is appropriate for these students to look at the relationships among animal populations as an introduction to the study of human populations. One strategy is to pick a native animal and investigate that animal's ability to adapt to its environment. In the northern regions of the country, a favorite is the beaver.

Understanding the interdependence of the various creatures in the natural environment, trappers can prolong their catch from an area as well as contribute to hunters' and fishermen's well being and conservationists' pleasures. The causal-loop diagram (figure 5.10) sums up the beaver story, clearly showing the interdependencies among animals and people.

Let's look now at the food and population quandary of the world as highlighted in a special insert of *Social Education* (Murphy) (see figure 5.11). However, the results are not what is either wanted or expected. The people most needing the food are not the people generally receiving it. Figure 5.12 suggests what is happening.

Several other factors, such as availability of transportation systems in the parts of the world where food is most needed and the number of government incentives to implement the green revolution in these

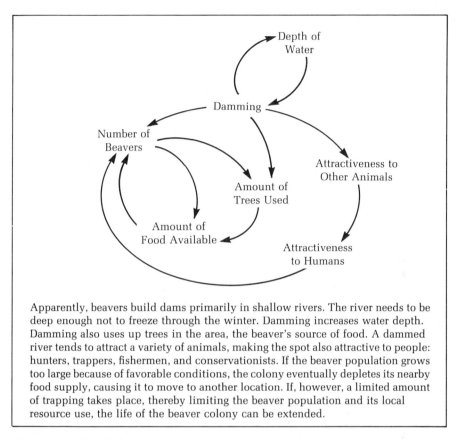

Apparently, beavers build dams primarily in shallow rivers. The river needs to be deep enough not to freeze through the winter. Damming increases water depth. Damming also uses up trees in the area, the beaver's source of food. A dammed river tends to attract a variety of animals, making the spot also attractive to people: hunters, trappers, fishermen, and conservationists. If the beaver population grows too large because of favorable conditions, the colony eventually depletes its nearby food supply, causing it to move to another location. If, however, a limited amount of trapping takes place, thereby limiting the beaver population and its local resource use, the life of the beaver colony can be extended.

Figure 5.10   Beaver story.

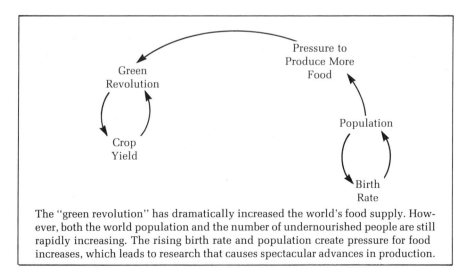

The "green revolution" has dramatically increased the world's food supply. However, both the world population and the number of undernourished people are still rapidly increasing. The rising birth rate and population create pressure for food increases, which leads to research that causes spectacular advances in production.

Figure 5.11   Initial food problem.

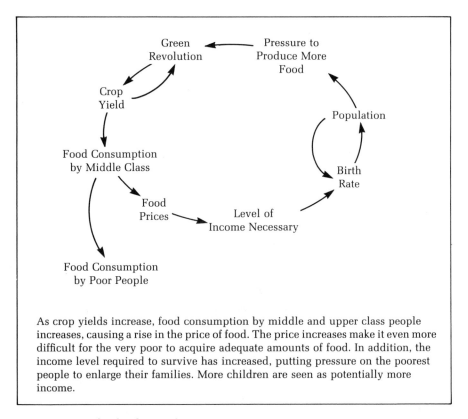

As crop yields increase, food consumption by middle and upper class people increases, causing a rise in the price of food. The price increases make it even more difficult for the very poor to acquire adequate amounts of food. In addition, the income level required to survive has increased, putting pressure on the poorest people to enlarge their families. More children are seen as potentially more income.

Figure 5.12   The food quandary.

regions, illustrate the complexity of the problem and the many interdependent elements. Figure 5.12 can be expanded to include all the factors understood and deemed important by the students studying the problem. The complexity of the diagram should not grow beyond the students' ability to handle such complexity. This tool then is a means for expressing increased insight and understanding as these are acquired by the students.

Endless numbers of examples fit the subject matter of the intermediate grade curriculum as well as the conceptual level of the children. As children build up a level of comfort with this method of analysis, they begin to apply it to all areas of the curriculum. In one sixth grade class the children developed the following diagram (figure 5.13) based on the classic book, *Mrs. Frisby and the Rats of NIMH* (O'Brien). The author's final comment was, "I felt bad about the title because it was a *people* race, and no sensible rats would ever do anything so foolish!" (O'Brien, p. 170).

The added symbols used in figure 5.13 and defined in figure 5.14, can be introduced at the fifth or sixth grade level. These symbols convey

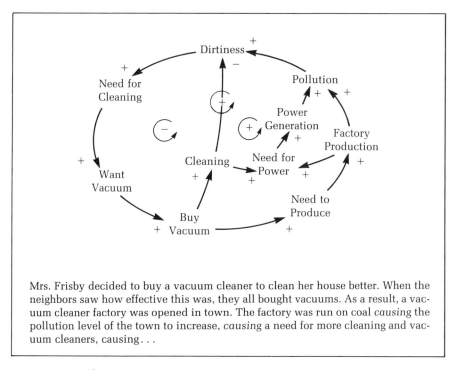

Mrs. Frisby decided to buy a vacuum cleaner to clean her house better. When the neighbors saw how effective this was, they all bought vacuums. As a result, a vacuum cleaner factory was opened in town. The factory was run on coal *causing* the pollution level of the town to increase, *causing* a need for more cleaning and vacuum cleaners, causing. . .

Figure 5.13   The rat race.

additional information about the behavior of the system (Roberts, p. 56). The symbols are the next step toward a more quantitative description of the situation under study. They are an intermediate step toward model-building through writing equations, introduced at the secondary level.

The Middle (Junior High) School Years

One of the social studies themes for the junior high school years is a broader view of people and problems. Building on the study of the food problem from the intermediate grades, a closer look at population growth is appropriate for these students. In addition, a more precise statement of the problem, looking carefully at the implication of changing numbers, makes for deeper understanding.

Figure 5.15 gives a simple causal structure for the world population problem. To understand the implications of this problem, the students can simulate population growth over a period of years using a chart such as figure 5.16. Let's start in 1975 when the world population was about 4 billion and the net birth rate was (and still is) 0.02. That is, 0.02 persons

Symbol	Meaning
(Arrow) (Tail) (Head)	The arrow is used to show causation. The item at the tail of the arrow *causes* a change in the item at the head of the arrow.
+	The + sign near the arrowhead indicates that the item at the tail of the arrow and the item at the head of the arrow change in the *same* direction. If the tail *increases*, the head *increases*; if the tail *decreases*, the head *decreases*.
−	The − sign near the arrowhead indicates that the item at the tail of the arrow and the item at the head of the arrow change in the *opposite* direction. If the tail *increases*, the head *decreases*; if the tail *decreases*, the head *increases*.
(+) or (+)	This symbol, found in the middle of a closed loop, indicates that the loop continues going in the same direction, often causing either systematic *growth* or *decline*, behavior that unstably moves away from an equilibrium point. This is called a *positive feedback loop*.
(−) or (−)	This symbol, found in the middle of a closed loop, indicates that the loop *changes* direction, causing the system to *fluctuate* or to *move toward equilibrium*. This is called a *negative feedback loop*.

Figure 5.14. Definitions of Causal-Loop Symbols.

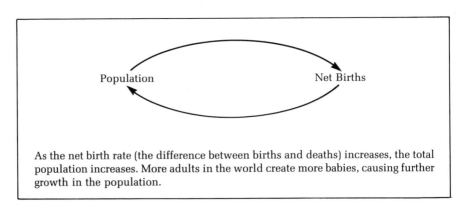

As the net birth rate (the difference between births and deaths) increases, the total population increases. More adults in the world create more babies, causing further growth in the population.

Figure 5.15 Population growth.

are added to the population each year for each person alive. 0.02 of 4 billion is 0.08 billion persons. The number of people added to the population between 1975 and 1976 was 0.08 billion. The population figure for 1976 was then 4.08 billion persons. With the same net birth rate continuing, the number of people added to the population between 1976 and 1977, rounded to two places, is again about 0.08 billion, and so on through the table.

Time (years)	Population (people)	Net births (people/year)
1975	4.00 (billion)	0.08 (billion)
1976	4.08	0.08
1977	4.16	0.08
1978	4.24	0.08
1979	4.32	0.09
1980	4.41	0.09
1981	4.50	0.09
1982	4.59	0.09
1983	4.68	0.09
1984	4.77	0.10
1985	4.87	0.10
1986	4.97	0.10
1987	5.07	0.10
1988	5.17	0.10
1989	5.27	0.11
1990	5.38	0.11

Figure 5.16.   Population Simulation, 1975–1990.

Students could continue filling out this chart for as long as necessary to understand the implications of a 0.02 net birth rate. However, if the birth rate should change, several of the numbers would need to be recomputed. It is unlikely anybody would be enthusiastic about such a task. Moreover, really to "see" what is happening, the numbers should be graphed as done in figure 5.17. If instead of carrying out the simulation and graphing by hand, a computer performs the simulation, the task becomes effortless.

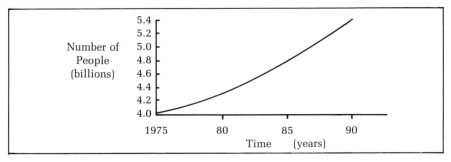

Figure 5.17   Hand-generated population growth.

Several choices are available for instructing the computer to perform these calculations. A spreadsheet program, as described in chapter 4, can be used. A program can be written in almost any computer language, such as BASIC or Pascal, to complete the arithmetic, or a special-purpose language for writing computer models can be used. Tasks are often more easily performed using specifically designed tools; the same is true with computers. One tool developed for writing computer models of this type is called DYNAMO, standing for DYNAmic MOdels (see resource section).

To convert the causal-loop diagram pictured in figure 5.15 to a computer model the computer needs to be instructed to "fill out" the chart in figure 5.16. The computer model, written in DYNAMO and using shortened English words, is:

POP.K = POP.J + (DT)(NBIRTH)

　　Population (people)

NBIRTH.KL = POP.K*NETBR

　　Net Births (people/year)

NETBR = 0.02

　　Net Birth Rate ($\frac{\text{persons/year}}{\text{person}}$)

The above "sentences" can be read:

The POPulation today (.K stands for "today") is equal to the POPulation the last time the census was taken (.J stands for "the last time the census was taken"), plus the Net BIRTHs over the time since the census taking (DT standing for "over the time since census taking or Difference in Time").

The number of new people, Net BIRTHs, added to the population between this census and the next census is determined by the current POPulation times ("*" standing for multiplication) the NET Birth Rate. NET Birth Rate is 0.02 per year.

The three lines of computer language above constitute a computer model that instructs the computer to simulate the world population over some specified period of time.

If Macintosh computers are available to the students, there is a more advanced, easier-to-use simulation language called STELLA, an acronym for Structural Thinking, Experiential Learning Laboratory with Animation. STELLA is based on DYNAMO but takes advantage of the graphics capabilities of the Macintosh. Figure 5.18 shows the population model as a student would develop it on the Macintosh. Population is represented by a picture of a tank (the square) to represent a quantity that accumulates. Net_Births are represented by a pipe controlled by a valve to represent a rate of flow. The cloud at the end of the Net_Births pipe says that this model is not going to try to explain where babies come from! The circle above Net_Birth_Rate represents a constant value, a value that does not change during the simulation run.

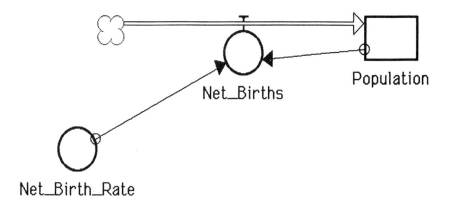

Figure 5.18 Diagram of a population model using STELLA.

Figure 5.19 shows the graph that the simulation generated, running the model from 1975 to 2000.

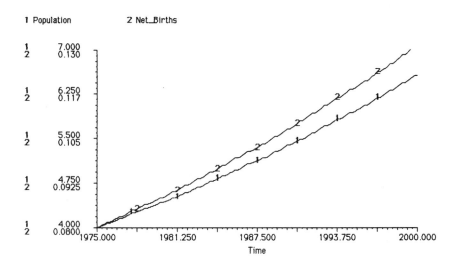

Figure 5.19 Graph generated by the population model using STELLA.

The line in figure 5.19 labeled with "1s" is the population (in billions of people). The line labeled with "2s" is Net_Births (in billions).

Figure 5.20 shows the population model as a picture and as a set of equations. The table shows the simulation run in tabular form. The square representing population is now filled in, showing the animation part of STELLA. The filling-in occurs as the simulation is taking place. The very small pictures, on the far left side of figure 5.20 constitute the menu of options from which the model-builder may choose while constructing a model.

File Define Windows Display Specs Run

POPULATION MODEL

Net_Births

Population

Net_Birth_Rate

Equations

Population = Population + Net_Births
INIT(Population) = 4.00
Net_Births = Population*Net_Birth_Rate
Net_Birth_Rate = 0.02

Table

Time	Population	Net_Births
1984.000	4.780	0.0956
1985.000	4.876	0.0975
1986.000	4.973	0.0995
1987.000	5.073	0.101
1988.000	5.174	0.103
1989.000	5.278	0.106
1990.000	5.383	0.108
1991.000	5.491	0.110
1992.000	5.601	0.112
1993.000	5.713	0.114
1994.000	5.827	0.117
1995.000	5.944	0.119
1996.000	6.063	0.121
1997.000	6.184	0.124
1998.000	6.308	0.126
1999.000	6.434	0.129
2000.000	6.562	0.13

Figure 5.20   A Macintosh screen divided into three windows.

This is a very simple illustration of a computer model. The same principles are followed for constructing a model of any level of sophistication. The elements included in figure 5.12 of the world food problem could be added to this model. Then such questions as "How much of a price increase can people of a certain income level bear?" or "What effect on the total system does a change in the birth rate have?" can be studied instantaneously with a simulation model.

Students do not have to build their own models to study such questions. There are some commercially available programs that provide models allowing the user to ask such "what if" questions. *Demo-Graphics*, described in chapter 2, is one example. The problem with using someone else's model is that the model becomes a "black box." The person using the model often accepts the assumptions (the model "sentences") as valid. It is sometimes difficult to determine these assumptions in commercial software unless the manual accompanying the program is explicit.

If information about the nature of the model is not included with the software, it can be an illuminating experience for both teacher and students to attempt to determine the model's structure and assumptions. Some strategies for doing this include the following:

1. Run the simulation many (approaching 100) times to determine random events and relationships among variables.

2. Test the model with extreme decisions, and see if the simulation still behaves reasonably.

3. Run the model, changing only one decision and keeping all other variables the same. This can be followed by then changing two decisions to get an understanding of their impact on each other. An excellent model for this was developed by Friel (1983).

4. Evaluate the simulation in terms of information available in the literature. This provides motivation to students to research the literature to determine if the literature supports the behavior exhibited by the simulation.

5. If appropriate, have the students act as "experts" and evaluate the behavior of the simulation based on their experiences. *Lemonade* is a simulation where students might have "real-world" experience.

6. Invite a guest expert to class — a local authority on the subject — and have him or her discuss simulation runs of the model.

The interesting aspect of these suggestions is that they are all used by research teams to validate models built as aids to decision making.

When students build their own models, however, they make the assumptions, examine the validity of the assumptions based on how the model acts, and restudy the problem if their mental and computer models do not seem to match reality. This process allows students to use the computer in its most powerful mode, as an extension of their minds.

Tools such as databases and graphing packages provide static representations of problems whereas computer model-building and simulation allow for active statements of problems. The latter approach focuses on creating more useful tools. The student molds the tool to his or her vision, theory, and needs. As knowledge and understanding of a situation increases, the tool can be more finely tuned for a particular problem. In this role of tool-maker the computer surpasses traditional tools; creating more appropriate tools is a higher-level use of the machine. The student, or any user, through continuous refinement of the tool, is provided with a more powerful intellectual problem-solving aid.

Model-building and Simulation at the High School Level

Social studies teachers may not have the mathematical skills to build elaborate models. However, there are many schools where mathematics teachers have incorporated model-building and simulation into their courses (Choate, 1983). In such cases the problems chosen to study inevitably come from the social studies area. However, if the causal-loop diagramming tool has been integrated into social studies courses (see figure 5.21), it seems appropriate for the social studies and mathematics teachers to combine skills and expertise. Together they can begin to bridge the separation between qualitative and quantitative approaches to problem solving. Figure 5.21 shows how one class used causal-loop diagramming to facilitate a discussion of the drug problem at its private school.

The problem was the increasing number of students taking drugs. The students identified four reasons for this situation as shown by the four positive (⟳ +) feedback loops in figure 5.21.

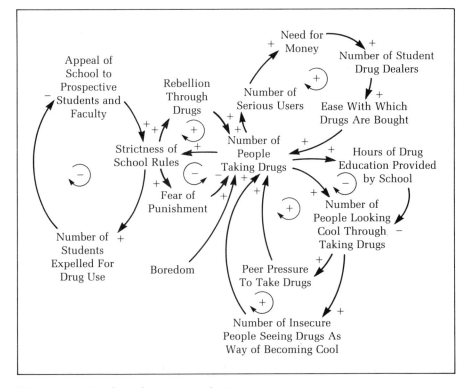

Figure 5.21   Student drug-use analysis.

1. As the number of serious drug users increases, their need for more money causes some of them to become campus drug-dealers, which makes drug acquisition easier for others.

2. The more people there are on drugs, the "cooler" drug taking becomes, increasing peer pressure to participate.

3. Drug taking is seen as a way for insecure people to look "cool."

4. As the amount of drug taking increases, the school's rules become stricter, causing drug taking to provide a means for rebelling.

The students then went on to suggest changes in parts of the system which might begin to lower the number of students on drugs. They identified two possible strategies.

1. As the school rules become stricter, more people fear punishment, causing fewer people to take drugs.

2. The increase in drug taking causes the school to provide more hours of drug education, causing the "looking cool through taking drugs" to decrease, the peer pressure to take drugs to decrease, and eventually the number of people on drugs to decrease.

The students also suggested that an increase in the strictness of school rules causes an increase in the number of students expelled, probably causing the attractiveness of the school to potential students and faculty to decrease.

The real learning from such an analysis is the appreciation of the complexity of the problem and the unlikeliness of there being only one correct solution. The students acquire an understanding of the delicate balance of the system involved, as well as the ability to understand how all the pieces of such a system fit together using such analytical tools.

The second example is from an economics course where the students actually built the computer model and started using the model for analysis. The problem the students chose to study was the effect on football and the National Football League (NFL) of the establishment of the United States Football League (USFL). The initial analysis led the students to develop the diagram in figure 5.22.

Figure 5.22 presents the scenario before the establishment of the USFL. Figure 5.23 is the students' analysis of the situation afterwards. The computer simulations suggested one football league would be bankrupt in ten years — not a bad prediction! This analysis very likely holds true for other sports as well and probably for other economic areas.

Of particular interest to the social studies teacher was the means by which students collected information for analysis. The students contacted each league office as well as local newspaper and television

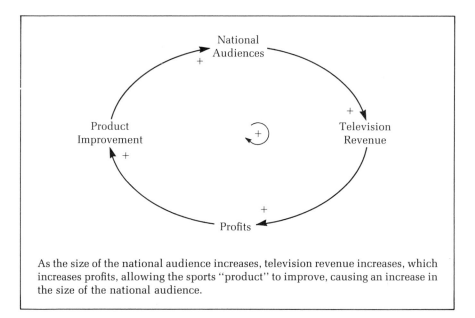

As the size of the national audience increases, television revenue increases, which increases profits, allowing the sports "product" to improve, causing an increase in the size of the national audience.

Figure 5.22   Sports economics, part I.

people. The students were involved in an economic study of genuine interest to them. They quickly realized the usefulness of simulation models in a situation of complexity. The students had learned the system dynamics approach the previous year in an applied mathematics course. The content from the areas of math and social science, which do not usually meet at the secondary level, provided these students with a useful problem-solving tool.

Looking back over this chapter, note that the computer does not usually enter the model-building and simulation scene until the secondary school level. The computer should only be used when it is an appropriate aid to problem solving. For the first nine or so school years the focus is on developing the skills needed for understanding problems. The computer enters only at the end of the process. This parallels the time allocation that occurs in the application of simulation in actual problem-solving situations. Typically more than three fourths of professional time is spent in understanding the problem, identifying the causal relationships and feedback loops, and collecting data about the behavior of the problem over time. If all this is not done thoroughly first, the resulting computer model is likely to be invalid. An invalid model is useless, whether it be a computer model or a mental model! The integration of model-building and simulation into the social studies curriculum is thus a gradual process over the K–12 years, with concepts and simpler tools long preceding actual computer use.

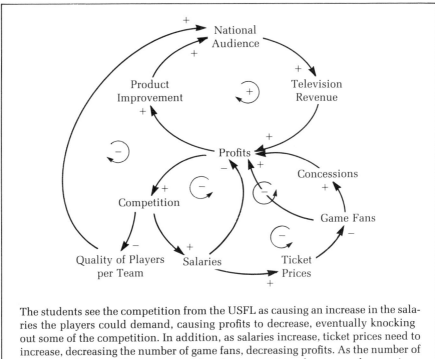

The students see the competition from the USFL as causing an increase in the sala-ries the players could demand, causing profits to decrease, eventually knocking out some of the competition. In addition, as salaries increase, ticket prices need to increase, decreasing the number of game fans, decreasing profits. As the number of game fans decrease, the amount sold at the concessions decreases, also causing profits to decrease. Finally, the increased competition decreases the number of quality players available per team, eventually decreasing the size of the national audience, changing the first, rosy picture to a more precarious projection.

Figure 5.23 Sports economics, part II (with competition).

References

Choate, J., "System Dynamics at Work in the High School Classroom," *Class-room Computer News*, vol. 3, no. 3 (1983) 65.

Friel, S., "Lemonade's the Name, Simulation's the Game," *Classroom Compu-ter News*, vol. 3, no. 3 (1983) 34–39.

"In Search of a Scope and Sequence for Social Studies," *Social Education*, vol. 48, no. 6 (April 1984) 249–73.

Murphy, E.M., "Food and Population: A Global Concern," *Social Education*, vol. 48, no. 5 (May 1984) 337–56.

Roberts, N.; Andersen, D.; Deal, R.; Garet, M.; and Shaffer, W., *Introduction to Computer Simulation*. Reading, Mass.: Addison-Wesley, 1982.

PART II

The Past, the Present, the Future

The Evolution of the Computing Machine

The twentieth century has been hailed as an age of change that has been dramatically accelerated in the last three decades by the invention of the computer. Computers played important roles in making the calculations needed to build the atomic and hydrogen bombs; they sit in every missile pointed toward the Soviet Union, and in every Soviet missile aimed at the United States. A computer is being used to write this paragraph — and most likely is used in your school for everything from scheduling students to keeping track of library books. Computers are widely viewed as the technology of the next millennium. Futurists such as Alvin Toffler suggest that computers are at the forefront of the "third wave" technology that is rapidly transforming the society in which we live. We are now on the fourth "generation" of computers, with each generation changing hundreds of times more rapidly than the previous one, and each generation foreshadows even further previously unpredicted changes.

Since the first Eisenhower–Stevenson election, computers have assisted in predicting election results and have influenced election strategies. Computers now record our bank balances, determine our credit ratings, and inventory our grocery stores. The automobile industry is terminating workers while robots on the assembly line begin to install in automobiles computers to navigate via satellite, monitor the function of the engine, and bleep out courtesy messages to passengers who forget to close their doors.

As social studies teachers we have observed the coming age of the computer, and some of us have already begun to master the technology in our homes and in our classrooms. As educators, however, we have the further commitment to help our students both comprehend and utilize this potent tool so central to this generation. One way is to understand how computer technology evolved over the centuries, with many scientists, often limited by the available technology of their times, playing major roles. The development of computers parallels the evolution of many other inventions and the technologies these fostered. Let us guide our students through the past, help them to comprehend the present, and prepare them for the future by making them aware of these repeating patterns of technological change.

*In every major field of endeavor there are pioneers — genuises like Leonardo da Vinci — who have the imagination to invent the future but live in a society bound by its limited technology.

*In most fields there are the folk heroes — people like the Wright brothers — who are responsible for new inventions and whose commitment to their ideas eventually results in a breakthrough that brings popular acclaim and acceptance of their innovation.

*For every recognized innovator there are usually scores of unhonored and unsung people whose work has either helped others achieve or who simply never got credit because they were not at the right place at the right time.

*Historically, governments have played major roles in developing those technologies seen to have national consequence and/or military significance.

*Most new technology gradually affects everyday people. Initially, limited to the inventors or agencies involved in its creation, the technology next moves to business and government. Eventually it is made less expensive by mass production, allowing ordinary people to afford it. The technology has come into its own when, as with the telephone, people can no longer understand how they managed without it.

The History of Computing

The need to quantify experience dates back to the days when our ancestors were emerging from the jungle and veldt. Fingers and toes undoubtedly were the first means used to count objects. Somewhere in prehistory, pebbles or stones were most likely used to keep records. This along with the use of a leather strip to string a necklace of beads sometime about 4,000 years ago resulted in the invention of the abacus.

Figure 6.1. The abacus, one of the earliest calculating devices, is still used in many parts of the world.

The word *abacus* is derived from the Arab word for "dust", and thus provides a clue regarding its origins. In the East, abacuses have been in continuous use since 2,000 years before the birth of Christ. This ingenious instrument, in the hands of a skilled user, can be faster than the desk calculator widely used in the 1940s.

Many ancient civilizations are known for their use of calculating devices to predict the arrival of the seasons. The Sumerian calendar changed from a thirteen-month lunar calendar to the twelve-month solar calendar about the time Sumerian society turned from a dependence on hunting to agriculture. Priestly scientific classes emerging in Sumer and many other ancient societies developed amazingly accurate means for calculating the summer and winter solstices. Ancient remains from even so primitive a society as the one populating Stonehenge, England, in the seventeenth century B.C. reveal that they functioned like a primitive calculator marking the location on the horizon where the sun rose and set during the summer and winter solstices.

The intricate computing devices available today result from continuous technical development primarily in western Europe. Before the sixteenth century, Europe's science and technology had not eclipsed the wisdom of the ancient world. It was in the seventeenth century that Galileo, Kepler, Newton, Leibniz, Descartes, and Pascal — giant figures in the development of geometry, calculus, logic, physics, and astronomy — advanced the frontiers of knowledge. As these sciences fed into and were fed by developing technological knowledge, the base for the industrialization of the modern world was established.

It is beyond the scope of this work, however, to delve into the history of modern science. Let us limit ourselves to the development of calculators and computers, outgrowths of many of these earlier achievements. This story begins with a little known figure in Germany, Wilhelm Schickard, inventor of the first known calculator. Schickard's instrument was destroyed in a fire, and he as well as his family died in the ravages of the Thirty Years War. Enough evidence remains, however, to credit this professor of Hebrew, mathematics, and astronomy with the creation, in 1623, of a calculating machine that could multiply and divide as well as add and subtract. Two letters from Schickard to Johannes Kepler describe the machine in enough detail to have allowed the construction of accurate working models.

It is unlikely that Blaise Pascal (1623–1662), born in the year Schickard invented his calculator, even knew anything about Schickard. Pascal, himself, might never have invented his calculator, had it not been for his father's bad luck. Raised in the stimulating environment of Paris, Blaise taught himself geometry, proved one of Euclid's theorems, and participated in the discussions of learned societies before the age of thirteen. Due to financial difficulties, the elder Pascal was forced to work in the provinces as a tax agent. In his new position much of M. Pascal's time was consumed in the dreary addition of long lines of figures in the eight different French coins then in use. At the age of seventeen, Blaise was taken away from his preoccupation with writing a concise study of the entire field of mathematics to help his father. To avoid doing these

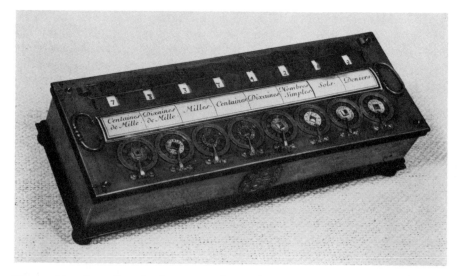

Figure 6.2. Pascal's calculator was devised to expedite the tedious task of adding long lines of figures.

tiresome sums, Blaise began work on a machine that would do them accurately and effortlessly. In its completed form it was about the size of a shoebox.

The machine had no problems either adding or subtracting. It could also multiply by doing a series of additions, and divide by carrying out a series of subtractions. Though their calculator was much admired and praised, the Pascals were unable to sell the fifty they built fast enough to turn a profit. Blaise Pascal lost interest in the device, busied himself with higher mathematics until the age of thirty, and became a religious recluse until his death nine years later.

Pascal's attempt at perfecting an all-purpose calculator was carried on by another child prodigy, also a mathematician and philosopher, Gottfried Wilhelm Leibniz (1646–1716). In constructing his calculator, Leibniz worked from Pascal's model. He improved on it, making multiplication and division possible as separate operations and not (as in Pascal's calculator) as adjuncts to addition and subtraction. The basic design of Leibniz's computing device was so good that slightly revised and simplified models of it were still being used during the 1930s, nearly 300 years after the appearance of the prototype.

The Basic Differences Between Calculators and Computers

Despite their achievements, Schickard, Pascal, and Leibniz had moved the world in the direction of making only calculators, not computers. To be sure, the two have some common functions — both, for instance, have input-output mechanisms for feeding data into the machine and for retrieval. Both instruments perform arithmetic functions such as addition and subtraction, though computers can perform far more complicated mathematical operations than even the most sophisticated calculator. The important difference between the two is that computers have control units that monitor the order in which the calculations take place. The control unit of the computer is unique in that it responds to its own previous calculation. For instance, the program might call for the computer to subtract a number from another *if* the first number is larger, but to add the numbers *if* the first number is equal to or smaller than the second number. When a mechanism with its own scanning of the results of previous calculations could decide what the next operation would be, it became a computer. Until that time, it remained a calculator. One way of understanding this concept is to think of playing checkers against a calculator as opposed to playing against a computer. While a calculator conceivably could write out the number of the spaces for a few opening moves, it cannot possibly adjust its own actions according to moves made by its opponent. A computer, however, can be programmed to respond to every move its opponent might make.

Charles Babbage; A Man Ahead of His Time

The first man to understand the differences between calculators and computers and to attempt to build the latter was Charles Babbage (1791-1871). Much like Pascal and Leibniz, Babbage exhibited signs of genius in early life. Unlike the others, Babbage is remembered only for his work on what he called his "Difference Engine," and its successor, the "Analytical Engine." Most of Babbage's adult life was spent in pursuit of his dream to make working models of these devices. The vain attempt to construct what would have been the world's first computer cost Babbage his wealth, health, and family. The great irony of Babbage's life was that, given the technology of his time, it was impossible to create a working model of a computer.

At the age of 32, Babbage concocted a design for his Difference Engine. Babbage envisioned this invention to calculate "a series of numbers following a mathematical law by a series of mechanical operations" (Zientara, p. 15). His plan was good enough to convince the prestigious Royal Academy to advance him £1,500. Ultimately the British government advanced Babbage a total of £17,000. Nevertheless, Babbage's workmen were unable to produce gears and sprockets capable of the precise measurements his machine required. When his chief engineer abandoned the project, Babbage himself lost interest. Rather than give up completely, however, Babbage began to work on an even more complicated device. While the first project was designed to be programmable for just one set of mathematical operations, the new project was to be capable of solving any conceivable arithmetic problem!

In planning his Analytical Engine, Babbage conceived the basic architectural design of the modern computer. Information was fed to an input device by way of punched cards. This idea was borrowed from Joseph Jacquard, a French weaver who used perforated cards to control the patterns woven by his mechanical looms. The machine's arithmetic unit (which Babbage called his "mill") then performed the required calculations, in the order dictated by the control unit. A memory (which Babbage called his "store") consisted of 1,000 registers, each capable of holding up to a fifty-digit number. This memory was designed to hold the intermediate numbers (while the machine was still completing its calculations) as well as the end product. The control unit performed the task of reading results from the previous calculations to determine the next operation. (Babbage was fully aware that the control performed a unique function, and referred to the process it performed as "the machine eating its own tail.") An output mechanism to communicate the end product to the operator completed the five essential elements which appear in modern computers. While each of these five procedures is indispensable to computers, it was the control unit which made Babbage's conception particularly significant:

Figure 6.3. With his calculating "Engines," Charles Babbage had conceived the basic design of the modern computer.

A machine that is to have the power to carry out any algorithmic [a sequence of mathematical operations] procedure whatever, must be able to use the intermediate results obtained at any stage to decide which of a number of possible sequences of operations to follow from then on, as required by the algorithm. . . . Babbage envisioned what he called the *control* unit, which would supervise continously the flow of operations and make these decisions automatically as required. The unit would cause the appropriate data to be extracted from the store at the appropriate time and transfered to the mill. The intermediate or final results would be returned from the mill to the store, and be presented to the mill, by means of perforated cards or otherwise, the statement of the operation to be performed next. It would thus ensure that the sequence was performed in the order required (Moreau, p. 17).

While Babbage conceived the idea of the modern computer, he did not have the technology to carry out his plans. His workmen could not make cogs and wheels with the required precision. Telephone switches, vacuum tubes, and, of course, computer chips were a long way from being invented. Thus, Babbage's machine was destined for failure. Babbage died at age eighty, broken and all but forgotten, but he has since been widely acclaimed as the father of the modern computer. Thomas Aiken, another pioneer in computer architecture who appeared on the scene a century after Babbage, recognized his great debt to the eccentric Englishman by noting that if Babbage had lived seventy-five years later, he (Aiken) would have been out of a job.

George Boole and Binary Math

What Charles Babbage did for the conception of the computer, another Englishman by the name of George Boole (1815–1864) did for its mathematical operations. Like the other innovators, Boole showed signs of brilliance at an early age. Hampered by poverty, he tried to prepare himself for a position in the Church of England by learning five languages, beginning with Greek and Latin. Boole's real love was mathematics, and before he was forty he had published a work that later led Bertrand Russell to exclaim: "Pure math was discovered by George Boole." Boole laid the foundations for binary math, which later became the mathematics used to structure and program computers.

Boole's most significant contribution to the development of the computer was in furthering ongoing work that attempted to:

1. show that all mathematics can be reduced to logic and therefore all logic to mathematics; and

2. identify a minimum number of key words that extended the classical (from the ancient Greeks) boundaries of logic. These words are:
    AND
    OR
    IF THEN
    NOT
    From classical logic, the following is usually accepted as a proof of truth:

    > If only mammals nurse their young,
    > AND whales nurse their young,
    > Then whales are mammals.

If the first sentence above is called sentence A, the second sentence B, and third sentence C, the above three sentences can be expressed as:

> If A is true,
> AND B is true,
> Then C is true.

If either A or B is not true, then C is not true (or false). Given these logical statements, all the possibilities presented here can be shown in a truth table, where T stands for "true" and F for "false" (or "not true"):

A	B	C
T	T	T
T	F	F
F	T	F
F	F	F

Looking at another one of Boole's key words:

    If Sam buys a ticket,

    OR Sam has a pass,

    Then Sam may go to the movies.

These sentences may be reduced to:

A	B	C
T	T	T
T	F	T
F	T	T
F	F	F

Instead of using the symbols T and F to represent these logic statements, 0 (for F) and 1 (for T) can be used. The "AND" table (the first example) can be shown as:

A	B	C
1	1	1
1	0	0
0	1	0
0	0	0

This suggests that the mathematics and logic being dealt with can be represented in a binary system, which is a system composed of two elements such as 0s and 1s. The binary system (base 2) works the same way the decimal system (base 10) works. Instead of having 10 symbols (0, 1, 2, 3, 4, 5, 6, 7, 8, 9) with which to calculate, there are only 2 (0, 1). So:

Base 10	Base 2
0	0
1	1
2	10
3	11
4	100
5	101
6	110
7	111
8	1000
9	1001

and so forth. For people who have been taught to calculate in base 10, base 2 appears unmanageable. For a machine designed to represent things as on or off, or as the presence or absence of electricity, the binary system is a necessity.

The combination of the concept of binary mathematics and the natural characteristics of electricity came together in more recent times to contribute to the development of today's computing machines. Electricity must have closed paths, usually wires, in order to flow. In any situation where electricity is being used, a break in the elements or circuits that conduct the electricity stops its flow. This flow/no-flow situation can also be thought of as a binary condition. The rules of logic, an important aspect of mathematics, can be represented by the presence or absence of electricity in a computing machine.

From the Census to IBM

An important breakthrough in designing more versatile calculators was made in the United States and makes a good case for the adage that "necessity is the mother of invention." It had taken the U. S. Bureau of the Census until 1887 to analyze and publish the results of its 1880 poll. By this time, much of the information was already outdated, and the Census Bureau was the object of much ridicule. Determined to avoid another fiasco, the Bureau sponsored a competition to find a faster method for analyzing the data collected in the 1890 census. The winner was Hermann Hollerith (1860–1929), an engineer with a degree from Columbia University and a former employee of the Bureau. The ingenious device Hollerith invented was a machine that electronically counted cards punched with codes signifying answers to the questions asked in the census, such as age, sex, country of origin, and religion. These cards were then run over cups filled with mercury. Wherever a hole was punched, the needle would drop through to complete an electric circuit, and a corresponding clock-like device was moved up one unit. At the end of each day's run, the numbers for each category were recorded on a separate sheet, the counters were set to zero, and the next batch of punched cards were prepared. An equally ingenious method was devised for sorting these cards after the original census was counted. If the Census Bureau wanted to see, for instance, how many college educated women were recent immigrants, the lid of an electronically operated sorting box opened, as cards indicating one of these characteristics passed by. The machine was then set to collect cards with the other characteristic. With the help of Hollerith's efficient invention, the 1890 census was tabulated in six weeks.

After his highly acclaimed success with the Census Bureau, Hollerith decided to go into business for himself. He formed the Tabulating

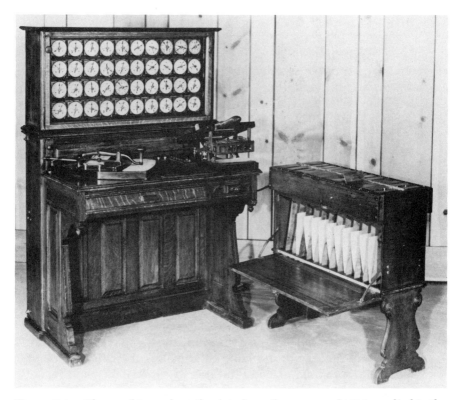

Figure 6.4.   The need to analyze the data from the census of 1890 resulted in the development of the Census Analyzer by Hermann Hollerith.

Machine Company, which provided businesses with a variety of different data processing machines. In 1911, Hollerith merged his company with two others to become the Computing-Tabulating-Recording Company, and upon stepping down three years later he was succeeded as president by Thomas J. Watson (1874–1956). Following several mergers, Watson changed the name of his company to International Business Machines. Under Watson's dynamic leadership, IBM pioneered in building computers and dominated this field for over thirty years.

Incidentally, Hollerith had fallen out of favor with the Census Bureau. The Bureau then hired James Powers to tabulate census results in 1910. Using advanced designs of Hollerith's machine, Powers subsequently formed his own company, which competed with IBM in supplying office equipment. Through a series of mergers, Powers's firm became Remington Rand. For a brief time in the 1950s Remington led IBM in business computers and even won the contract for the 1950 census. The rivalry has continued to the present with IBM now dominating the computer business.

Inventing the First Modern Computer

In the years immediately preceding and following World War II, the modern computer was invented. The technological advances leading to the development of these computers seem to have been made quite independent of each other by a number of different people using a variety of approaches. Perhaps it was only coincidence — being the right person at the right time — that brought recognition and fame to one person rather than another. On the other hand, maybe it was far more than luck that gave Princeton scientist John von Neumann the recognition implicit in the casual naming of the first generation computers "von Neumann machines." Perhaps a case could also be made for calling them Charles Babbage, or even Konrad Zuse, machines.

Konrad Zuse was a young German engineer who, in 1938, conceived the idea of using telephone relay switches to make a computer-like calculator based on binary math. His workbench was the living room of his parents' apartment in Berlin. With the aid of a friend in 1940 at the outbreak of the war, Zuse sought government support to develop this technology. The government, however, believed the fighting would be over before Zuse's devices could aid the war effort. As a civilian engineer in a German airplane factory Zuse was able to put his home-built electric relay computer to work. He used it to make calculations needed to help reduce the problem of wing fluttering in war planes and rockets. Zuse eventually opened a factory employing twenty workers to make his complex calculators. As the war drew to a close and the Russians were invading the outskirts of Berlin, Zuse fled to Switzerland with one of his Z-4 models. After the war he entered into negotiations with both IBM and Remington Rand. Neither of these two industrial giants were interested in developing Zuse's patents. Left on his own, Zuse himself formed a successful company that built and sold computers.

While Germany was turning a deaf ear to Konrad Zuse's plans for a binary computer, the British had a crew of young scientists cracking the secret German military code. Thanks to the Polish underground, a copy of the German coding machine, Enigma, was smuggled into England early in World War II. The British government set a team of its top mathematicians to work on cracking the code. Under the direction of Alan Turing, this team built several computer-like electronic devices capable of reading instructions at the then unheard of rate of five thousand characters per second. Impressive as they were, these decoders cannot be considered computers. They were designed or programmed for only one purpose, and could be converted to perform some other task only with great difficulty.

Working more or less in isolation at the time World War II began, an obscure science professor at Iowa State College began experimenting with ways to make calculations easier for his twenty graduate students. He claimed to have resolved some basic design problems in developing

Figure 6.5. John Atanasoff and Clifford Berry developed a calculating machine that used binary numbers, vacuum tube circuits, and stored programs.

such a machine, including the use of binary numbers, stored programs, and vacuum tube circuits. In 1941, John Atanasoff and an assistant, Clifford Berry, were pictured in a local paper with a calculating machine which they said would be ready in about a year. Atanasoff also wrote several theoretical papers describing the machine and the logic that would make it work. Atanasoff attracted some attention and several visits from John Mauchly who later engaged in similar work.

Bell Labs and Harvard-IBM

Meanwhile, several other U.S. physicists, mathematicians, and engineers were working on computer-like projects. Using telephone relay switches, Bell Laboratories mathematician George Stibitz built a binary adder over a long weekend in 1937. In his spare time, Stibitz created binary dividers and multipliers. Stibitz estimated he could build a binary computer for $50,000, but was derisively asked why anyone would want to spend that much money to build a machine just to do calculations. When finally given the signal to proceed, Stibitz built five different models. The first one was used by three different teams at Bell Labs. Called the complex calculator, this device achieved brief fame when it was hooked up by telephone lines to a convention of mathematicians at Dartmouth College, New Hampshire, in 1940. Mathematics problems were sent by phone to the Bell Labs, and answers were relayed back in less than a minute. Stibitz followed with four other versions of his complex calculator, each more sophisticated and computer-like than the previous. By the time Stibitz completed number five in 1946, however, other teams had constructed more powerful and flexible computers that overshadowed the innovations of the Bell Laboratories team.

While still a graduate student at Harvard, Thomas Aiken (1900–1973) drew up plans for a computer that so impressed his mentor that he sent Aiken to see Tom Watson at IBM. Watson not only decided to bankroll this project at a cost of $500,000, but also gave Aiken some of his top engineers. The result was a calculator of immense proportions, weighing five tons, measuring fifty-one feet long and eight feet high, and containing 800,000 different parts. Data was fed into it using punched cards, and wheels were turned with electronic impulses — ten to a complete revolution. The clanking of its thousands of gears and electric relay switches caused a deafening amount of noise, and the heat they generated melted the several tons of ice needed each day to control the temperature. By modern standards, this computer was extremely slow — requiring up to eleven seconds to do division. Completed in early 1944, it was dubbed the "super brain" but is better known as Mark I. Later versions, including Marks II, III and IV, did valuable work for the Navy and Air Force until the early 1950s. Though a marvel for their day, these computers were eventually overshadowed by better designed machines, whose binary math and vacuum tubes achieved far greater speed and computing capacity.

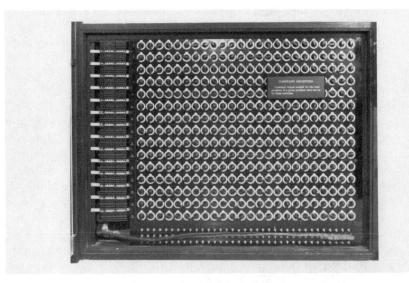

Figure 6.6.   Thomas Aiken's computer was dubbed "super brain".

Figure 6.7.   John von Neumann is given a major share of credit for designing the prototype computer.

The "von Neumann Machines"

The immediate forerunner of modern computers was developed at the Aberdeen, Maryland, U. S. Army Ballistic Research Laboratories, associated with the Moore School of Engineering of the University of Pennsylvania. This project was given its start by solving the U.S. Army's problem of computing trajectories of artillery firing-tables under varying conditions. For example, Army engineers knew that the rarefied atmosphere at the high point of a shell's trajectory could come close to doubling the range of the shell. Seven hundred seventy-five different calculations were needed for each of 3,000 possible projections. Even with 100 employees using hand calculators, the Army was unable to make significant progress in completing these tables.

To speed up the computations, the army assigned a young math professor, Herman Goldstine, to the Aberdeen project. Goldstine was fortunate to have John Mauchly (1907–1980) and J. Prospect Eckert to work with when he arrived. Mauchly had learned a great deal about computer design from John Atanasoff. Eckert, only twenty-two, was already an expert on vacuum tubes, which were used in radios. These tubes required far less electricity than the cumbersome electric relay switches Aiken and Stibitz had used in their projects. Work on the Electronic Numerical Integrator And Computer (ENIAC) began in 1943 and was not finished until after the war. First unveiled to the public in February, 1946, ENIAC covered about as much floor space as the Mark I and weighed twenty-five tons, but with its 18,000 vacuum tubes calculated 500 times faster than the Harvard-IBM machine.

Before ENIAC was even completed, the men who designed it realized its major failings:

1. its memory was so short it could only hold twenty ten-digit numbers;

2. it required manual interventions to complete programs; and,

3. it could take several days to reprogram.

Work on a design that would correct these deficiencies had begun when another scientist joined the Moore-Aberdeen staff. While waiting for a train, John von Neumann met Goldstine. It was a lucky meeting. From his work on the hydrogen bomb project in Los Alamos, von Neumann understood the need for making thousands of computations involving innumerable variables. He listened with increasing fascination while Goldstine described the work being done at Aberdeen and decided to join Goldstine's team. Always a quick learner, von Neumann soon understood the essentials of the ENIAC project. When it came time to draft the final proposal to correct the design, von Neumann did most of the writing though he was still dividing his time between Aberdeen and Los Alamos. Many of the ideas in the proposal did not originate with von Neumann; nevertheless, von Neumann's name was widely associated with the forceful arguments advanced there. Subsequent computers built along the lines of this proposal have been called "von Neumann machines." In Princeton, New Jersey, where von Neumann personally supervised the project, his computer was dubbed the "Johniac."

The three major design features that distinguished subsequent "von Neumann machines" from the earlier computers were vastly expanded memories, greater flexibility in reprogramming, and ability to perform operations following instructions from their own internal memories. In the following passage, von Neumann addressed these issues:

> Since the orders that exercise the entire control are in the memory, a higher degree of flexibility is achieved than in any previous mode of control. Indeed, the machine under control of its orders, can extract numbers (or orders) from the memory, process them (as numbers!), and return them to the memory (to the same or other locations); i.e. it can change the contents of the memory — indeed this is its normal *modus operandi*. Here it can, in particular, change the orders (since these are in the memory!) — the very orders that control its actions. Thus all sorts of sophisticated order-systems become possible, which keep successively modifying themselves and hence also the computational proceesses that are likewise under their control (Bernstein, pp. 72–73).

Von Neumann's influence on computer architecture was furthered in 1946 and 1947 by a series of seminars and papers on computer design.

During those two years von Neumann and his colleagues at the Moore School generously shared their insights and solutions in the immensely difficult task of designing computers and computer programs. It is much to the credit of these technological pioneers that they upheld the best tenets of the scientific tradition to make their knowledge available to all rather than hide it away for commercial exploitation.

If, on the other hand, developing computers was thought of as a competition between different groups of scientists at different universities or corporations, Cambridge University, U.K., might be declared the winner. Under the direction of Maurice Wilkes, fresh from his seminars with von Neumann, the Cambridge group completed their computer in 1949. It took von Neumann himself considerably longer. Rebuffed by Eckert and Mauchly, who together started a commercial computer business, von Neumann began his project at Princeton's Institute for Advanced Study. In the atmosphere of a private university with no wartime or marketing deadlines to meet, it took the von Neumann group five years to complete their Electronic Discrete Variable Automatic Computer (EDVAC). With but slight variations its design was widely copied, and later even the copies were copied, while the original outlived its competition and served faithfully until 1962. In the meantime, Eckert and Mauchly ran into financial difficulties and were on the verge of bankruptcy when they were invited to organize Remington Rand's computer division. With Mauchley and Eckert in command, Remington's computer division briefly bested its old rival, IBM, and was used to compute the 1950 census. Despite their success, Mauchly and Eckert never completely reconciled themselves to the fact that von Neumann was given the major share of credit for designing the prototype computer. In a statement made just a few months before his death in 1980, Mauchly complained:

> History is certainly going to change its view of me and Eckert and lots
> of other people. We think it will change in respect to who did what,
> so as to reflect the part we really played in the invention of the computer (Zientara, p. 48).

Generations

In the forty-odd years since von Neumann, Eckert, and others built the first modern computers, further development of this significant invention in speed, accuracy, reliability, and efficiency has accelerated at an exponential pace. Students of this development have provided us with a schema of five different generations of computers, each based on a different technology.

By modern standards, the first generation computers of the 1940s and 1950s were slow, bulky, hot, unreliable, and expensive to run. They required large rooms to house them, experts to operate them, tons of ice to cool them, and prodigous amounts of electricity to power them. Furthermore, these computers could perform but 1,000 calculations per second compared to 100 million for modern computers.

The main cause of the problems that plagued the first generation was the vacuum tube technology on which they depended. These tubes took time to warm up, ran hot, used much electricity, occupied a good deal of space, and were fairly expensive to replace. It is not difficult to imagine the headaches that 130,000 such tubes could create if housed in one computer.

The invention of the transistor in 1947 by three Bell Lab scientists, J. Bardeen, W. Braittain, and W. Schockley, paved the way for a new generation of computers employing solid-state technology. To say the least, theirs was "a fundamental invention." Even the relatively crude early transistors were one two-hundredth the size of the smallest vacuum tubes. Transistors also generated less heat and required less electricity than vacuum tubes; and they were far faster, more efficient, reliable, and inexpensive. Despite these significant advantages, transistor technology was not really perfected until the late 1950s. The second generation of computers is said to have begun in 1959 with the use of transistors in the central processors. Though still slow by modern standards, second generation computers were 100-fold faster than their vacuum tube ancestors, and their memory 250 percent longer.

Third-generation computers began appearing in 1963 as integrated circuits printed on silicon chips replaced the second generation's transistors. This new process had engineers design large diagrams of computer circuitry; the diagrams were then photographed. The photographs were miniaturized one-hundred fold and more, and the microscopic pictures were photoengraved onto minute silicon chips. The chips were then wired together, mounted on circuit boards, and installed in computers. This microcircuitry process increased computer speed from some 100,000 calculations per second to 100 million. In fact, since 1948, computer speed has been increased by a factor of ten every five years, a rate of increase that has actually accelerated with the passing of time.

Meanwhile, procedures for mass-producing silicon chips were developed and constantly improved, driving the price for these intricate devices to affordable mass market levels. From the private realm of military scientists, computers have come to enjoy an ever larger circle of users. Branching out to other government agencies, and then adopted for commercial purposes, computers have come to invade almost every facet of corporate life from processing payrolls to recording proxy votes. With the increased miniaturizing and decreased costs of computers in the 1970s, they have found their way into the daily lives of most Americans. Today computers find an endless variety of uses, ranging from toys to missiles, from business machines to recreational equipment, from mining coal to forecasting the weather.

Figure 6.8. Microcircuitry and silicon chips have made computers affordable to an increasing number of users.

Even as this is being written, the fourth-generation computers are being produced by precision lasers etching the ciruitry of room-sized computers onto single silicon wafers. While the chips of the third generation held thousands of transistor circuits, wafers are now being designed to hold millions. The increased speed and memory of these wafers allow these new computers to simulate air flow around an entire plane, break codes, forecast weather, and find new sources of energy. According to experts, the country that first masters this technology will have a decided competitive advantage over other countries in terms of military as well as commercial development. Right now, the race is between the United States and Japan.

While we may still be contemplating the winner of the race to the fourth generation, computer engineers are busily laying the groundwork for a fifth generation. Fifth-generation computers involve the development of artificial intelligence (AI). At this stage, computers are programmed to think in terms of symbols rather than numbers. Using this method, scientists hope to make the breakthrough to a truly intelligent computer that can think instead of merely react in accordance to its programmed instructions. Some students of the field believe that the computers themselves will take over, designing increasingly intelligent computers that will in turn design even more intelligent machines.

One thing is certain. The world continues to change at an exponential rate as microchips get smaller and computers faster, more powerful, and more intelligent. There will be new computer-based technology affecting our lives not only as teachers and students but as parents, citizens, and consumers. The world in which we were raised is quite different than the world our children will live to see. In the next chapter we look at other new technologies and the issues being created by these technologies. The eighth chapter looks further into the future, presenting the thinking of Alvin Toffler and other visionaries.

References

Bernstein, J., *The Analytic Machine.* New York: William Morrow, 1981.

Evans, C., *The Micromillennium.* New York: Washington Square Press, 1979.
Goldstine, H.H., *The Computer: From Pascal to von Neumann.* Princeton, New Jersey: Princeton University Press, 1972.

Moreau, R., *The Computer Comes of Age.* Cambridge, Mass.: MIT Press, 1984.
Zientara, M., *The History of Computing.* Framingham, Mass.: C.W. Communications, 1981.

The Potential of Technology

Personal computers are the major innovation of this decade, and their use has yet to be entirely realized. This chapter considers new and potential applications of technology in the field of artificial intelligence and in the related areas of video and telecommunications. Several resulting issues that have implications for the social studies curriculum are explored. The chapter concludes with a scenario of a future that is enhanced by the presence and use of technology.

Artificial Intelligence

Computers can now read books for the blind. Machines exist that can recognize a person's voice and respond to a spoken command. Expert systems can help a physician make a diagnosis or an oil company locate oil reserves. A limited number of responsive tutors (computer-aided instruction programs that can provide "thoughtful" responses to student errors) exist in experimental settings. Robots, performing low-level tasks, are in use in many industrial settings, while scientists search for ways to make them more intelligent. Computers are being used as "smart machines" that exhibit artificial intelligence, or AI.

Artificial intelligence involves using computers to carry out tasks that are considered intelligent if done by humans. AI, as a field of study within computer science, emerged in the mid-1950s. The early 1960s saw the "dawn" of the age of AI, with enthusiastic claims being made about the possibilities for creating intelligent computers. The "dark ages" followed, with the earlier predictions seemingly unattainable. In the 1970s there was a resurgence of interest, and the number of successes in the field have steadily, though slowly, increased.

What are the difficulties? Brains and computers are very different. While many people would like computers to be able to do what brains do, it has been possible only in very simple and clearly defined areas. Computers have not proven to be successful in solving problems that involve insight, ambiguity, or poorly-defined objectives.

Artificial-intelligence research involves investigation in a variety of areas, including game playing, pattern recognition, problem solving, natural-language comprehension, and robotics. AI techniques are the basis of expert systems, and such techniques are now being applied to database systems.

Expert systems are designed to store and use the accumulated knowledge of a particular human speciality. With the increasing growth in knowledge, the limited number of "specialists" in any knowledge field and the years of training needed to become an expert, people find it desirable to develop a mechanism for accessing and using such accumulated knowledge. For example, an expert system called MYCIN, developed at Stanford University to assist doctors in making medical diagnoses, has been under continuous development and use for several years. Given the results of specific medical tests and described symptoms, the program can narrow the field of possible ailments. The program asks the questions of the doctor, seeking evidence to support or refute possible diagnoses. If the doctor cannot provide certain information, the program may defer drawing a conclusion until such information is provided.

Unlike expert systems, database systems, as discussed in chapter 4, are intended to store relatively static knowledge. In the expert system dealing with medical diagnosis, knowledge needed to make better and more effective decisions is constantly changing. Dynamic knowledge and heuristic relationships must be continually re-evaluated. A database system on a similar topic provides access to the articles and books written on a particular disease and does not need continual re-evaluation beyond the addition of the latest entries.

The effectiveness of a database system depends on how easily it can be searched. Unlike a library where a librarian can help a person search for information, a database system requires that the user have a complete understanding of how to find the needed information. The computer does not help the person determine how to search or for what. Database systems offer a great deal of knowledge but have very little "sense" about a user and how she or he is functioning in the database environment, thus making it difficult for the novice to use a database system. This also encourages individuals to specialize in the development of skills that then qualify them as "information brokers."

With the application of natural language techniques to searching a database, use of such systems by a broad cross-section of the public becomes more realistic. Databases can be designed to help the user understand what she or he is looking for and to keep track of particular directions in the search process. For example, if a search is being made for George Washington, should articles that refer to President Washington or G. Washington be included? Currently such distinctions are the responsibility of the user. Furthermore, a database system has no contextual understanding so it cannot distinguish between Washington the president and Washington the state and cannot make assumptions about the inquirer's information needs.

Since expert systems reach conclusions through the use of logic and experience similar to human reasoning, they can be designed to provide a "human window." In other words, expert systems can examine their own behaviors and report to humans how they reached their conclusions. AI researchers stress the importance of this aspect of expert systems — it permits humans to monitor and control machine behavior.

Video Technologies

Video technologies include television, videotape, and now videodisc. The current educational focus is on the combined use of video and computers. Broadcast television and videotape involve one-way transmission, and their use by the viewer is essentially passive. As earlier experiments with educational television suggest, video and television are not generally useful as pedagogic tools when used alone. They lack the capabilities for interaction and, consequently, for user control. The combination of computers with video permits the element of control that is essential to the learning process.

During the last twenty years techniques have been developed to create interactive videotapes. Control devices have been developed that work with computers and permit the use of programs designed to direct videotapes to "branch" to specific locations on the tape. An example of this is a series of videotaped court trials available to law students. The purpose of these materials is to increase the student's understanding of when it is appropriate for one lawyer to object to another attorney's line of questioning during a trial. At several points during the trial, the student must make a decision with regard to such a situation. If the student's decision is correct, the tape proceeds; if incorrect, the tape "branches" to the place on the tape where the explanation is given of why the student's decision was inappropriate.

Another example is the use of this technology to simulate flight. The student assumes the role of pilot and is asked to make a series of decisions during a trip. At each decision point, the implications of that decision are shown to the student by branching to the appropriate place on the tape. For example, one decision involves deciding where to land given information on weather conditions, amount of fuel, and location of airports. A poor decision would show the student the consequences of that decision, such as an emergency landing or a crash. The student can rewind the tape and experiment with other decisions. The combination of motion picture, explanatory text, and student interaction makes for a powerful learning environment.

These are interesting applications, but they clearly have not become commonplace in education. Videotapes have limited applications because of the time it takes to locate information on a tape, the costs to produce tapes, and the requirement for additional equipment to make the tapes interactive. As an alternative, videodiscs are providing some new options.

A videodisc looks like a very shiny, silver-colored record. Information, in the form of text, pictures, and sound, is recorded as a series of indentations or pits on the disc. Most commonly, this pattern of pits is read by a low-powered laser beam, translated into electronic impulses, and decoded to produce audio and video signals (Butler).

Unlike videotape, the life of a videodisc is potentially unlimited since nothing touches the videodisc when it is read.

There are 54,000 tracks on a disc. Each track, considered as one 360-degree rotation of the disc, is equal to one frame of a motion picture. A videodisc player reads thirty frames per second, the standard rate for

Figure 7.1   A videodisc.

television. The videodisc player can also read one spiral track continuously, accomplishing the same thing as freezing a motion picture frame.

Because each frame is assigned a number, videodiscs have the ability to access randomly any frame within seconds. This is a major improvement on videotape where random access is awkward because of the need to wind or rewind the tape to change locations. In addition, videodiscs may be slowed down for slow-motion sequences or speeded up for scanning. A videodisc has two sound tracks that permit incorporating speech and music, dialogues in two languages, or explanations at two different levels of complexity.

The storage capacity of this small silver platter is remarkable. The 54,000 frames provide as much storage as 600 carousels of slides or information found in approximately 180 books. A complete videodisc, if played linearly from beginning to end, takes about thirty minutes to view.

The real educational power of the videodisc is realized when it is combined with computer control. Given the videodisc equipment, which costs between $500 and $1000, and a computer, the additional hardware needed for interaction between a videodisc player and a computer starts at about $150. Furthermore, the knowledge required to put the videodisc player under computer control is relatively minimal.

Over the same time-period that videotapes and videodiscs have been explored as educational tools, computer-aided instruction (CAI) has been developing (see chapter 2). CAI has progressed slowly. Programs were initially written for large computers with poor graphics capabilities and with high costs per student, both in terms of computer time and course development. It is clear, however, that several educational benefits emerge from this kind of material.

1. CAI allows for the creation of student-paced, self-teaching materials.

2. Many different paths through these materials are possible to support different learning styles.

3. CAI is effective for disciplines requiring of all students a minimum knowledge-base such as U. S. History.

4. The possibility of immediate feedback provides a supportive learning environment for certain educational tasks.

5. The ability to have pre/post, self-scoring, and recording tests is particularly convenient for certain kinds of materials.

6. CAI can be more motivating than books to some students if it is well designed and highly interactive.

7. If the teacher has written the material, or can access the program, it is possible to keep the material very current, something that can be costly when relying just on books.

Again, education has not been dramatically changed by the availability of personal computers and CAI. Will the combination of the new videodisc technology and personal computers with greatly improved graphics capability and lowered costs affect education?

Three possible ways currently exist for combining computers and videodisc players:

1. two monitors, one connected to the computer, one to the videodisc player, with the interface box between;

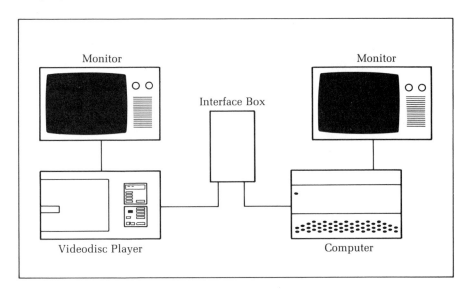

Figure 7.2 Interactive computer-controlled videodisc system.

2. one monitor, connected to both machines, on which computer-generated information is overlayed onto the videodisc image;

3. one monitor with a controller that switches back and forth between the two machines, displaying each machine's output separately on the monitor.

Under the broad definition of education, some very meaningful applications already exist for these combined technologies. The U.S. Navy has produced a course to train people to repair the complex electronic equipment now used on ships. The videodisc displays a picture of the particular piece of equipment to be studied. The computer then presents the problem. The student proceeds to diagnose the problem and repair the equipment, "peeling back" layer after layer of the equipment as necessary by pointing to places on the monitor. The student concurrently gives repair instructions to the computer. Tutorials are available if mistakes are made. Students may try as many different repair strategies as they wish. The computer and videodisc respond by showing and telling the results of each decision. This training, if actual equipment and ships were used, would be cost-prohibitive as well as potentially dangerous. In some sense, the complexities of our world today demand this kind of educational support.

In the area of health, an extremely sophisticated system to train people in cardiopulmonary resuscitation has been developed by the American Heart Association. The system includes a computer, videodisc, and manikin. The process is introduced by a doctor shown on videodisc, practiced by the student on the manikin, and monitored by the computer. If the rhythm, hand placement, or compression used to resuscitate is not within appropriate bounds, the computer signals the student, and the doctor makes suggestions. The student can select different training segments and repeat them as many times as desired. The entire training process is controlled through a series of program menus. Students appear to learn the process in considerably less time than when working with human instructors.

In the realm of precollege education several applications have been carried out. The Minnesota Education Computer Consortium (MECC) has developed a high school economics course using computers and videodiscs. The motivation was to provide such a course to high schools without an economics faculty. A commercial company has produced a disc to allow high school students and parents to "tour" colleges from their own high school. In addition to pictures of the colleges, information about admission requirements and financial aid is included.

An experimental project (a combined effort of two school districts and a computer company) is currently underway to produce a completely interactive videodisc system, including a programming language. The goal of the project is to create middle school problem-solving units using content from the physical sciences as presented through videodisc/computer materials. Currently the major use of the videodisc is motivational; interaction to the extent of the Heart Association project is difficult to achieve.

As with every new technology, problems exist that limit videodisc usefulness:

1. Both videodisc and computer hardware and software are incompatible across manufacturers.

2. The production of videodisc materials is costly because of the high fidelity of the medium.

3. Because of the random-access characteristic of videodiscs, the planning for a videodisc is very different from planning for a film or a videotape, which are always shown linearly from beginning to end. Traditional scripting is no longer an adequate tool; flowcharts are

more appropriate. Producers must work with a different kind of team, now including computer programmers and instructional designers.

4. The videodisc is still primarily a read-only medium. Once a videodisc is produced, changes cannot be made, unlike videotapes and computer programs. Thus, for the present, videodiscs are best used for subjects like history that do not change significantly over time, although the ability to revise videodiscs will no doubt soon be available.

5. As can be seen in figure 7.2, much equipment is required for interactive videodisc courseware. This necessitates perhaps more space and money than most schools today have available.

Telecommunications and Network Technologies

Tele is the Greek word for "distant." Telecommunications means communicating information over some distance. Telecommunication devices in common use throughout the world include telephones, telegraphs, radios, and televisions. Information, in the form of words, pictures, or sounds, is currently transported by means of wire, airwaves, microwaves, satellites, and laser beams. One key to the rapid advances in almost instantaneously accessing and transferring information is the development of computer telecommunications networks.

The analogy of people travelling to information travelling is useful for gaining insight into information transfer. To get from Boston to Colorado Springs, for example, a person might travel via a taxi from home to the airport, transfer to an airplane to Denver, then to a bus to Colorado Springs, and perhaps finally to a taxi to hotel lodgings. Information sent via a computer network from Boston to Colorado Springs might travel from a personal computer in Boston via telephone lines to a large central computer, by cable to a communications satellite sending station, by microwave to the satellite and back to a receiving station, by cable to another computer, and finally by telephone lines to a personal computer in Colorado Springs.

Since some routes are busier or more expensive than others, at several points along the way decisions are made about the fastest and cheapest route. These decision points for information travel are called nodes. Here electronic information is collected, destinations are considered, and information is then dispersed along the most expeditious route. An analogous but clearly slower information system is the pneumatic message system in Paris. If people wish to send messages to another part of the city they can use the pneumatic tube system. They place their message in a tube, located in a post office, hotel, or other public building, and indicate its final destination. The tube goes to a collection station. A person looks at the final destination and chooses the fastest next tube in which to place the message. For many years this was the easiest way to send information around Paris.

Transfer of information electronically, or of electronic data, is timed in terms of baud rate or bits per second. The word *baud* was taken from a man named Baudot, one of the early communications pioneers. Personal computers usually send and receive information at 300 or 1200 bauds, or 300 or 1200 bits per second (a bit being one electrical impulse). It is possible to send information at even higher speeds such as 9600 bauds. However, for such transfer high-quality connection lines are necessary to prevent errors in information sent. Telephone lines are generally not of high enough quality to go beyond 1200 baud. If an organization requires faster information transfer, dedicated lines are used, that is, lines not used for or by anyone else.

Networking means the connecting together of two or more computers. Networking can be done at many levels, from several computers linked together in one room, to computers in one or several buildings, to global networks where large and small computers at widely separate locations are in communication with each other.

Room-wide networks have been available almost since the mass production of personal computers. The reasons for linking all the computers together in a single room include allowing all the machines to share in the use of peripheral devices such as printers and disk drives. This avoids the necessity of having multiple copies of software, each copy needing to be loaded individually into each computer; it also cuts down on hardware costs. In a classroom, such a network permits teachers to monitor students' work from a central location as well as communicate individually with students.

The next level in networking is to link together all the computers in one or several buildings of a school system (or company). Such networks are usually referred to as local area networks (LAN). At this level of networking, the challenge is to integrate the use of different kinds of computers and peripherals. Students or faculty should be able to sit down at any computer on campus and continue their work using whatever software they wish.

Linking computers can be accomplished by using existing telephone lines, laying cables, or accessing a cable television channel. A leader in this effort, Brown University, chose to lay its own cables to connect its on-campus buildings as well as its more distant teaching hospitals. Known as BruNet, this network is one way Brown is working to solve the problems in computerizing a college campus. One of Brown's areas of experimentation is with a totally computerized classroom. One lecture hall contains sixty Apollo computers, one for each student and one for the lecturer. The same information can be sent to each machine by the instructor for demonstration purposes, or each student can try things on his or her own, during the same class period.

One Greater Boston public school system is also involved in setting up a local area network. It currently plans to connect all its school buildings in the network, using a local cable television channel. The director of planning began by having a terminal placed in every principal's office to provide each principal with access to data such as student and staff records on the central computer. In addition terminals are placed in all buildings for student use, since the central computer has available the largest amount of software. As the system develops, other possible uses include establishing an electronic mail system, thus allowing all of the school's population to communicate quickly with one another, and a database including evaluations of all school materials.

The most comprehensive level of networking is referred to as global networking, implying the linking together of computers on a potentially worldwide basis by employing telecommunications. Chapter 3 (in the discussion on databases) suggests some of the ways in which global-level networks offer exciting educational potential. In addition to accessing large databases, global networks can be used for teleconferencing and computer conferencing.

Teleconferencing is similar to a radio talk show with pictures. The National Diffusion Network, a division of the Federal Department of Education, is experimenting with teleconferencing as a means of diffusing exceptional education projects. The teleconference is publicized well in advance for a particular day. The project creators assemble at a sending station. Each project leader is given twenty minutes to explain and demonstrate his or her project. Viewers, located at a receiving station, are then invited to call in with questions.

A broader use of global networking is computer conferencing. Here a predetermined group of people communicate via computer to accomplish a specific task. Tasks can vary from something as unstructured as communicating about educational uses of computers to tasks as focused as joint authoring of a book. Protocols for each group need to be determined. Such matters as frequency of dialing into the conference (once a day, once a month), how individual contributions are identified, who of the group has final editing power, how issues are resolved (by consensus or voting), and whether new people can be added to the conference — all such matters must be resolved at the outset.

Many educational applications can be envisioned. Students from different parts of the world living in very different environments can be brought together for appropriate projects. Currently a pilot project, funded by the Carnegie Corporation, is linking a Cambridge, Massachusetts, public school with two New York City schools. The three classes held an on-line teleconference to inaugurate the project. The students talked about special school events and shared reactions to a movie about Russian schools they had all recently seen. This classroom hookup is part of a larger project involving American and Russian educators who are studying the potential of telecommunications in educational settings. The eventual goal is to link together classrooms in the U. S. and U. S. S. R. for joint projects.

There are many educational links already occurring all over this country. New Jersey has a very advanced telecommunications educational system hosted by the New Jersey Institute of Technology. New York is in the process of linking together all its public educational institutions. Massachusetts, Maine, and New Hampshire are meeting to extend to their whole region the small projects that are occurring in many individual schools — and so on across the country. Students are interacting with experts. Joint newsletters and papers are being "published" by students in different locations on topics of common interest. Teachers are accessing expert advice about educationally related problems from consultants in many different locations, usually in much less time than when using the mail or telephone systems.

Teleconferencing as described here, however, usually involves costs that might slow its implementation. To participate all users often need to subscribe to the same on-line service such as *CompuServe* or *The Source*. This involves membership costs and computer access-time fees.

Another way to accomplish similar kinds of communications is through private-message systems (PMS). Anyone with a telephone, computer, modem with an autoanswer, and bulletin-board software (there are many versions in the public domain) can establish a PMS. Such a system can be limited to certain individuals or open to the public. The initiator might assume all the costs of disks and electricity, or these may be shared among the participants. Either way, the costs are usually lower than subscribing to a service.

Some educationally oriented message systems are already functioning. One is the *Kid's Message System* and another is *The Turtle Bulletin Board* focusing on Logo. Many of these systems operate across the country. A good source for finding out about them is through local computer user groups.

There are, of course, problems associated with PMSs. Each PMS involves the use of one computer, one modem, and one telephone number. Callers therefore encounter many busy signals in their attempts to dial-in. Telephone lines vary in quality across the country. Poor quality lines can result in the transmission of inaccurate information or in the loss of information. However, the PMS is a relatively low-risk way to experiment with electronic communications. *Online Today*, June, 1984 (pp. 12–18), explains in detail how to start a PMS.

Resulting Issues

Several issues are raised by the use of computers and other new technologies in educational settings. It seems appropriate for the social studies teacher to consider where and how these issues should be considered in the curriculum. The issues can be loosely grouped under the following headings: thinking machines, equity of access, crime/ethics, privacy of information, the potential for human isolation, and information overload.

Thinking Machines

The central issue with regard to artificial intelligence is whether a machine can think or not. It raises both technical and ethical concerns. Indeed, for many people, whether machines can think is really a question of whether machines are human. While machines are not human, the evidence to date indicates that at some future time machines will be able to perform at levels of sophistication that can be classified as "true" thinking.

How will the thinking machines be used? Programs such as the medical diagnosis program can become a routine part of doctors' diagnostic tools. Indeed, there may come a time when physicians, as part of a medical insurance program, are required to "consult" with such a program. This suggests that one way such systems may be used is in symbiotic relationship with their human counterparts. Human thinking will improve because of its interface with computer thinking.

Science fiction writers, such as Isaac Asimov in *I, Robot*, suggest that thinking computers will quietly take over and run all aspects of human lives. Such machines may even be so clever that humans will continue to believe that they control the decisions that govern their well-being. This suggests that systems are going to move beyond human thinking and will be used in spite of their human counterparts.

A great deal of controversy continues in the field of AI. Some scientists suggest that there is less danger in machines taking over than in humans becoming dependent on machines. Some scientists stress the capabilities of computers as potentially better decision-makers than humans, while others focus only on the limitations. There is still disagreement about what constitutes AI and at what point intelligence is truly demonstrated. Finally, debate continues on whether machines should eventually be limited in what they can perform.

Equity

The issue of equity of access to equipment and information revolves around differences based on gender and socio-economic level. Evidence suggests that females are not gaining equal access to technology. Pre-college advanced computer courses, beyond the first year of programming, tend to be almost entirely male. When Stevens Institute of Technology in New Jersey required all freshmen to purchase a computer, their next freshman class dropped from 25 percent to 13 percent female. Disturbed by this, Stevens Institute surveyed the parents of accepted female candidates. Parents who were questioned almost unanimously suggested they did not believe that their daughters had serious career intentions and therefore the added college expense of a computer was not justified. Computers are still seen as male math-machines. David Moursund, editor of *The Computing Teacher*, feels "that the nature of our society puts extra barriers in the path of a woman who seeks a professional career in science and math-related areas" (p. 4).

Economic-based inequities are another area of concern. Upper-middle-class families, over the past five years, have certainly spent more on hardware and software than lower-income families. This is one of the major arguments for the immediate need for mass purchasing of hardware for precollege use. However, it is not at all clear today if the home market will continue to grow, level off, or decline, making this initial concern shrink in its potential to create a class gap. Besides income-generated gaps, differences in exposure to technology have been found based on region of the country and type of community (for example, urban versus rural — the South has been found to have the lowest amount of equipment in precollege settings). One area where inequities of access to equipment have not been found is in race, although concern has been expressed that minority students, slower learners, and non-math, non-science students generally are exposed, when using computers, only to drill and practice applications.

Some solutions to these equity problems might be addressed by giving thought to the physical placement of computers and the reasons for their use. For example, when computers are placed in one room, the computer laboratory thus created tends to become "male turf." Surveys suggest that computers placed in the teaching classrooms tend to be more equally used by boys and girls. Girls seem to prefer using applications programs, such as databases and word processors, while boys prefer to write programs. The social studies curriculum is therefore a perfect environment for promoting equity of use. Students need to become sensitive to different preferences of the sexes. A social studies unit where the students look at such things as sex biases in software, sex preferences, and different emphases in value sets can make important contributions to the ability of men and women to work harmoniously as adults in the work environment.

The home is still a major source of educational inequity in general and in technological exposure in particular. Involving parents is important, especially in the lower socio-economic communities. Workshops should be offered in both using computers and career awareness; computers should be loaned for weekend home-use; parents should be encouraged to volunteer for such activities as staffing computer rooms, running courses, and helping with computer clubs.

Crime/Ethics

A third issue raised by these technologies involves identifying new areas for potential unethical or criminal uses of computers. The most blatant problem involves software piracy, the illegal copying of software. Educators as well as students are guilty of committing this crime. In a survey conducted by *Electronic Education*, half of the teachers questioned felt free to make additional copies of a piece of software to allow them to use it with more than one student. Because this illegal activity is so wide spread, a group of people representing educators, publishers, and manufacturers, organized by the International Council for Computers in Education, came up with a set of guidelines that is now being adopted by many educational groups. The full text can be found in the September, 1983, issue of *The Computing Teacher*. In summary, the committee recommends:

1. Both educators and industry have a responsibility to insure that the copyright laws are observed. The current interpretation of this law allows software owners to:

    – make a backup copy of a computer program for archival purposes only, destroying that backup when the original is no longer in use;

    – alter the software, if necessary, to get the program to run on the machine for which it was purchased.

2. Educators are responsible for both observing the law and educating their students on the law.

3. The ICCE committee encourages publishers to:

    – provide a free or inexpensive backup copy of all software sold;
    – provide on-approval purchases;
    – provide multiple-copy pricing and network pricing to take into account situations where only one copy is needed for several users or classroom situations.

Another kind of computer-related crime is the illegal accessing of electronic information. Laws have been passed to cope with this in only about half the states. The problem is augmented by the fact that when this involves students, the press tends to make them heroes. Schools must make students cognizant of the fact that illegal access to information and stealing of computer time are crimes or, where not crimes, extremely unethical. This is similar to stealing telephone time by making illegal long distance calls — acknowledged as wrong but not taken very seriously until the telephone company started to identify and stop offenders.

Figure 7.3 Bloom County. ©1983, Washington Post Writers Group, reprinted with permission.

As suggested by the cartoon above, the social studies teacher has many strategies for presenting these issues in class. Exercises for students in Kohlberg-type dilemmas, values clarification, and role-playing are all suggested in the August/September, 1984, issue of *The Computing Teacher.*

Privacy of Information

What constitutes privacy of personal information? Privacy involves insuring individuals the right to know what information is stored about them, who has access to the information, and how the information is to be used. On an individual level, this includes the right to decide what personal information should be shared with others. On a societal level, privacy involves the right to withhold information.

What controls have been developed to support informational privacy? Several legislative acts have been instituted at the federal level, some of the more important being the Privacy Act (1974), the Freedom of Information Act, the Fair Credit Reporting Act (1974), the Family Education and Right to Privacy Act (1976), and the Right to Financial Privacy Act (1978). Each of these acts addresses various concerns about privacy. Additional controls have also been enacted at the state levels.

With the increasing use of networking and the growth of telecommunications capabilities, the issue of privacy of information is one that should be addressed by the social studies teacher. This will help heighten students' awareness about the kinds of information individuals provide about themselves. It also sensitizes them to the informational demands of society and how they, the students, might take some control of the information stored about themselves.

Potential for Human Isolation

Another issue often brought up when considering the use of computers in education is the increased isolation of students as they interact with machines instead of people. There is little current evidence to support this concern, but there are also few studies and not enough elapsed time to look at long-term effects. Along this same line is the difficulty in producing high quality computer-aided instructional materials. The result, then, for students who do spend a meaningful amount of time using CAI is that they are trapped at the lowest level, the knowledge-acquisition level, of learning. These students rarely get to use the computer as a problem-solving tool; they rarely control the computer. In addition, the teacher has less control over the materials with which his or her students are interacting because of the difficulty of modifying software. However, there are benefits related to CAI as suggested earlier in this chapter.

Information Overload

A final area of concern is learning to cope with the possibility of information overload. Having access to such information sources as databases and expert systems provides the potential for obtaining huge amounts of information on any identified problem. The psychological implications and the sense of loss of control over the ability to make reasonable decisions are potential problem areas. Schools need more and more to prepare students for the different world that is evolving.

Scenario of an Educational Setting Using These Technologies

Below is a scenario of what it might be like to be a student in a world enhanced by the presence of multiple applications of technology.

The first thing Marjorie does every morning is to check her electronic mailbox for her school tasks for that day as noted by herself and her teacher. Today she notices there is nothing requiring her presence in school until the noon meeting of her play group. She therefore spends the morning at her computer going through the next unit of her mathematics curriculum, finishes her analysis of *Much Ado About Nothing* and sends it to her teacher's mailbox, and polishes her contribution to the school district's newsletter by running a final spelling and grammar check, sending that also by electronic mail to the editor.

Having completed these tasks, Marjorie decides to walk to school. Planning her arrival perfectly, her first activities are lunch and recess followed by her play group meeting. Marjorie then has just enough time to go through a videodisc presentation reviewing the rules and strategies of soccer. Checking her messages once again, she sees she has a meeting with her computer simulation group who are setting up a community on a nearby planet, a play rehearsal late in the afternoon, and a meeting in two days with her study group on the settlement of Southern California. She decides to let her mother know via the electronic bulletin board that she will be home late. At the same time, she orders supper from the local take-out restaurant to be picked up at 7:30 p.m.

Her major afternoon task is to check in on her computer conference. She is involved in a project attempting to understand better the phenomenon and problems of homeless teenagers across the United States. The conference group is composed of students from five major U.S. cities, two professors of sociology, plus a social worker and a religious leader from each of the five cities. The twenty-two members of the conference group are first attempting to define the problem clearly by collecting data. The group's final goal is to build a computer simulation model of the problem, which they can then use to help generate recommended actions.

Having spent longer than she should reviewing the information left by her conference mates, she has just enough time to run through another portion of the interactive videodisc on touring in Spain (she hopes to be part of the exchange program this year). Left undone is the search of the Library of Congress database on publicly available videodiscs of historic documents relating to the settlement of Southern California. That will have to wait for tomorrow.

Does this scenario sound futuristic? Not very. All the technologies are readily available and currently used in many situations, some even educational. The costs might still be high, the human interfaces might not be as friendly as people would like, but everything is well within the realm of possibility. As educators, we need to take responsibility for directing the use of these new tools in our environment.

References

Butler, M., "The Record with a View — Videodisc," *Information Technology Newsletter*, vol. 2, no. 3 (1983) 7–18.

Electronic Learning, vol. 4., no. 3 (November/December, 1984).

Moursund, D., *The Computing Teacher*, vol. 11, no. 8 (September, 1983).

The Computer Future

In the past few years there has been a growing awareness that the United States, Western Europe, and Japan are rapidly undergoing a transformation as a result of recent technological developments. While technology has always acted as an agent of change, the growth of computer technology has had an extraordinary effect on society in the past decade and will induce even more rapid changes in the years ahead. These developments have propelled us into a new era known by a number of different names. Sociologist Daniel Bell used the term "the information society." Others have called it the "post-industrial society," and futurist Alvin Toffler coined the term "the Third Wave."

Whatever the name of this new age, computers are either directly or indirectly responsible for most of the advances of the past four decades. These advances are profoundly affecting our lives, homes, playgrounds, and offices. Not only is technology altering the physical features of those familiar institutions, but also changing the nature of society — the ways in which we travel, do our work, and participate in government. While changes in these tangible areas are significant, the more subtle transformations in how we think of ourselves and how we relate to one another may be more profound. This chapter shows how computers are and will be changing our physical environment, our social institutions, and finally our relationships with others. The authors draw upon the work of futurists such as Alvin Toffler and Paul Frude to help social studies teachers understand these changes and incorporate futurists' insights into their curriculum.

Computers in Our Daily Lives

Perhaps the most awesome and frightening aspect of the new technology revolves around the primitive need for survival and the age-old quest for supremacy. Early computer prototyes provided the mathematical calculations to create the first hydrogen bombs. Subsequently, computers in one form or another have been used in every aspect of the arms race. Following the instinct of grabbing the biggest stick, both the U.S. and the U.S.S.R. have built ever more powerful weapons, which in the long run have made both sides less secure. Whether computers ultimately help save this planet or speed it on its way to Armageddon is yet unknown. However, this chapter is confined to discussing non-military applications of computer technology.

Automated payrolls have introduced the computer into the lives of workers in all fields. The airlines long ago computerized their reservation systems. The mainframe computers used for these purposes were frequently upgraded and replaced by smaller and more efficient computers. Subsequently computers have been adapted for thousands of other uses by industry ranging from keeping track of inventory to developing new products; from billing customers to testing advertising strategies; and from making mailing lists to locating bad credit risks.

The advent of solid-state transistors, silicon chips, and vastly improved miniaturizing techniques have allowed the development of microprocessors with a previously unimaginable degree of accuracy, efficiency, and speed in computing. According to Christopher Evans, if equally spectacular advances had been made on the automobile, Rolls Royces would be selling today for $2.50 and getting one million miles per gallon! With these improvements, computers are serving a whole host of new functions including word processing and electronic mail, creating data banks, reading price labels at supermarket check-outs, making possible digital watches and hand calculators, and of course, creating ever more complex games, tutorials, and simulations. Meanwhile microchips are used in many such common objects as clock radios, washing machines, and video cassettes, bringing the computer in direct contact with millions of Americans.

Computers and Work

The computer has provided the latest means of automating the traditional assembly lines, such as robots in the automobile industry to cite but one example. At Chrysler, General Motors, and Ford plants throughout the nation, robots spot-weld and spray-paint automobiles. In addition, robots cut out and stamp standard parts on dies that other robots were instrumental in developing and shaping. In this process, workers on the now antiquated assembly lines as well as skilled painters, welders, and tool-and-die makers are replaced. Labor leaders see these computers threatening to cause massive lay-offs. Using the September, 1984, settlement with General Motors as an industrial model, unions have sought job-security funds for retraining and early retirement to protect their members.

While computers have been responsible for technological unemployment, they have also been helpful in forming many new American industries. According to John Naisbitt's *Megatrends*, the United States has already crossed the boundary line from an industrial to an informational society. A full 65 percent of working Americans are engaged in some form of communicating information, up from 17 percent in 1950. These new positions include programmers, teachers, bureaucrats, lawyers, writers, and technicians. While automobile, steel, coal, and rubber producing factories were once considered the bellwether of American industrial production, today only about 12 percent of the work force are engaged as factory workers.

Furthermore, the computer revolution has changed the nature of manufacturing. With the automation of many assembly line jobs, those that remain are far less tedious and impersonal. Consider the new Hewlett-Packard plant in Colorado as an example — 40 percent of its employees are engineers, programmers, clerks, and informational workers. Instead of the deafening roar of the assembly line, Hewlett-Packard workers stand at work stations decorated according to their own tastes, playing songs of their choice. Instead of a single punch-in clock registered to regulated shifts, workers negotiate their own hours in a flex-time schedule subject to their obligations both inside and outside the plant.

Computers in the School and Home

Computers have entered the schools at every level from preschool to postgraduate. They not only schedule students and record their grades, but also help teach in the classroom. Increasingly usable educational software is helping teachers and students by providing skill-and-drill exercises, tutorials that teach important concepts, simulations that help students understand the dynamics of a subject matter, and tools with which to create their own learning environments.

Computers were originally brought into the home as microprocessors to activate games. Now they serve as word processors, as aids in filing income-tax returns, correcting spelling mistakes, organizing Christmas card lists, and teaching children. Harnessed to modems, these home computers may be linked to the stock market, local weather stations, and several different data banks. The technology now exists to link these home computers to interactive television for such purposes as shopping. Computers can also protect homes with burgler and fire alarms appropriately connected to police and fire stations. Computers are also used to activate video cassettes, monitor phone calls, pay bills, and balance checkbooks. In the classic progression of the adoption of a new technology, computers have already served as a novelty and a luxury for the well-to-do, and for most they are now a necessity. The family without a computer in the not too distant future may consider itself deprived, just as many Americans would feel if they did not have at least one color television and two toilets. Futurists see computers as the core of the twenty-first century home organized around centers for family entertainment, eating, cooking, working, and sleeping. The computer's electronic switching devices will be used for such things as distributing heat from solar-energy-storage units as needed, and channelling the house stereo to provide the most appropriate music to each of the various centers.

New Relationships

Daily comforts aside, many futurists see the home as the new workingplace for white-collar professionals. Once only artists and writers had the privilege of working at home. Now with home terminals connected to computerized offices, interactive television allows a wide range of workers to hold conferences with other professionals or entrepreneurs in their "electronic cottages." Futurists have predicted that up to 20 percent of the workforce will eventually work out of their own homes. This will have an important effect on mass transportation and save millions of people up to two hours of commuting time each day.

Using the same computer and interactive television that connects workers to their offices, high school students could be connected to a lecture, lab, or virtually any classroom activity at any level. Modern fiber-optic techniques allow simultaneous transmission of 1,000 messages, and can put the "electronic cottage" with its modern television equipment in touch with local and county officials. With this technology, each home computer terminal can serve as a broadcast studio, allowing home participation in school committee deliberation and in town meetings. Experiments with such fiber-optic home broadcasting systems have already been undertaken in Japan where their value has been demonstrated. There is no reason why this concept cannot work in the U.S., where participatory town meetings have been the hallmark of this democracy for some three hundred years.

Societal Changes

Of course no one can predict with absolute certainty the ways in which "the future" will no longer be "what it used to be." We can, however, reduce the margin of error by first looking at the past, then at the present, and then attempt to project into the future. We have now looked at some of the recent tendencies in the change of such material entities as the work force, the office, the assembly line, and the house. Little if anything, however, has been said about how the changing material condition of our lives will affect how we interact with others and restructure our societies and values.

Agricultural Societies

Fortunately, futurist Alvin Toffler provides us with very useful guideposts by which to distinguish between what he calls first- and second-wave technologies. By examining the prevailing ideologies of these periods and showing how they related to the technological infrastructure, Toffler establishes a firm basis from which to project the outlines of the new society called the Third Wave.

Toffler describes the First Wave as the agricultural communities that some 9,000 years ago began to replace the foraging and hunting societies that preceded them. Toffler's Second Wave is the industrial societies that came into being in mid-eighteenth-century England. The shift from an agricultural to an industrial society involved profound changes in the way people lived and worked.

The dominant occupation in the agricultural wave was planting and harvesting to produce food and fiber for the people. Even with the relatively efficient agriculture in eighteenth-century America, it took nine farmers to sustain one person not engaged in agriculture. This figure is appropriate for the great ancient civilizations as well. All of them required a predominantly agrarian society to support a relatively small political and economic elite.

In this agricultural society, the main sources of energy were replace-able: wood burned for heat; the energy of humans, animals, wind, and sometimes water converted into other forms of power. The family farm in general was the productive unit, and the extended family the main social organization. This family or clan involved three and even four genera-tions living in close proximity. The family not only served as the major productive unit, but also functioned as school, hospital, and old-age home. The simple division of labor in that era was between young and old, male and female. Goods were produced not for a distant market, but for home consumption.

Even though political control, in theory, could and often was imposed from the top down, the social and economic life remained decentralized. Sometimes, or even frequently, the local lord, church, or national leader took goods from the village, or even dragooned young men to fight in their wars. While these interruptions were often trauma-tic, they were just that — interruptions of an ebb and flow of life over an agricultural civilization that varied less in substance than in form for the vast majority of people the world over from one century to the next for some 7,000 years.

Industrial Society

The Second Wave, in the form of the Industrial Revolution, began in England about three hundred years ago. Over the course of three centuries, machines replaced workers, mass production replaced the work done in the home and the farm, and in approximately one-quarter of the globe agricultural civilization was uprooted.

Where workers once labored in the fields producing their own food, men and women now are employed by others to produce for a mass market. While the major source of energy in the pre-industrial society was renewable, industrial societies have tended to deplete the forests, pollute the air, and strip the earth of its minerals. While producers and consumers in pre-industrial societies were close relatives, industrial producers work for an unseen consumer known vaguely as "the market." From these simple examples we can readily see the implications of industrial technology not only on people's occupations, but also on the underlying structure of their society.

The extended family, adapted to rural agriculture, gave way to the nuclear family of industrial societies. As the family rid itself of such appendages as aging grandparents, it dropped many of its former functions. Today children are sent to schools for their education, to prepare them to play their roles in industry as willing and pliant workers. Instead of being cared for at home, the old are sent to nursing homes, and the sick and women in labor to hospitals. The mentally retarded are institutionalized, and the criminal imprisoned rather than banished. Children now meet and mate on the free-market of love rather than by prescribed rules and according to the more practical considerations of their parents. They move out of their parents' homes to form independent productive and consumer units as soon as they can afford it.

The corporation, Alvin Toffler claims, replaced the family and village as the dominant societal organization. It was granted a gift of unlimited life and the same legal rights and privileges under the law as individuals. Society was standardized, centralized, and synchronized for the benefit of the mass market. People were placed on standard time, given standard hours, vacations, and fringe benefits. Schools and colleges insisted on standardized tests. According to Toffler, children were concentrated in schools, criminals in prisons, and the insane in asylums. Production was centralized in crowded factories; businesses bought each other out and formed great oligopolies, monopolies, and cartels, that concentrated capital in the hands of a few. Large central banks were organized to pump capital into business. Nation states, created in Europe out of a mass of mini-states (350 in Germany alone), provided businessmen with a huge market. Political power was centralized in the hands of presidents, prime ministers, kings, politburos, and central bureaucracies.

The driving force that brought most agrarian countries under the political and/or economic control of industry was economics. The need or desire for raw materials and markets coupled with superior military power imposed industrial market networks on agricultural economies. The West went to the Middle East for its oil, to Indochina and Brazil for its rubber, to Peru for its tin, and to Cuba for its sugar. In their wake, the industrialized countries left disrupted colonial economies and a harvest of bitterness and despair. Much to their subsequent regret, the industrialized nations developed their economies on the false assumption that there was an unlimited supply of inexpensive fuel and raw materials that could always be appropriated in a buyers' market.

Post-Industrial Society

Alvin Toffler gives several different reasons that (in his words) "the society that made the factory into a cathedral" is dying. One reason is the growing awareness that the imagined limitless supply of raw materials is running out. Another is the evidence that industrial societies are "poisoning the well" with their industrial waste. Nevertheless, the great progress that has been made in science over the the past decades offers hope for people in the post-industrial society. In the new "green revolution," scientists can splice genes that produce hardy plants that yield increased production without requiring expensive fertilizers and irrigation. We can farm and harvest almost unlimited amounts of food from the ocean, certainly enough to feed the entire world today. New industries are developing in such fields as molecular biology, oceanomics, space science, data processing, and petrochemicals.

The electronic cottage, already considered a new work-center in future society, may also form the basis for a new family structure. Just as industrial societies destroyed the economic base of the extended family, the electronic cottage allows the work unit to become the basis for reviving the nuclear family. Rather than spending hours commuting to and from jobs, workers in the post-industrial society will give new vitality to their neighborhoods. In addition, the post-industrial society will allow for a wider acceptance of alternative life styles such as communal and extended families, thus providing many options to the nuclear family of the industrial society. A key concept of Toffler's is the sense of alienation in a society where producers never see the consumers who buy their products. In the post-industrial society, he predicts a great increase in the number of people producing their own goods — growing some of their own food and sewing their own clothes — to a much greater extent than now.

Post-industrial thinking, Alvin Toffler believes, has already begun to displace industrial ideology. Standardization, centralization, and concentration, once valued in the industrial economy, are no longer virtues in the post-industrial age. *Small is Beautiful*, the title of a popular book by economist E.F. Schumacher, heralds post-industrial concepts such as finding economic systems that fit people's needs, rather than the reverse.

The new economic order can be a combination of concentrated, centralized, and efficient along with the local, decentralized, and personal. The franchise movements, for example, which allow the advertising and capital of the modern corporation to be harnessed to the individual freedom and initiative of the local entrepreneur, represent an example of this new synthesis.

The decentralizing tendencies seen in the work place, represented by electronic cottages and fiber-cable communities, may well be the indices of a similar political trend. Local groups are being formed for a host of different purposes, as any school superintendent knows who tries to close a school, or any state highway official learns who tries to build a connector road in a residential neighborhood. Local groups are also getting together to save historic buildings, to preserve wetlands, to oppose new industries, and hundreds of other local concerns. They are part of a worldwide trend of single-issue groups, making it far more difficult to maintain the consensus that kept the old political machinery running. More seriously, separatist movements are plaguing the nation-state the world over. Besides Northern Ireland, Biafra, Pakistan, and Bangladesh, there are the Basques in Spain, the Corsicans in France, even the Scotch in Great Britain, and of course the French in Canada.

The Third World, as we have seen, was once no more than an economic appendage to industrial nations' markets while serving as a continual supplier of inexpensive raw materials. The post-industrial third world societies will be both more independent of their old colonial masters and able to profit from post-industrial technology: Toffler calls it "Gandi with a satellite." The post-industrial technology, which made a second green revolution possible, also has created generators running on human waste that can supply enough electricity to satisfy the needs of a small village. Other innovations, such as artificial ecosystems in which shrimp and chickens are fed each other's waste products, provide viable alternatives to the now discredited big steel mill concept of industrial society planners such as W.W. Rostow.

Eliza and Her Sisters

Since the beginnings of recorded time there have been myths, children's stories, and folk tales recounting relations between people and inanimate objects. As Sir James Frazier informs us in *The Golden Bough*, for primitive man "the world in general is animate, and trees and plants are no exception to this rule. He thinks that they have souls like their own and treats them accordingly" (Frude, p. 104).

Rocks, trees, clouds, sun, moon, and stars, all once believed to have human characteristics, often served as the object of supplication. For untold centuries human characteristics have been attributed to statues and puppets. Right to the present, inanimate objects such as dolls and portraits or photographs of people are sometimes treated as if they could understand and react. We even occasionally catch ourselves talking to an automobile that will not start or to a pot that has boiled over. It therefore is hardly surprising that computers with interactive programs may sometimes be treated as if they have human characteristics. What astonishes, however, is the extent to which computers are being used as a substitute for human interactions, and people's readiness to accept the substitution of computer programs for interpersonal relationships.

In the 1960s, Joseph Weizenbaum wrote a program which he aptly called ELIZA in honor of the heroine of the play *My Fair Lady*. Programmed along Rogerian principles of reflecting the patient's feelings, ELIZA gives a reasonable facsimile of a therapist responding to a client. The following interview between Weizenbaum's program and a client produces a startlingly realistic dialogue (Note: the computer's statements are underlined):

Men are all alike.

In what way

They are always bugging us about something or other.

Can you think of a specific example

Well, my boyfriend made me come here.

Your boyfriend made you come here

He says I am depressed much of the time.

I am sorry to hear that you are depressed

It's true, I am unhappy.

Do you think coming here will help you not to be unhappy

I need some help, that much seems certain.

What would it mean to you if you got some help

Perhaps I could learn to get along with my mother.

Tell me more about your family

My mother takes care of me.

Who else in your family takes care of you

My father.

Your father

You are like my father in some ways.

<u>What resemblance do you see</u>

You are not very aggressive but I think you don't want me

to notice that.

<u>What makes you think I am not very aggressive</u>

You don't argue with me.

<u>Why do you think I don't argue with you</u>

You are afraid of me.

<u>Does it please you to believe I am afraid of you</u>

My father is afraid of everybody.

<u>What else comes to your mind when you think of your father</u>

Bullies.

<u>Does that have anything to do with the fact that your</u>

<u>boyfriend made you come</u> (Weizenbaum, pp. 474–480).

An even more dramatic indication of computer power is its use in detecting suicide risks. From 1966 to 1970, in University of Wisconsin hospitals in Madison, computers were used to interview and identify potentially suicidal patients. According to the program developer, Dr. John Geist, the majority of those interviewed said they preferred talking to computers than conversing with trained interviewers. Geist speculated the reason was that patients felt computers to be non-judgmental. Furthermore, Geist reported that the computers did a far better job in predicting potentially suicidal patients than clinicians. The computers were successful in identifying 70 percent of all suicidal cases while the clinicians succeeded only in identifying 40 percent.

Futurists have pointed to several areas of human interaction, such as preliminary screening for psychiatric care, where computers can replace humans. In other areas of medicine as well, computers have proven successful in preliminary interviews and making useful diagnoses. In fact, studies have revealed that computers are better than doctors at screening patients, avoiding jargon, and exuding warmth and friendliness. They have more time for patients, and supposedly can make more astute and objective diagnoses than trained professionals. We, however, doubt that the A. M. A. would agree with these conclusions!

We have already seen what role CAI can play in the schools of the future. Certainly, computers can store far more knowledge than any teacher and undeniably have far more patience. Some futurists predict that computers eventually will replace the classroom teacher. A technology that can hook together twenty home-bound students and a teacher can also eliminate the need for all to come to school — except of course, for the pleasure, sometimes ignored by futurists, of interacting directly with one another.

Computer Intimacy

Futurist Paul Frude has taken a careful look at where we are now and the direction in which we are heading. This has led him to make some of the following predictions. Using a short and long run scenerio Frude looks for computers to gradually replace people in physically demanding, disagreeable, and purely routine labor. He sees the computer providing an interactive environment for workers, using as an example a "talking forklift truck." In the long run Frude thinks that computers will do almost all of the work performed by humans — giving people inordinate amounts of leisure time. Apparently Frude thinks this will not create special problems because the computers will provide people with such entertainment as three-dimensional, computer-simulated games, computerized fights between famous boxers from history, interactive video games, old movies, and television shows.

Conclusions

It is clear that mankind is standing on a computer-induced threshhold. On the one hand computers have helped develop nuclear weapons and are programmed to play a crucial role in firing them at enemy targets. With this technology, both the U. S. and the U. S. S. R. are capable of annihilating one another and producing a "nuclear winter" that would probably destroy life on this planet as we know it. On the other hand, computers have helped develop a technology that can potentially feed all of the earth's population, and provide a comfortable, labor-free existence for the world, if not within our life time, perhaps in the lifetime of our students.

However, even if we achieve this Utopia, there may be serious liabilities: namely, will something very much related to the quality of life remain in a universe where there is no need for productive work and no incentive to finding truly human companionship? When machines are made that can do all the things once only people could do, there will be perhaps no further use for human beings. The challenge for all of us, therefore, is to see that computers do not become instruments of mass destruction and that computers are used in life-enhancing ways that do not decrease the need for human interaction but that make interactions more meaningful.

References

Evans, C., The *Micro Millenium*. New York: Viking Press, 1979.

Frude, N., The *Intimate Machine*. New York: The New American Library, 1983.

Masuda, Y., *The Information Society as Post-Industrial Society*. Washington, D.C.: World Future Society, 1981.

Naisbitt, J., *Megatrends*. New York: Warner Books, Inc., 1984.

Toffler, A., *Future Shock*. New York: Random House, 1970.

Toffler, A., *The Third Wave*. New York: William Morrow and Company, Inc., 1980.

Weizenbaum, J., "Contextual Understandings of Computers," *Communications of the ACM*, vol. 10 no. 8 (August, 1967) 474–480.

Stages of Educational Change Involving Innovation

Information about the causes, nature, and ammunition of the microcomputer revolution has now been presented. The authors hope the reader, at this point, has joined the revolution on the side of integrating technology into the classroom. What then can the reader do as he or she rises to a position of leadership? This last chapter presents an overview of the process of change in a typical school. Understanding this process will provide the reader with a sense of how best to help his or her school system take advantage of these educational innovations.

Research suggests that schools, over a certain time period, are accepting the need to integrate computers into their programs (Becker). Previous research, from the era of open classrooms, has suggested that school personnel seem to go through a consistent set of stages during the process of integrating an innovation (Hall and Loucks, Cory). These four stages of innovation, applied to the microcomputer phenomenon, can be briefly stated as:

1. Beginning awareness — a few staff members are knowledgeable about computers and begin to experiment with computers in their classrooms.

2. Spread of acceptance — more of the staff and administration verbally acknowledge the importance of the innovation and back this

acknowledgment by providing some funds for educating teachers in the new technique or technology.

3. Rise in comfort level — people become genuinely excited about the technology; more people try things out in their classrooms; there is more sharing of experiences and mutual support.

4. Impact on the curriculum — strategies for teaching are changing as well as the content in some areas. Attempts to evaluate student learning occur.

Beginning Awareness

The process usually begins either with an innovative teacher using a computer in his or her classroom or with an administrative decision to purchase a small number of machines and software packages. The beginning use of technology generally causes two things to happen: an immediate increase in the nervousness and fear in those people not yet involved and an eventual increase in allocation of funds for similar purchases. Figure 9.1 presents a description and causal-loop diagram of this process.

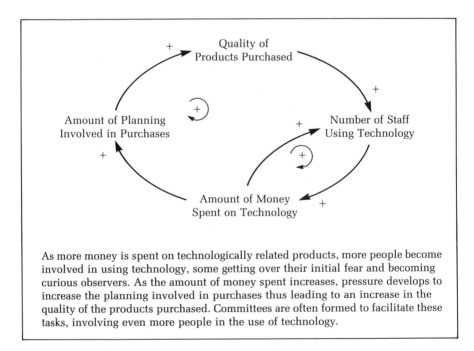

As more money is spent on technologically related products, more people become involved in using technology, some getting over their initial fear and becoming curious observers. As the amount of money spent increases, pressure develops to increase the planning involved in purchases thus leading to an increase in the quality of the products purchased. Committees are often formed to facilitate these tasks, involving even more people in the use of technology.

Figure 9.1   Initial stage of introducing technology.

Each arrow in figure 9.1 indicates some passage of time. For some school systems the time for increasing pressure for additional budget allocations might be as little as one budget cycle. For other schools, because of general lack of funds and low community, staff, and student awareness, this might take three to five years. Again, the time it takes different systems to organize committees to the point of functioning at a reasonable level of decision-making also varies.

Spread of Acceptance

The next stage involves an awareness of the need for training staff in the use of technology. Training usually begins with short in-service sessions provided by the teacher who happens to have more experience or by a local consultant or parent (figure 9.2). This initial amount of training almost always produces frustrations because of its brevity and shallowness.

People's abilities to cope with an accelerating rate of change increases. Eventually the staff comes to understand that education in the area of technology, during their professional lifetime, is an ongoing process. Again each arrow in figure 9.2 represents the passage of time,

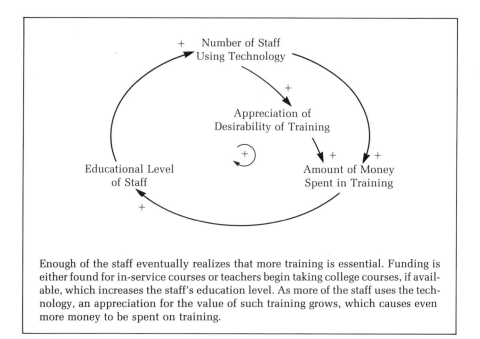

Enough of the staff eventually realizes that more training is essential. Funding is either found for in-service courses or teachers begin taking college courses, if available, which increases the staff's education level. As more of the staff uses the technology, an appreciation for the value of such training grows, which causes even more money to be spent on training.

Figure 9.2   Effect of training on use of technology.

which differs within a range of several years for different school systems. Such factors as availability of technologically knowledgeable people and attitudes of teachers influence the time delays that occur.

Not considered in either figures 9.1 or 9.2, but clearly important in the larger picture are the budget pressures that build up as the ratio of hardware and software expenses to total educational budget increases. Spokespeople for an expanded sports program, more enrichment activities, or additional staffing begin to regain the attention of the decision-making board. These will appear a few years down the road from the beginning of computer acquisition in any given system.

Rise in Comfort Level

Figure 9.3 represents the third stage in a school system's acceptance of technology.

Teachers stop sweating when they confront a computer. In fact, sign-up sheets for weekend and vacation use of computers become necessary. Teachers begin to purchase home computers using a variety of excuses such as, "It's for the children."

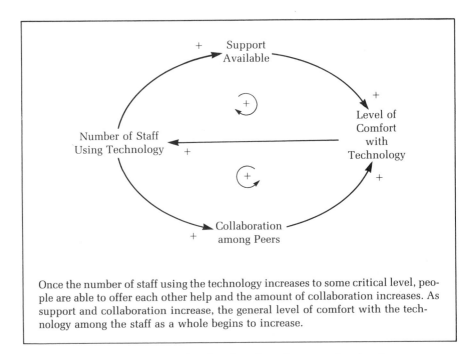

Once the number of staff using the technology increases to some critical level, people are able to offer each other help and the amount of collaboration increases. As support and collaboration increase, the general level of comfort with the technology among the staff as a whole begins to increase.

Figure 9.3   Changes in use of technology based on comfort level.

Impact on Curriculum

The final stage in the adoption of technology suggested by the literature involves the impact on the curriculum. When an innovation is first introduced, whether it be computers or a new style of teaching such as team teaching, the new idea is not suddenly put into practice in the classroom. Stages of acceptance, understanding, and use by teachers involve all the above steps. This last stage, shown in figure 9.4, explains how teachers move from learning about the innovation to actually changing the way they teach and think about the learning process.

When computers are first brought into classrooms, teachers tend to use them in the most obvious ways as they build their level of comfort with the technology. Such uses as drill-and-practice or instructional games that clearly fit into their normal lesson plans are often used first. Next, perhaps a teacher might try to use a tool package and have several students build a database that enriches the current unit of study.

One social studies class decided they wanted to identify real problems of both their school and town at the same time they put their computer skills to work. The class decided on these two problems: that of students and staff who forget to turn off their automobile headlamps (a problem on dark early-winter mornings); and the accessibility of town public-buildings to the handicapped. The class created databases for both situations. Students entered the license-plate numbers of all people using the school parking-lot. As soon as a lighted headlamp was reported, the person owning the car was immediately contacted. For the second problem, data were collected on a variety of measurements of all public buildings. Such information regarding width of doors and ramp access was collected with the cooperation of all students. The availability of the database was advertised in the local paper. Now when a handicapped person needs information, it is readily available.

Should the evaluation of the effect of the innovation as shown in figure 9.4 be negative, change in the opposite direction results. There is *less* collaboration among colleagues, *less* impact on the curriculum, causing *less* evaluation to occur. However, the evidence to date almost entirely suggests some positive result from using computers in the schools. Students require less time to learn materials, enjoy learning more, are more attentive to the task for longer time periods, and work more effectively in groups (Molnar and Deringer).

Other changes in attitude, generally representing a more balanced view of technology, occur in this last stage of acceptance. School people become more thoughtful critics of software because they have had more experience using it in their classrooms. In addition, because of increased education and interest in computing, teachers become exposed to more software. Getting a new program up and running is itself easier because of increased skills and more relaxed attitudes. The full impact of the

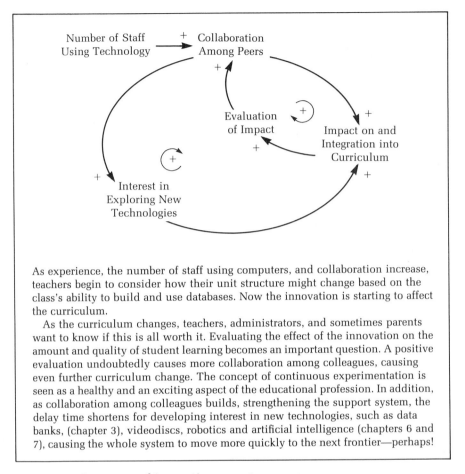

As experience, the number of staff using computers, and collaboration increase, teachers begin to consider how their unit structure might change based on the class's ability to build and use databases. Now the innovation is starting to affect the curriculum.

As the curriculum changes, teachers, administrators, and sometimes parents want to know if this is all worth it. Evaluating the effect of the innovation on the amount and quality of student learning becomes an important question. A positive evaluation undoubtedly causes more collaboration among colleagues, causing even further curriculum change. The concept of continuous experimentation is seen as a healthy and an exciting aspect of the educational profession. In addition, as collaboration among colleagues builds, strengthening the support system, the delay time shortens for developing interest in new technologies, such as data banks, (chapter 3), videodiscs, robotics and artificial intelligence (chapters 6 and 7), causing the whole system to move more quickly to the next frontier—perhaps!

Figure 9.4   Last stage of innovation acceptance.

meaning of the information age will be clearer as teachers gain experience in accessing and manipulating information with the aid of computers. The appreciation of having computerized information available, in the same sense as the need to have libraries available, is better understood.

Figure 9.5 puts together all the pieces described above to show the whole process, over time, of acceptance of an innovation such as computers. If the intermediate goal of a school system is to increase the number of staff using computer technology, figure 9.5 clearly indicates four key elements: the educational level of the staff, the quality of the products purchased, the staff's level of comfort with the technology, and the amount of money spent on the technology. These elements (circled in figure 9.5) are shown by their linking arrows to have a direct influence on the "Number of Staff Using Technology."

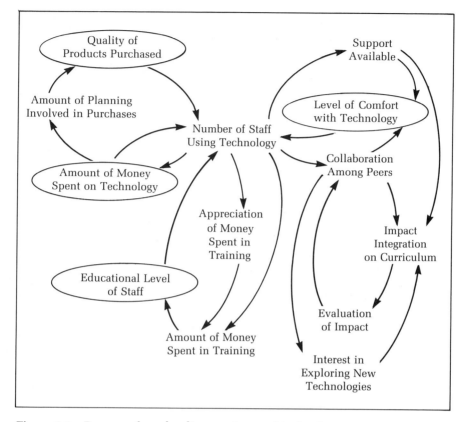

Figure 9.5   Process of a school's acceptance of technology.

A Social Studies Teacher's Special Contribution to the Acceptance of New Technology

The literature supports the claim that everyone eventually gets to stage four in the above process. Accepting this, let's look at the special role a social studies teacher can and should play as his or her school works through these stages. The following discussion is not what the authors believe should happen, but rather the kinds of activities we have observed in school systems.

At some time during stage one, a system-wide computer committee is formed. This is usually composed of teachers and administrators, and in some cases, interested or knowledgeable citizens. *One of the members of this committee* should be a social studies teacher.

The committee is formed because decisions need to be made requiring the support of the school staff and often of the general public as well. These decisions fall into two areas: expenditure of reasonably large amounts of the school funds for hardware, software, and teacher training;

and curriculum decisions. The curriculum decisions often fall into three general categories producing the following scenarios:

Scenario 1: Every student must be computer literate (usually not clearly defined) before graduation. This can be done most efficiently by developing for several grade levels units that are reasonably short in duration and require small amounts of hardware. A relatively common combination of topics is: an introduction to the Logo programming language for grade four, an introduction to the BASIC programming language for grade seven, and several electives for high school including word processing and the Pascal language. These satisfy a common general definition of computer literacy that often includes:

–Teaching a programming language, which gives students a sense of control over the machine.

– Word processing, which demonstrates the use of the computer as a powerful tool.

The first scenario reflects a school system at stage one of innovation acceptance. Very few people in the system are seen as having any computer competence, and the allocation of machinery becomes a political issue. Developing short units, which are easy to prepare teachers to teach, and making them system-wide, fulfills the perceived current needs. Since the plans in the first scenario generally ignore social studies, the social studies teacher on the committee should push for the release of a small amount of funds for computers moveable from class to class so that teachers willing to experiment in their classrooms have some computer access. In addition, one of the best investments in the use of hardware is to allow teachers to take the equipment home. These travelling computers can be earmarked for borrowing as well; this begins to move the school system towards stage two.

Scenario 2: Give the hardware to those teachers requesting it. The allocation decision is based on the commitment shown by the teacher. This commitment is demonstrated by the amount of training the teacher has acquired and the thoroughness of the proposal for the computers requested.

Scenario two is more suggestive of a stage-two system where the desirability of teacher training has become recognized. The social studies teacher on the committee has the responsibility to make sure some proposals are submitted for use in the social studies curriculum area. One effective way to motivate such proposals is to identify a social studies leader at each educational level. It is important that this person gets the exposure and training necessary to write a proposal for the committee. The social studies committee member might very well be the first to develop a proposal.

Social studies people are also excellent contributors to designing in-service courses. Someone with a strong liberal arts background is usually able to take a more balanced view of technology, of its impact both on the classroom and on society. Such a person is more inclined to include discussions of ethics and equity and feelings. A broader view of computers generally results in a more interesting in-service course — one not entirely focused on one application or just programming.

Scenario 3: Look carefully at the K–12 curriculum and try to match currently available software with teaching objectives. Then, as these computer applications are evaluated, determine curriculum changes based on the new learning possible or otherwise needed for different ages and for different learning styles.

Scenario three represents the kind of decision made by a school system that has already entered stage four. At this point the major issue might be the allocation of hardware, still a scarce resource. A national survey (Becker) suggests that optimal use of computers, in terms of hours in use per day, occurs when the computers are placed in a laboratory setting. However, this requires signing up in advance by the teacher. This is reminiscent of renting films at the end of one school year for use during the next. If the teacher slightly changes the order of topics, or the timing of presentation, the film's arrival is inopportune. The laboratory works well for programming classes, which are scheduled on a regular basis anyway, or as an open room for word processing. To allow genuine integration into the curriculum, one computer or several must be available when needed.

The other choice for allocating hardware is to place it in classrooms as needed. In some cases this would require permanent locations for a number of machines. In other situations several machines would be required for one unit for perhaps one or two months. The social studies committee person is most qualified to make the other committee members recognize this.

Having computers as a permanent part of the classroom facilitates both integrating computers into the curriculum and integrating the various topics of the curriculum as a whole. As an example, a first grade class in the Greater Boston area has the luxury of having two computers in its classroom on a permanent basis. As the teacher designs her unit about foods, the following things occur because of the availability of the computers:

1. A grocery corner is set up as it had been in previous years, but this time one of the computers is used as a cash register. A program is written by the student teacher that allows the student cashier to type in the "universal bar code" of each item and the quantity purchased. When the student customer's order is rung up, the computer produces the total dollars spent. The amount of money given by the customer is then entered and the computer returns the amount of change required. As the first grade students help design the cash-register program, they understand why universal bar codes were developed.

2. Arithmetic enters the unit when money is counted for change and when the customer estimates the total cost to judge if he or she can afford the purchases.

3. Several language arts activities are involved with the unit. The "biggest shopping list in the world" is created using a database program and entering all the foods the children can think of for each letter of the alphabet. The list is printed and hung from the ceiling. A recipe file is created using *Bank Street Writer*, a word processing package. Stories and poems about food are dictated by the children to the teacher, then printed and shared.

4. A database is designed to create a classification system for the foods in the grocery story, bringing science into the unit. The children create food pictures for scrapbooks as they learn Logo, integrating art and science.

These four occurences together provide one example of how the computer acts as a catalyst in the classroom for creating interdisciplinary units.

Other stage four type decisions also require the input from a social studies person. These might include the discussion to form a computer science department for the high school. If such a proposal is made, the social studies person should be involved in structuring such courses as "Computers in Society" or "The History of Technology." These courses can be offered by either the social science or computer science department but should be developed, and probably taught, by a social studies teacher.

A further point is that the tendency of the computer committee's agenda to dominate the overall set of school concerns must be kept in control. Computers are not going to replace a need for the traditional basic skills — at least not entirely. In fact, high-level reading skills are often needed to understand technological literature. And certainly high-level writing skills are needed to eliminate poor technical writing. Moreover, social studies people need to make sure the school system, along with society in general, does not get caught up in a technological fix — a belief that advances in technology will cure all of society's ills.

Finally, it seems that the discussion of teaching programming — what language, where in the curriculum, and to which students — is ongoing. The social studies committee member might want to become involved in these discussions. Briefly, Logo is the language created by Seymour Papert at M. I. T. and Wallace Feurzeig at Bolt Beranek and Newman over a decade ago. The purpose of this project, sponsored by the National Science Foundation, was to develop a language readily accessible to beginners and without an upper limit for sophisticated programmers. Because children from kindergarten up can learn to program using Logo, the language has swept the country.

BASIC is another language almost always taught in schools. BASIC's popularity stems largely from the fact that it is the native language of personal computers. Almost every major manufacturer includes BASIC at no extra charge. BASIC is also the language that has traditionally been taught at the high school level. Therefore, if there is a computer teacher around, he or she undoubtedly knows BASIC.

The third language currently found at the secondary level is Pascal. There are two reasons for Pascal's appearance on the scene. First, it was designed as a teaching language to force students into good programming habits. Good programming habits are very similar to good composition habits. Writing, whether a program or a composition, should be readable. Moreover, the work should be easily altered by the author or a collaborator. Finally, a piece should be written in small sections, following problem-solving procedures that break a large task into smaller parts — something like outlining and then writing one outline section at a time. Second, Pascal is currently the language chosen for the college advanced placement exam for high school students. Schools concerned with having advanced placement courses available usually have one in Pascal. For a more detailed discussion of programming languages, see the *Practical Guide* (Coburn).

One major argument for teaching programming is that programming allows the user the maximum sense of control over the machine. To be able to instruct the machine to do something — eventually something of use — has the appearance of control. In addition, some of today's more sophisticated application packages, such as dBase II, require some programming knowledge to use fully. However, people in the field of artificial intelligence are working to make the machine more intelligent — that is, more able to respond to human language. As this field progresses, the need for most people to program in today's sense will disappear. Moreover, for students not going on for post-secondary education, merely having a brief introduction to programming may be useless.

If a student obtains employment with a bank, for example, at about the time the bank makes a decision to put a personal computer on every desk, that high school graduate is invaluable to the bank if he or she has a high level of comfort with several different kinds of applications, such as word processing, spreadsheets, and databases. The social studies curriculum provides fertile ground for exposure to applications packages (chapters 3 and 4). The social studies teacher might therefore act to temper other committee members' overwhelming enthusiasm for the absolute need to teach every student to program. An appreciation of and ability to use a variety of applications packages may be more important for students, even for an introductory exposure.

The social studies teacher should possess all the elements needed to act as the catalyst for meaningful curriculum change. These elements include both an understanding of the needs of the individual in the coming generation as well as a vision of society's needs. The authors hope this book has given the reader the information and ideas necessary to become a leader in these exciting times.

References

Becker, H., *School Uses of Microcomputers*. Issue Nos. 1–5, Baltimore, Md.: The Johns Hopkins University, 1983–84.

Coburn, P.; Kelman, P.; Roberts, N.; Snyder, T.; Watt, D.; and Weiner, C., *Practical Guide to Computers in Education*. Reading, Mass.: Addison-Wesley, 1982.

Cory, S., "A Four-Stage Model of Development for Full Implementation of Computers for Instruction in a School System." *The Computing Teacher* (November 1983) 11–16.

Hall, G. and Loucks, S., "Teacher Concerns as a Basis for Facilitating and Personalizing Staff Development," *Teachers College Record*, vol. 80, no. 1 (September 1978) 36–53.

Molnar, A. and Deringer, D., "Edutainment: how to laugh and learn." *IEEE Spectrum* (June 1984) 114–118.

Appendix

Social Studies Microcomputer Courseware Evaluation Guidelines

Stephen A. Rose, Allan R. Brandhorst, Allen D. Glenn, James O. Hodges and Charles S. White

This document was produced by the Ad Hoc Committee on Computer Courseware Evaluation Guidelines for the National Council for the Social Studies. The authors are: Stephen A. Rose, Chairperson, University of Northern Iowa at Cedar Falls; Allan R. Brandhorst, University of South Carolina at Columbia; Allen D. Glenn, University of Minnesota at Minneapolis; James O. Hodges, Virginia Commonwealth University, Richmond; and Charles S. White, Indiana University at Bloomington.

Social-studies educators at all levels are employing the microcomputer in a variety of instructional settings. Many social studies educators have little difficulty locating microcomputer hardware that can be used effectively in the classroom. Unfortunately, the same cannot be said about courseware ("software" designed for use in a course of study). While a multitude of educational courseware is available, identifying that courseware most useful for achieving social studies goals and objectives is often problematic. Even the existence of numerous generic courseware evaluation instruments has not made things easier, primarily because these instruments do not focus on the specific goals of the social studies. It was in response to this concern that the National Council for the Social Studies developed guidelines to evaluate and select social-studies-related courseware.

These guidelines contain three broad categories of questions — knowledge, skills, and values. The implied criteria in the questions have been drawn from the "NCSS Social Studies Curriculum Guidelines," "Curriculum Guidelines for Multiethnic Education," and "Essentials of the Social Studies." Collectively, these documents outline a variety of roles the social studies play in preparing youth for full participation in society. Social studies, for example, should specify goals that go beyond the acquisition of academic content and seek to develop learners who have the personal, social and intellectual skills needed for both citizenship and effective participation in society. Moreover, it is essential that social studies programs have students develop a realistic picture of themselves, examine their own values and value systems, and increase their reading, writing, thinking, and speaking skills. Additionally, the social studies curriculum should help students understand and appreciate cultural diversity throughout the world and develop the capacities for working cooperatively with others. Lastly, social-studies education is directly concerned with the development of students' understanding of the body of knowledge developed and refined by historians and social scientists. This includes important facts, concepts, generalizations, and skills that permit students to explain and describe social phenomena affecting their lives.

Computer courseware materials must be evaluated carefully in two stages. First, educators need to determine whether or not a particular set of materials is appropriate for use in the social studies classroom. These guidelines address that need: they contain criteria derived from the goals and purposes most appropriate to social studies. Second, while judging the value of a set of computer courseware as it relates to the goals of social studies, educators must also confront technical and instructional issues. There are many excellent evaluation guidelines already available for this purpose, including the *Evaluator's Guide to Microcomputer Based Instructional Packages* published by MicroSift and *Guidelines for Evaluating Computerized Instructional Materials* by the National Council of Teachers of Mathematics. These and other such evaluation instruments are identified at the end of this document.

The two-stage evaluation process described above, with one stage focusing on the courseware's relationship to the overall goals of the social studies and the other on the technical/instructional issues, is an integral process. By assuring that both stages receive careful attention, the social studies educator should be able to determine whether a particular set of computer courseware should be used, and if so, where and how. The final goal is the selection of computer courseware that meets the instructional goals and objectives of a particular social studies teacher.

Social Studies Microcomputer Courseware Evaluation Guidelines

The guidelines are organized around three areas — *Knowledge, Skills, and Values* — each of which contains organizational descriptors. A checklist has been included to help evaluators monitor the extent of emphasis a courseware package places on each criterion. The checklist contains four headings — Strong Emphasis (SE), Moderate Emphasis (ME), Inadequate Emphasis (IE), and Not Applicable (NA). When using the checklist, it is important to realize that the breadth of criteria in this document and the variety of courseware on the market preclude a single courseware package from meeting all the standards in these guidelines.

Knowledge

Social studies educators at all levels have rejected curricula based exclusively on the behavioral and social sciences. Instead, they have adopted a broad-based curriculum that not only addresses the concerns of those academic disciplines but concentrates on the personal and social concerns of the student, as well as the multicultural and normative concerns of society.

SE	ME	IE	NA	
				Significant Characteristics
				1.01 Validity
				Does the courseware emphasize currently valid knowledge from one or more of the social sciences?*
				1.02 Accuracy
				Does the courseware present a true and comprehensive body of content, free of distortion by omission?
				1.03 Reality Oriented
				Does the courseware's content deal with the realities of today's world in terms of its flaws, strengths, dangers, and promises?
				1.04 Significance of Past and Present
				Does the courseware deal with important concepts, principles, and theories of modern society? Does it present significant ideas that convey the excitement of the past, present, and future?
				1.05 Bias
				Does the courseware avoid bias and/or stereotyping with regard to gender, ethnicity, racial background, religious affiliation, or cultural group?

*History is included in this classification.

SE	ME	IE	NA	

When unfamiliar customs and institutions or different ethnic groups and cultures are dealt with, are they presented in an unbiased and objective manner?

Content Emphasis

1.11   Issue Analysis

Does the courseware engage students in analyzing and attempting to resolve social issues? Is a data base provided, and does it contain information of sufficient depth and breadth for students to make realistic decisions? If not, can the data base be expanded by the teacher or student?

1.12   Pervasive and Enduring Issues

Does the courseware focus on problems and/or issues that are socially significant? Do the materials demonstrate the reciprocal relationships among the social sciences, social issues, and action?

1.13   Global Perspectives

Does the courseware help students develop a global perspective? Are students assisted in recognizing the local, national, and global implications of the problems being examined and their possible solutions?

1.14   Development of Society

Does the courseware develop knowledge and insights into the historical development of human society? Do the facts, concepts, principles, and processes presented offer direction in organizing a study of human behavior? Does it help students understand: how modern societies develop the role of central institutions and values of national societies and those of the world community?

1.15   Multiculturalism

Does the courseware help develop an understanding of the diversity of cultures and institutional arrangements within American society and in other societies within the global community? Does it provide a rational explanation for customs and other distinctive aspects of daily life arrangements that are explored? Does it contribute to the students' acceptance of the legitimacy of their own cultural identity as well as that of others?

1.16   Personal/Social Growth

Does the courseware help students understand their own development and capabilities, as influenced by their families, peer groups, ethnic groups, media, and the society at large?

Skills

Social-studies education should provide students with the opportunities to develop, practice, and use a variety of thought processes and skills. Students should have opportunities to probe, to extract knowledge from experience, to think and to communicate their findings and conclusions, both orally and in writing. They should learn how to learn — to develop self-direction in gaining meaningful knowledge and employing it effectively. The social studies program should develop the student's ability to make rational decisions. In order to accomplish this, it is essential that students acquire skills in critical thinking, inquiry, information processing, and problem solving.

SE	ME	IE	NA	
				Intellectual Skills
				2.01 Inquiry and Problem Solving
				Does the courseware pose problems which require students to use the methods of inquiry? Specifically, are students given practice in: identifying and defining problems, formulating and testing hypotheses, and arriving at valid generalizations?
				2.02 Critical Thinking
				Does the courseware foster the development of critical-thinking skills of distinguishing between fact and opinion, detecting slant and bias, determining cause and effect, and evaluating the reliability of sources?
				2.03 Higher Cognitive Levels
				Does the courseware help students develop and/or reinforce the thought processes of analysis, synthesis, and evaluation? Do students encounter material that helps develop their understanding of the relationship between elements and how these elements fit together as a whole? Are students given opportunities to use information to construct new communications? Are students asked to make judgments based on appropriate criteria?
				2.04 Divergent Thinking
				Does the courseware encourage divergent thinking which allows students to provide a variety of answers for difficult questions?
				2.05 Concept Formation
				Does the courseware present a broad range of illustrations, models, and examples appropriate for helping students image, dissect, conceptualize, define, or recognize relationships between patterns or concepts?

SE	ME	IE	NA	

Decisionmaking Skills

2.11 Processes

Does the courseware develop decisionmaking skills of identifying alternatives, establishing criteria to evaluate alternatives, evaluating alternatives in light of criteria and making decisions? Are students given the opportunity to re-test, re-interpret, and re-organize their beliefs about facts and values?

2.12 Learning Environment

Does the courseware and its accompanying materials create a social environment populated by believable characters confronting difficult circumstances and choices?

2.13 Choices

Does the courseware require the student to make choices, and are those choices then used as data for reflection?

2.14 Information Base

Does the courseware's data match the kind of data that would be accessible by citizens outside the instructional context? Is the courseware flexible enough to allow the alteration and addition of information, so that students can practice making decisions under a variety of factual and value circumstances?

2.15 Consequences

Does the courseware confront students with realistic consequences (for themselves and for others) of decisions they are required to make in using the courseware?

2.16 Assessment

Does the courseware and its accompanying materials assist the teacher and the student to assess the latter's skills and abilities in decisionmaking?

2.17 Degree of Certainty

Does the courseware provide experiences in making decisions under conditions of uncertainty? Does the courseware help the student recall the basis on which decisions were made and to make revised decisions informed by new understandings?

Information-Processing Skills

2.21 Orientation Skills

Does the courseware foster the development of map and globe skills?

2.22 Chronology and Time Skills

Does the courseware provide students practice in

SE	ME	IE	NA

interpreting chronology and applying time skills, i.e., sequencing events and trends, and identifying and using measures of time correctly?

2.23 Graphic Data Skills

Does the courseware help students develop skills of reading and interpreting, constructing, and drawing inferences from graphs, tables, and charts?

2.24 Gathering and Processing Data

Does the courseware provide opportunities for students to develop skills in locating, organizing, interpreting, and presenting data?

2.25 Content Reading Skills

Does the courseware facilitate the development of the student's word-attack skills and the ability to read on the literal, interpretative, and applied levels?

2.26 Communication Skills

Does the courseware or its accompanying materials foster adequately developed communication skills and provide opportunities for communicating effectively orally and in writing?

Cooperation and Participation Skills

2.31 Interaction

Does the courseware and its accompanying materials require groups of students to work together? Do the learning tasks require a division of labor? Does successful completion of the tasks require shared information?

2.32 Cooperation

Does the courseware and its accompanying materials reinforce the importance of, and provide support for, cooperation in resolving conflicts over contradictory facts and values?

2.33 Social/Political Participation

Does interaction with the courseware and its accompanying materials enhance the student's ability to participate effectively in the social and political processes of his/her school and community?

2.34 Follow-up Activities

Does the courseware or its accompanying material offer suggestions for activities that follow logically from the use of the courseware? Does the courseware allow students to experience vicariously the positive and negative consequences, the costs and benefits, the frustrations and satisfactions of taking action?

Values

The cultural pluralism characterizing American society makes value conflicts inevitable. These conflicts are particularly evident in debates about solutions to complex social problems confronting our society. Effective participation in resolving these problems requires people who have rationally developed their own value system and are proficient at making defensible value decisions.

Social studies education should provide ample opportunities for students to rationally examine value issues in a non-indoctrinating environment. Additionally, it should promote the reflective examination of value dilemmas that underlie the personal and social issues that students confront in their everyday lives.

SE	ME	IE	NA	
				Societal Orientation
				3.01 Influence of Values on Behavior Does the courseware help students develop an understanding and appreciation of the influence of beliefs and values on human behavior patterns?
				3.02 Procedural Values Does the courseware help the student identify and develop an appreciation for values that underlie substantive beliefs and procedural guarantees expressed in this nation's fundamental documents?
				Valuing Processes
				3.11 Beliefs Does the courseware require the student to identify his or her own beliefs, to make choices based on those beliefs, and to understand the consequences of the choices made?
				3.12 Conjoint Reflection Does the courseware require conjoint reflection on feelings, behaviors, and beliefs?
				3.13 Defensible Judgments Does the courseware support a process of value analysis by which learners can make rational, defensible value judgments?
				3.14 Feedback Does the courseware track the process students use in making value judgments and provide useful feedback with respect to its quality and improvement?

Systems for Evaluating Technical and

Instructional Courseware Issues

Computer Library Media Consortium for Classroom Evaluation of Microcomputer Courseware, 1983. San Mateo County Office of Education, 333 Main Street, Redwood City, CA 94073. Phone (415) 363-5400. (A three-page untitled evaluation reporting form.)

Dennis, J. Richard. *Evaluating Materials for Teaching with a Computer,* includes "Courseware Evaluation Worksheet." The Illinois Series on Educational Application of Computers, No. 5e, Department of Secondary Education, University of Illinois at Urbana-Champaign, 1979.

Douglas, Shirley and Gary Neights. *A Guide to Instructional Microcomputer Software,* includes "Microcomputer Software Evaluation Form." Instructional Materials Service Programs, Pennsylvania Department of Education, Box 911, 333 Market Street, Harrisburg, PA 17108. Phone (717) 783-2528.

Evaluating Instructional Computer Courseware; Materials Review and Education Center, Division of Educational Media, Department of Public Instruction, Raleigh, NC.

Evaluation Guide for Microcomputer-Based Instructional Packages. Developed by MicroSift, The Computer Technology Program, Northwest Regional Educational Laboratory. Published by International Council for Computers in Education, Dept. of Computer and Information Science, University of Oregon, 1982.

Heck, William P. et al. *Guidelines for Evaluating Computerized Instructional Materials.* The National Council for Teachers of Mathematics, Inc., Reston, VA, 1981.

Rosenstock, Robert, Norman Dodl and John Burton. *Education Microware Assessment: Criteria and Procedures for Evaluating Instructional Software.* Education Microcomputer Laboratory, Room 400, War Memorial Gym, Virginia Tech, Blacksburg, VA 24061. Phone (703) 961-5587.

Smith, Richard A. (ed.). *Guidelines for Software Evaluation,* Department of Technology, Houston Independent School District, Houston, TX (a four-page questionnaire).

Glossary

Alphanumeric A set of characters made up of both letters and numbers.

Binary system A mathematical number system made up of two elements, usually represented by 0 and 1.

Baud rate A measure that indicates the time requirements for transferring electronic information. The dimension is bits per second.

Board The part of the *computer* containing chips, wires, and other electrical components. A computer has a main board, usually called the mother board, and special purpose boards for additional tasks like communicating with a printer.

CD-ROM (Compact Disk - Read Only Memory) Similar to an audio compact disk, this device can store 550 million pieces of information on a less than five-inch-round disk. Used with a computer, the information on the disk can be accessed randomly.

Central processor (CPU — Central Processing Unit) The part of the *computer* that controls what the computer does. Often the largest chip on the mother board.

Computer An electronic device that manipulates symbolic information according to a list of precise instructions called a *program*.

Computer-assisted instruction (CAI) Sometimes called computer-aided instruction. Preprogrammed computerized teaching materials including drill-and-practice, tutorials, simulations, and educational games.

Computer-based materials See *Computer-assisted instruction*.

Computer-based tools General purpose computer materials designed to facilitate specific tasks such as record keeping, writing, or accounting.

Computer conferencing Several people conducting a topical discussion over time from different geographic locations using a central computer's storage and retrieval capacity.

Computer links *(networks)* An electronic communication system connecting *computers* to each other to enable them to share resources, like printers, and transfer information to and from each other.

Computer model A representation of a real-world system with the aid of a *computer*.

Courseware Educational *software*, usually accompanied by a range of ancillary materials.

Database A body of related information, usually accessible by a computer.

Database management system (DBMS) A software package that allows a person to store and manipulate data in a variety of ways.

DBMS See *database management system*.

Documentation The collection of manuals and instructions that explain the use and applications of a given piece of hardware or software.

Drill-and-practice *Software* that primarily drills students on factual material or the application of algorithms.

Electronic information service A company that sells *computer*-based information.

Electronic mail Sending and receiving information with the aid of a computer.

Field The part of a database *record* that contains a unique piece of information such as a name or address.

File A category name used when talking about information storage:

> **Text file** *Alphanumeric* information stored for use by people, such as letters or essays, in contrast to files stored for use by computers, such as programs.

Database file The general subject (topic) of a database that is composed of individual *records*.

Hardware The collection of physical devices that make up a *computer* system such as the computer, disk drives, and printers.

Integrated circuits One of the lowest-level parts of a *computer*, containing computer logic in the form of electronic components.

Interactive video A medium that delivers video displays, such as television, tape players, and disk players, and is designed to allow the person viewing the display to participate.

LAN Local area networks where several computers in a building or small geographic area are connected for purposes of communications.

Microchip The smallest complete unit of a *computer*.

Microcomputer A *computer* that is designed around a microprocessor.

Model-building Replicating the functioning of a system by constructing a simpler version of that system, usually using mathematics, for purposes of analysis.

Mode The particular environment in which a computer user is working. Used to distinguish between entering text, usually referred to as the edit mode, or printing text, called the print mode.

Modem Short for MOdulator/DEModulator, this device allows for communications between computers over telephone lines by converting a computer's digital signal to audio tones and then back to digital signals for the computer at the other end.

Network The communication links, such as cables, satellites, and microwaves, that allow two or more computers to pass information among them.

Nodes Centers, usually in the larger cities, where electronic information from an information network is collected and dispersed.

Port An input/output place on a *computer* to allow peripherals, such as *modems* and printers, to communicate with the computer.

Private message system An electronic mail system initiated by an individual or group which is independent of the commercial electronic service bureaus.

Program The list of instructions that tells a *computer* how to perform a given task.

Programmer The person who writes instructions for a *computer*.

Query The software that allows a user to find out particular information from a large computerized *database*.

Record One entry of a larger *database*. For example, information about one country in a database on Africa is a *record* in that database.

Silicon chips *Computer* chips made primarily from the raw material silicon.

Simulation Using a *computer* to imitate the behavior of a system using a model of that system for purposes of playing games or experimentation.

Simulation game See *simulation*.

Simulation model See *simulation*.

Software The *computer programs* that allow the computer to function in specific ways.

Telecommunications Communications over some geographic distance.

Teleconferencing Discussions, on an ongoing basis but for a specified reason, among a group of people with the aid of *networked computers* or terminals.

Template A premade design for a general purpose software package; for example, one setting up the *fields* to be used for a particular *database* application.

Text file See *file*.

Truth table A way of visually showing classical logic that also defines the basic logical operations of a *computer*.

Tutorial *Software* that teaches and tests students on a particular body of knowledge.

Videodisc A record-like object which can contain video, graphics, and text.

Word processing Using the computer to imitate a typewriter.

Resources

Researched and compiled by Evelyn J. Woldman

Introduction

The information in the section to follow reflects an extensive database sampling of the resources available to the educator interested in Computers and the Social Studies. Included is information on Associations and Organizations, Publications, On-Line Networks and Databases, Software, and Resource Centers.

In each of these sections, great care was taken to make the information as current, up-to-date, and complete as possible, in order to serve the reader coming from either a technological or a social studies background. Data, however, is in constant flux and, as a result, some information may have changed.

We hope that this resource section provides the social studies educator with some new ideas, inspirations, and phone numbers for further involvement in the field of Computers and the Social Studies.

Resources Contents

Associations and Organizations

The listings below reflect organizations that would be of interest to both the educational-technology and the social studies educators.

American Educational Research Association (AERA)
1230 Seventeenth Street, NW
Washington, DC 20036
(202) 223-9485

AERA is an organization of university researchers as well as public school educators at all levels and has a special interest group for members interested in computer-assisted instruction. Publications include: *Educational Researcher; Educational Evaluation and Policy Analysis; American Educational Research Journal; Review of Educational Research;* and *Review of Research in Education* (an annual volume).

Association for Computing Machinery (ACM)
11 West 42nd Street
New York, NY 10036
(212) 869-7440

The ACM deals with all aspects of computing. The two sections of ACM that deal specifically with instructional computing are the special interest group on computer uses in education (SIGCUE) and the elementary and secondary sub-committee of the education board. Publications that may prove useful are: *Computing Reviews; The ACM Guide to Computer Literature; Covering Curricular Recommendations; and Teacher Certification.* The SIGCSE (Computer Science Educators) are another special interest group under this organization. Other publications include the *ACM Guide to Computer Science* and the *SIGCUE Bulletin.* The latter is especially helpful for educators.

Association for Educational Communications and Technology (AECT)
1126 Sixteenth Street, NW
Washington, DC 20036
(202) 466-4780

AECT promotes the effective use of media and technology in education. It supports a special committee on microcomputers and a division for information systems and computers and offers Techcentral, an educational electronic network which includes a microcomputer program database, bulletin boards, and electronic mail. AECT's purpose is to increase understanding and information-sharing of educational computing and its use in basic skills education.

Publications: *Educational Communication and Technology Journal; Journal of Instructional Development; Tech Trends.*

Guide to Microcomputers; Learning with Microcomputers; Equipment Directory of Audio-visual Computer and Video Products; Software Quality and Copyright; Issues in CAI (book and videotape).

An annual conference is held which offers approximately 150 sessions in educational technology.

Association for the Development of Computer-Based Instructional Systems (ADCIS Headquarters)
409 Miller Hall
Western Washington University
Bellingham, WA 98225
(206) 676-2860

This association advances the use of computer-based instruction and management by facilitating communication between product developers of CAI materials. Its members include elementary and secondary school systems, colleges and universities, and businesses and government agencies. ADCIS maintains several special interest groups active in educational technology.

Publications: *The Journal of Computer-Based Instruction; ADCIS Newsletter;* annual conference proceedings.

International Communications Industries Association
3150 Spring Street
Fairfax, VA 22031
(703) 273-7200

ICIA is a trade association that advocates the use of educational technology. ICIA offers information on funding for classroom computer-use through its market-research program and through updates in its newsletter. Its annual equipment directory of audio-visual, video, and microcomputer products gives details on microcomputer hardware and other technology.

International Council for Computers in Education (ICCE)
University of Oregon
1787 Agate Street
Eugene, Oregon 97403
(503) 686-4414

The ICCE is an international organization for computer using educators. The ICCE has published over twenty booklets and monographs on the instructional use of computers. ICCE also has special interest groups (SIG). It serves computer science teachers, videodisc/microcomputer users, computer coordinators, and teacher educators. Available from ICCE is a booklet entitled *Computing in the Social Studies Classroom* by Allen Glenn and Don Rawitsch. ICCE has several policy statements available; among those included are: (1) a code of ethical conduct for computer using educators; (2) a statement on networking and multiple machine software. Write for further information.

National Council for the Social Studies (NCSS)
3501 Newark Street, NW
Washington, DC 20016
(202) 966-7840

NCSS is the national organization for social studies educators at all levels. In addition to concerns in its own field, NCSS has become involved in the field of technology and the social studies as well. NCSS is interested in the use of simulations and other computing programs for teaching social studies. NCSS recently prepared a booklet titled *Computers in the Social Science Classroom*. Its journal, *Social Education*, often includes articles on educational computing.

Recently, NCSS has begun to sponsor pre-convention workshops on computing at its national meetings. In addition, the Council has approved a set of software evaluation guidelines for social studies software (see appendix), and several committees are collaborating on the development of a policy statement on the role of computers in the classroom.

National Education Association (NEA)
1201 Sixteenth Street, NW
Washington, DC 20036
(202) 822-7200

The NEA is a national organization serving teachers. They publish a newsletter, *NEA Today*, that frequently includes articles on educational computing. In addition, the NEA has started the NEA Educational Computer Service, which provides a comprehensive guide to courseware.

National Education Computing Conference (NECC)
ICCE — University of Oregon
1787 Agate Street
Eugene, OR 97403
(503) 686-4414

The National Education Computing Conference runs once a year. It covers instructional computing from K–college. The goal is to provide a forum for discussion of the latest research and practical applications on computers in education. NECC is a refereed conference.

SIG-CASE
c/o NCSS
3501 Newark Street, NW
Washington, DC 20010
(202) 966-7840

SIG-CASE is a special interest group within the National Council for Social Studies focusing on computers and social education. The group serves to identify powerful applications of computer technology in the field and to share information about projects and materials among the membership of the National Council.

Publications

The Publications section consists of five major parts. The first part is Periodicals, which includes some periodicals which are strictly technological, some which are strictly on the social studies, and a few which may be technological in nature but include frequent contributions of interest to the social studies educator. The second part is Articles, the third part is Indexes, the fourth Books and the fifth Papers.

It should be noted that some of the material in this section reflects in part a search done on the ERIC database and some of the abstracts may contain paraphrasing from that search.

Periodicals

Byte
McGraw-Hill
70 Main Street
Peterborough, NH 03458
(603) 924-9281

Byte offers technical information for the home computer user. The monthly magazine contains detailed discussions of new microcomputer hardware and software and includes exceptionally well-researched special-focus issues. Educators interested in developing their own programs may find this a valuable source of information.

Classroom Computer Learning
Peter Li Incorporated
19 Davis Drive
Belmont, CA 94002
(415) 592-7810

Classroom Computer Learning links computer-based instruction with traditional classroom teaching. Published eight times a year, it features teacher-developed classroom ideas, original programs, software reviews, and a two-sided pullout poster for classroom use. Manufacturers' product news and a calendar of educational computing events are included in each issue.

Computers in the Schools
The Haworth Press, Incorporated
12 West 32 Street
New York, NY 10001
(806) 742-2290 or (806) 794-4833

Computers in the Schools is an interdisciplinary journal devoted to the theory, practice, concerns, and issues surrounding the use of microcomputers in the school curriculum. It features articles on research, computer languages, software, hardware, educational psychology, and instructional and administrative applications. One thematically based issue is published annually.

The Computing Teacher
International Council for Computers in Education (ICCE)
University of Oregon
1787 Agate Street
Eugene, OR 97403
(503) 686-4429

The Computing Teacher publishes general and technical articles on the instructional uses of computers and on teaching about computers. Sent to members of the International Council for Computers in Education, it emphasizes precollege education and teacher training. Teachers in the field write most of the articles. It also includes sections devoted to programming suggestions, computing problems, software and book reviews, news items on conferences, projects and resource centers, and technological developments in computers. Regular columns include the Logo Center, Computers and the Teaching of English, and Computers and the Media Center.

Curriculum Product Review
Hanson Publishing Group
Six River Bend — Box 4949
Stamford, CT 06907
(203) 358-9900

Published September through May, under a controlled circulation, *Curriculum Product Review* features short descriptions of textbooks, sources for new materials, software and supplementary materials — all less than a year old. Topics include computer-assisted instruction (CAI), computer-managed instruction (CMI), curricula, and office and administrative materials for supervisors at the district level.

Electronic Education
Electronic Communications, Incorporated
1311 Executive Center Drive, Suite 220
Tallahassee, FL 32301
(904) 878-4178

Electronic Education informs school administrators and educators from middle school through college about the uses of technology in education. Articles cover technology's applications in the schools, new products, trends, and interviews with prominent people in the field.

Electronic Learning
Scholastic, Incorporated
730 Broadway
New York, NY 10003
(212) 505-3000

Electronic Learning provides non-technical introductions to educational computing applications. News columns report on innovations and official receptivity to computers in education. Experienced classroom educators evaluate commercial software and discuss the merits and faults of classroom software applications. Regular features include profiles of what various states are doing in computers, funding sources, computer applications for administrators, resource material on new software, hardware, books and curriculum products, regular reports on educational software producers, and teachers' suggestions for simple computer-based classroom activities.

Microzine
Scholastic, Incorporated
730 Broadway
New York, NY 10003
(212) 505-3000

Microzine is a bi-monthly magazine-on-a-disk for the Apple II series of computers. Each disk is two-sided with full-length programs designed for grades 4 through 8. Programs include utilities, interactive stories, special features, and a back page of puzzles, letters, games, and a computerized "Micro-strip" comic strip. Activities are often social studies related. A handbook and teaching guide are included with each disk.

Optical Information Systems
Meckler Publishing
11 Ferry Lane West
Westport, CT 06880
(203) 226-6967

This magazine assists readers in keeping abreast of videodisc, optical disc, CD-ROM, and other optical technologies such as laser cards, in addition to other computer and communication technologies. Each issue focuses on a particular topic of video application; for example, the role and use of instructional theory on the development of the videodisc as an educational, instructional, and training tool.

Teaching and Computers
Scholastic, Incorporated
730 Broadway
New York, NY 10003
(212) 505-3000

Teaching and Computers provides information and practical suggestions for integrating computers into the elementary classroom. It includes non-technical information about how computers work, teacher-developed lesson ideas, and information on new books, new software and hardware, and other resources. Ideas in all curricular areas, including social studies, are abundant.

Social Education
National Council for the Social Studies
3501 Newark Street, NW
Washington, DC 20016
(202) 966-7840

Social Education is the official publication of the National Council for the Social Studies. The journal features articles on current issues in the social studies, including a column in almost every issue on technology and the social studies. In addition, each issue includes an elementary school section, book reviews, NCSS news and events, and other features.

The Social Studies
Heldref Publications
4000 Albermarle Street, NW
Washington, DC 20016
(202) 362-6445

The Social Studies is a bimonthly publication which features articles of current interest to social studies educators. Included in almost every issue is at least one article based on computers and the social studies. Also included are book reviews.

The Social Studies Professional
National Council for the Social Studies
3501 Newark Street, NW
Washington, DC 20016
(202) 966-7840

The Social Studies Professional is the offical newsletter published by the National Council for the Social Studies. Sent to every member of the council, the newsletter includes current events in the social studies, a calendar of upcoming conferences and workshops around the country, news about the workings of the national council, advice to aid in the development of local council activities, and general articles/editorials describing current world situations about which the social studies teacher should be aware. Also included are listings of any noteworthy awards of local council members.

Articles

Choosing Computer Simulations in Social Studies
Mark C. Schug/Henry S. Kepner, Jr.
The Social Studies, (September/October 1984)
Heldref Publications
4000 Albermarle Street, NW
Washington, DC 20016
(202) 362-6445

This article deals with the appropriate use of simulations within the social studies classroom. The authors examine the whys of using simulation, the right time to use it in the curriculum, and finally go through the types of things to look for when choosing a simulation.

Computer Corner
Mollie L. Cohen
Social Education, vol. 48, no. 3 (March 1984), pp. 216–218
National Council for the Social Studies
3501 Newark Street, NW
Washington, DC 20016
(202) 966-7840

This article looks at the ways that the educator can use the computer in a social studies classroom as an information-processing tool. One example given is the use of a database to store and manipulate recorded data.

Computers in the Curriculum: Playing with History
Gwen Solomon
Electronic Learning (May/June 1986), pp. 39–43
Scholastic, Incorporated
730 Broadway
New York, NY 10003
(212) 505-3000

This article encourages use of software that stimulates inquiry and hypothesis formation and testing. Five geography programs are compared.

Creating and Using Data Bases in the Social Studies
Printout, vol. 3, no. 3 (May 1986), pp. 3–7
Datek Information Services, Incorporated
Box 68
Newton, MA 02160
(617) 893-9130

Student use of microcomputer databases in social studies is discussed.

Developing Your Own Microcomputer Courseware with Authoring Tools
James O. Hodges
Social Education (January 1985)
3501 Newark Street, NW
Washington, DC 20016
(202) 966-7840

This article is a synopsis of some of the more popular authoring tools on the market today. The author discusses the pros and cons of authoring languages and reviews the Courseware Authoring System and Apple Superpilot.

Five Ways to Use Databases in Social Studies
Robert Jackson
Teaching and Computers, vol. 1, no. 3 (November/December 1983), pp. 16–18
Scholastic, Incorporated
730 Broadway
New York, NY 10003
(212) 505-3000

This article is a comprehensive look at databases — what they are and how they can be used effectively in a social studies classroom. Specific curriculum examples are given.

Four Futures for Social Studies
Irving Morrissett
Social Education (November/December 1984)

National Council for the Social Studies
3501 Newark Street, NW
Washington, DC 20016
(202) 966-7840

This article examines four possible avenues in which social education will travel: (1) It will stay just the way it always has been; (2) it will move, albeit quite slowly, towards agreed-upon goals; (3) there is a new social studies to come but it has not come yet; (4) computers may be the catalyst to get the new social studies curriculum going.

From Social Studies to Social Science
Learning, vol. 3, no. 3 (October 1984), pp. 32, 38, 42
Learning Corporation
1255 Portland Place
Boulder, CO 80321
(303) 447-9330

Computers may help students delve further into social studies research topics. The role of the computer in database management is explored in this article.

Helping Students Deal with Computer Issues in Social Studies
Georgia Social Science Journal, vol. 6, no. 1 (Winter 1985), pp. 5–15
Georgia Council for the Social Sciences
Dudley Hall
University of Georgia
Athens, GA 30602
(404) 542-7265

The special responsibility of the social studies program is to help students understand the personal and social issues related to computer technology. Students must understand how computer technology influences us in our roles as consumers, workers, citizens, and family members.

Introducing Microcomputers into the Social Studies Classroom
Mary Furlong
Social Studies Review, vol. 22, no. 2 (Winter 1983), pp. 61–65
California Council for the Social Studies
616 Juanita Way
Roseville, CA 95678
(916) 786-6056

This article emphasizes the current need for teachers to keep up with the emergence of computers in the schools. The author looks at uses both instructionally and administratively. Also included is a list of organizations and resources that can help teachers get started.

Knowledge-Creative Learning with Data Bases
Beverly Hunter
Social Education, vol. 51, no. 1 (January 1987), pp. 38–43

3501 Newark Street, NW
Washington, DC 20016
(202) 966-7840

A nationally known expert on databases, Beverly Hunter applies database usage to social studies content.

The Learning Software Awards
Sherry Fraser
Classroom Computer Learning (Yearly)
Pitman Learning, Incorporated
19 Davis Avenue
Belmont, CA 94002
(415) 592-7810

This article is an evaluation of many disciplines and of what this magazine considers the best software at the current time. Social studies is one subject covered. Also listed are criteria used in the evaluation process.

Lemonade's the Name, Simulation's the Game
Susan Friel
Classroom Computer News (January/February 1983), pp. 34–39
Classroom Computer Learning
19 Davis Drive
Belmont, CA 94002
(415) 592-7810

This article describes the teaching of basic economic concepts through the playing of a simulation game.

Longstreet Social Studies Significance in Microcomputing
Louisiana Social Studies Journal, vol. 13, no. 1 (Fall 1986), pp. 22–27

This article discusses the reasons the microcomputer revolution merits attention within the social studies curriculum and stresses the skills social studies must help develop for students to deal with the impact of computer operations.

Microcomputer Capabilities in the Elementary Social Studies Program
Social Studies, vol. 76, no. 2 (March/April 1985), pp. 62–64
Heldref Publications
4000 Albermarle Street, NW
Washington, DC 20016
(202) 362-6445

How microcomputers can be used in the elementary social studies classroom to teach and reinforce new concepts, to relieve teachers of a variety of time consuming chores, and to motivate students to produce creative projects.

Social Studies Microcomputer Courseware Evaluation Guidelines
Stephen Rose, Allan Brandhorst, Allen Glenn, James Hodges, C. White
Social Education (November/December 1984)

National Council for the Social Studies
3501 Newark Street, NW
Washington, DC 20016
(202) 966-7840

This article is a checklist for the criteria used in evaluating a piece of social science software. It covers many skill areas in depth, for example: intellectual skills, decision-making skills, cooperation and participation skills, and more (see appendix).

Social Studies, Spreadsheets, and the Quality of Life
Larry Hannah
The Computing Teacher (December/January 1985–6), pp. 13–17
University of Oregon
1787 Agate Street
Eugene, OR 97403-1923
(503) 686-4414

The article describes the use of spreadsheets to analyze the "quality of life" based on a number of factors and using data available from several sources.

The Status of the Social Studies in the Public Schools of the United States: Another Look
Social Education, vol. 49, no. 3 (March 1985), pp. 220–23
National Council for the Social Studies
3501 Newark Street, NW
Washington, DC 20016
(202) 966-7840

In 1976 Richard Gross surveyed state social studies specialists and local supervisors to determine the status of the social studies. To determine whether the generalizations from his study are still applicable at this writing, a questionnaire was sent to the Council of State Social Studies Specialists. Results of the two studies are compared.

Teachers Using Technology
Charles White
Social Education, vol. 51, no. 1 (January 1987), pp. 44–47
3501 Newark Street, NW
Washington, DC 20016
(202) 966-7840

This article presents a series of scenarios of places around the country where computers are being used successfully in the social studies field.

Teaching Presidential Elections Through Simulation
Jack E. Cousins
The Social Studies, vol. 75, no. 4 (July/August 1984), pp. 172–177
4000 Albermarle Street, NW
Washington, DC 20016
(202) 362-6445

This article discusses the complexity of dealing with the presidential elections in the classroom. It then reviews several computer simulations dealing with presidential elections, including "Elect 1 and Elect 2," "Hat in the Ring: The Presidential Nominating Game," "Coalition: The Presidential Election Game," and "Hail to the Chief."

Teaming Up Social Studies and Computer Teachers
Electronic Learning, vol. 4, no. 7 (April 1985), pp. 16, 21
730 Broadway
New York, NY 10003
(212) 505-3000

This article describes a geography lesson that computer and social studies teachers present together to teach elementary and secondary school students about computers and to help them place the technology in a social context.

Technology and the Social Studies: Issues and Responsibilities
Richard A. Diem
Social Education, vol. 47, no. 5 (May 1983), pp. 308–310, 313
National Council for the Social Studies
3501 Newark Street, NW
Washington, DC 20016
(202) 966-7840

The article covers four basic themes having to do with computers and their impact on social studies. The themes include access to technology, control of the information generated, social responsibility as it relates to the technology, and cultural implications for all of the above.

Uses for the Computer in Implementing the Essential Elements of Social Studies
Southwestern Journal of Social Education, vol. 5, no. 1 (Spring/Summer 1985), pp. 9–14
Texas Council for Social Studies
Box 5427
Denton, TX
(817) 565-2296

This article examines the variety of computer software uses and possible effects they can have on social studies instruction using programs as mediating devices and tools. It concludes that the computer can assist implementation of essential objectives in the social studies curriculum.

Using Interactive Computer Techniques to Develop Global Understanding
Tama Traberman
The Computing Teacher, vol. 11, no. 2 (September 1983), pp. 43–50
ICCE — University of Oregon
1787 Agate Street
Eugene, OR 97403
(503) 686-4429

This article describes an eighth-grade teacher's use of the microcomputer to teach complex and abstract social studies concepts. Students learn to enter, store, and access data and to format numerical data. They also learn to upgrade, form tables, and display symbols. A real use of integration of social studies and microcomputers is described.

Using Microcomputers for Instruction in Humanities and Social Sciences, II
Barbara Pannwitt
Curriculum Report, vol. 13, no. 3 (January 1984)
National Association of Secondary School Principals
1904 Association Drive
Reston, VA

This report is the second of a three-part series on computer-assisted instruction. It reports on the use of computers in business education, English, social studies, foreign languages, bilingual education and ESL (English as a second language). Also included is an extensive discussion of the role of word processing in each of these areas.

Indexes

The Current Index to Journals in Education (CIJE)
Oryx Press
2214 North Central at Encanto
Phoenix, AZ 85004
(602) 254-6156

ERIC produces two indexes that are extremely valuable sources of information on microcomputers in education. The CIJE is an excellent source to use for locating journal articles. Using the subject headings "Microcomputers" and variations of the word "computer(s)", e.g. "computer literacy," "computer-assisted instruction," "computer simulations," many relevant citations can be found. Each entry is annotated.

ERIC Clearinghouse on Information Resources
Pamela McLaughlin, User-Services Coordinator
Syracuse University School of Education
Syracuse, NY 13210
(315) 423-3640

The ERIC Clearinghouse has user-service materials such as mini-bibliographies and ERIC digests available on the topic of microcomputers. It has a publications list of information-analysis products about current issues and developments in the microcomputer field and publishes a newsletter, ERIC/IR, updated several times a year. These items are available with a self-addressed, stamped envelope. In addition, a software package called *Microsearch* is available. This is being used to teach the concepts of on-line searches. It is marketed for the Apple II series.

Microcomputer Index
Data Base Services, Incorporated
P.O. Box 50545
Palo Alto, CA 94303
(415) 961-2880

This is a most important computer index for those interested in instructional computing. Available both in printed form and online through Lockheed's Dialog system, it is one of the few indexing services that deal solely with information on microcomputers. Approximately thirty-eight periodicals are indexed, including many of the popular microcomputing magazines not indexed anywhere else. Articles, books, hardware and software reviews, columns, and letters are all referenced. All articles are indexed under one or more subjects, and the abstracts are listed numerically and also arranged by magazine title.

Resources in Education (RIE)
U.S. Government Printing Office
Washington, DC 20402
(301) 656-9723

This is an ERIC publication. It is a unique abstracting service that indexes educational materials not accessible through any of the other indexes or abstracts. Most of the literature is unpublished. Types of documents included vary, and some examples are as follows: research reports, directories, resource guides, bibliographies, conference proceedings, and curricula. RIE has a wealth of information on microcomputers that can be located using the subject headings "Microcomputers" and variations on the word "computer" (see *Current Index to Journals in Education*).

T.E.S.S. — The Educational Software Selector
Epie Institute
Box 839
Watermill, NY 11976
(516) 283-4922

T.E.S.S. is one of the most comprehensive collections of computer related products on the market today. Sponsored by the Epie Institute, T.E.S.S. contains over 7500 product descriptions from over 600 suppliers. Entries include hardware, curricula, software, and other related computer products and include information on all major microcomputers commonly used in the schools. Entries are submitted from a national network of evaluators.

Books

Computers and Reading Instruction
Leo D. Geoffrion and Olga P. Geoffrion
Addison-Wesley (1983)
One Jacob Way
Reading, MA 01867
(617) 944-3700

One book in the Addison-Wesley *Computers in Education* series, it includes both philosophical and practical ideas on incorporating the fields of reading instruction and computers.

Computers and Teaching Mathematics
P. Kelman, A. Bardige, J. Choate, G. Hanify, J. Richards, N. Roberts, J. Walters, and M. Tornrose
Addison-Wesley (1983)
One Jacob Way
Reading, MA 01867
(617) 944-3700

This book is another in the Addison-Wesley *Computers in Education* series. It provides a practical approach to the integration of computers in the mathematics curriculum.

Computer Based Education in the Social Studies
Lee Ehman and Allen Glenn
ERIC Clearinghouse (1987)
Indiana University — Social Studies Development Center
2805 East 10th Street
Bloomington, IN 47405
(812) 335-3838

This book provides an overview of the trends and research and takes a look at some of the unresolved issues related to the integration of computers into the social studies classroom.

Computers, Education, and Special Needs
E.P. Goldenberg, S.J. Russell, and C. Carter
Addison-Wesley (1984)
One Jacob Way
Reading, MA 01867
(617) 944-3700

Another in the Addison-Wesley *Computers in Education* series, this book explores some of the issues central to working with people with special needs of all types.

Computers in the Language Classroom
Robert M. Hertz
Addison-Wesley (1987)
2725 Sand Hill Road
Menlo Park, CA 94025
(415) 854-0300

This text explores the uses and implications of computers as an aid to teaching English and foreign languages. Content includes programming suggestions, ideas for course development, and other useful applications.

Computing in the Social Studies Classroom
Allen Glenn and Don Rawitsch
ICCE (August 1984)
University of Oregon
1787 Agate Street
Eugene, OR 97403-1923
(503) 686-4414

This booklet is an overall look at the use of computers in the social studies classroom. It includes chapters on use, computer applications, location of materials, evaluation of current materials, and a discussion of the relevance of computers to the social studies curriculum.

How to Incorporate the Computer into the Social Studies Classroom
Tom Snyder Productions, Incorporated (1986)
123 Mount Auburn Street
Cambridge, MA 02138
(617) 876-4433

This booklet contains a very practical set of questions and answers posed by educators who want to start including technology in the existing curriculum.

Integrating Computers into the Elementary and Middle School
Nancy Roberts, Richard Carter, Susan Friel, and Margerie Miller
Prentice-Hall (1988)
Englewood Cliffs, NJ 07632
(201) 592-2000

Focusing on the elementary and middle school, this book describes classroom activities for integrating computers into all the discipline areas.

Introduction to Computer Simulation —
A System Dynamics Modeling Approach
Nancy Roberts, David Andersen, Ralph Deal, Michael Garet, William Shaffer
Addison-Wesley (1983)
Reading, MA 01867
(617) 944-3700

Designed as a thorough introduction to the field of system dynamics, this book is accessible to high school students and above. Explanations as well as many computer and non-computer exercises are included.

Microcomputers and Social Studies:
A Resource Guide for the Middle and Secondary Teacher
Joseph A. Braun, Jr.
Garland Publishing (1987)
New York, NY
(212) 686-7492

This book combines a bibliography of resources, software evaluation technique, a section on databases, and modern technology topics including artificial intelligence and ethics.

My Students Use Computers
Beverly Hunter
Reston Publishing Company, Incorporated (1984)
Reston, VA
(703) 860-8400

This book is a very practical guide to using computers with children in the elementary and middle grades. The author provides lesson plans with objectives, materials, and instructions. All subject areas are covered.

OMNI Online Database Directory
Michael Edelhart and Owen Davies
Macmillan (1985)
866 Third Avenue
New York, NY 10022
(212) 935-2000

The *OMNI Online Database Directory* is a reference book that provides evaluations of 1100 databases available for a personal computer. The directory provides uses and content of the databases as well as pertinent addresses. Updates are being made for each new edition. The book is arranged by subject, with references gleaned from books, newspapers, and periodicals.

Practical Guide to Computers in Education
P. Coburn, P. Kelman, N. Roberts, T. Snyder, D. Watt, and C. Weiner
Addison-Wesley (1985)
One Jacob Way
Reading, MA 01867
(617) 944-3700

The first book in the Addison-Wesley *Computers in Education* series. This is a general first reader in the field of computers in education.

School Administrator's Guide to Computers in Education
D. Cheever, P. Coburn, F. DiGiammarino, P. Kelman, B. Lowd, A. Naiman, G. Sayer, K. Temkin, and I. Zimmerman
Addison-Wesley (1986)
One Jacob Way
Reading, MA 01867
(617) 944-3700

This is another book in the Addison-Wesley *Computers in Education* series. It is a comprehensive guide to help administrators understand, prepare, and plan for the use of computers in the schools.

Teacher's Handbook for Elementary Social Studies
Hilda Taba
Addison-Wesley (1967)
2725 Sand Hill Road
Menlo Park, CA 94025
(415) 854-0300

This book is a general handbook for instruction in social studies at the elementary level. Included are Taba's views on how social studies curricula should be structured as well as many specific applications.

Ten Social Studies Lesson Plans
Scholastic, Incorporated (1987)
730 Broadway
New York, NY 10003
(212) 505-3000

This activity booklet includes ten fully developed lesson plans in various areas of social studies. Each lesson plan includes about three pages of text elaborating on the instructions as well as an accompanying disk with a program to enhance the lesson. The lessons are geared to grades 3 through 8.

Using Microcomputers in the Social Studies Classroom
Robert B. Abelson, ed.
Social Science Education Consortium, Incorporated (1983)
855 Broadway
Boulder, CO 80302
(303) 492-8154

This book is a compilation of articles and papers by some of the leading educators in the field of computers. The first chapter is a basic introduction to the computer; the second chapter discusses computer applications to the school setting; the third chapter discusses methods of evaluating software. The last chapter deals with the social and educational issues confronting educators who are using computers with children; it also includes a perspective on the future. Extensive bibliographies and resources are included.

Using Computers in the Social Studies
Teachers College Press (1986)
New York, NY
(212) 678-3929

This book provides a basic background on the impact of computers in the social studies field. It includes a chapter on how to use software effectively in the classroom and another on social issues created by the rapid growth of the technology.

Using Computers To Teach Social Studies
Gene Rooze and Terry Northrup
Libraries Unlimited (1986)
Littleton, CO
(303) 770-1220

This book emphasizes the use of software in the social studies classroom. It gives suggestions for software evaluation and describes the various tools and their uses to promote organization, analysis, writing, and reporting. There are over 200 software programs described covering all aspects of software.

Writing and Computers
Collette Daiute
Addison-Wesley (1985)
One Jacob Way
Reading, MA 01867
(617) 944-3700

This book outlines the problems and benefits of using the computer as a writing tool. It discusses what is difficult, what is challenging, and what is beneficial in combining the two. Finally, the book reviews the use of computers in various ways to enhance the writing process.

Papers

Analytical Criteria for Microcomputer-Based Simulation/Games
Roger Berg
Paper presented at the annual conference of the Social Science Education Consortium (June 8–11, 1983)

The paper presents evaluation criteria developed following extensive research along with the author's own experiences relating to microcomputer social studies simulation/games. The paper deals with a review of the research in seven areas: (1) definitions of microcomputer-based social studies simulation/games; (2) effectiveness of the games; (3) effectiveness of computer-based education, (4) methods for reviewing computer software, (6) instructional theories related to computer-based education, and (7) methods for reviewing social studies.

Computer Databases: Applications for the Social Studies. ERIC Digest No. 25
ERIC Clearinghouse for Social Studies (November 1985)
Boulder, CO

This ERIC digest examines the uses of databases in the social studies, including what a database is and how to use it, types of databases available for social studies classroom use, and the role this educational tool can play in achieving the goals and objectives of the social studies.

Computer Simulation in Social Science
David Garson
RIE (October 1985)
U.S. Government Printing Office
Washington, DC 20402
(301) 656-9723

From a base in military models, computer simulation has evolved to provide a wide variety of applications in the social sciences. General purpose simulation packages and languages such as Firm, DYNAMO, and others have made significant contributions toward policy discussion in the social sciences and have well-documented efficacy in instructional settings. With the microcomputer revolution has come a revival of computer simulation. The findings in this article reflect the state of simulation in the social sciences.

Developing Computer Literate Social Studies Teachers

Peter Martorella
National Council for the Social Studies (November 1984)
3501 Newark Street, NW
Washington, DC 20016
(202) 966-7840

Six dimensions of computer literacy for social studies educators to address are discussed in order to prepare them for teaching in the twenty-first century.

How to Think About the New Instructional Technology and Social Science Education: Making Proper Distinctions. Draft Number 2 (April 15, 1983)

Peter R. Senn
Paper presented at the annual conference of the Social Science Education Consortium (June 8–11, 1983)

A brief discussion of the need to define social studies is followed by methods for developing selection criteria for microcomputer programs in the social studies, a model for lesson development on a microcomputer, and evaluation criteria.

The Impact of the Micro on Social Studies Curricula or Computer Assisted Learning (CAL) in Economics, History, and Geography Curricula in England, Wales, Northern Ireland

Ashley Kent (June 1983)

Discussed in this paper are government initiatives for incorporating microcomputers into the schools in England, Wales, and Northern Ireland as well as the availability of and attitudes toward computer-assisted learning in secondary school geography, economics, and history.

Microcomputers in the Social Studies

James E. Davis and John D. Haas
Paper presented at the annual meeting of the Social Science Education Consortium (June 8–11, 1983)

This paper begins by evaluating the use of microcomputers at the elementary and secondary levels in the social studies curriculum. Also included is a list of publications and a checklist to help teachers to evaluate programs. Different types of computer programs are discussed (i.e., drill-and-practice, tutorial, and simulation). Also included are a set of appendices with useful resources, references, and other pertinent information for the social studies educator involved with the computer.

The New Information Technology:
Critical Questions for Social Science Educators.

Mary Hepburn
Paper presented at the conference of the Social Science Education Consortium (June 8–11, 1983)

This paper explores the role of social scientists and educators in an increasingly technological world. Presented for consideration are issues relating to the adaptation to change within education necessary to keep up with the technological revolution.

New Information Technology in Social Science Education: Viewpoints from Europe and the United States
Annual Conference of the Social Science Education Consortium (1985)
Athens, GA

Fourteen conference papers dealing with the effects of electronic information technology on social studies education.

Sex Equity in Computer Education: Concerns for Social Studies
Lynn Parisi (August 1984)

The issue of equal access to and use of computers by boys and girls is reviewed and evaluated from the perspective of social studies content, skills, and goals. Material is arranged in four sections, each introduced by a topic question. A thirteen-citation bibliography concludes the paper.

Online Networks and Databases

Most of the on-line services contained in this section are available on BRS (Bibliographic Retrieval Services) and Dialog. CompuServe and The Source are mostly for business and home use, but people in academic settings use them as well. ERIC (Educational Resources Information Center) is the most informative in terms of educational issues.

CompuServe
CompuServe Information Service
5000 Arlington Center Boulevard
Columbus, OH 43220
(614) 457-8600

CompuServe is a service offering a wide range of programs in information retrieval and communications. Representative of the types of information are financial, an electronic encyclopedia, shopping, banking, and text editing. Of particular interest to those in education are Grolier's "Academic American Encyclopedia" (full-text, searchable by key word). Also included are the files of EPIE as well as the MECC software catalog.

ERIC (Educational Resource Information) (Database)
BRS Information Technologies
1200 Route 7
Latham, NY 12110
(800) 345-4277

The ERIC database contains more than 500,000 citations covering research findings, project and technical reports, speeches, unpublished manuscripts, books,

and journal articles in the field of education. ERIC can be accessed through several on-line services including BRS (Bibliographic Retrieval Service — listed above) or Dialog which consists of over 250 databases. For Dialog information contact:
Dialog Information Services, Inc.
Marketing Department
3460 Hillview Avenue
Palo Alto, CA 94304
(800) 334-2564

Educational Resources Information Center (ERIC) (Network)
ERIC Processing and Reference Facility
4350 East/West Highway
East/West Towers, Suite 1100
Bethesda, MD 20814
(301) 656-9723

The purpose of ERIC is to bring the literature of education under bibliographic control for access by and dissemination to all levels of the educational community. The nationwide information network is composed of clearinghouses across the country that catalog, index, abstract, and distribute information about different topics in education. Information on the particular topics covered by the respective clearinghouses may be obtained from any of the clearinghouses listed below or from the ERIC processing and reference facility (see above). In addition, the clearinghouses listed below are directly involved with information on classroom computer use.

ERIC
Educational Resources Center
Office of Educational Research and Improvement
Washington, DC 20208
(202) 357-6088

ERIC Clearinghouse on Information Resources
Syracuse University
School of Education
130 Huntington Hall
Syracuse, NY 13210
(315) 423-3640

ERIC Clearinghouse on Elementary and Early Childhood Education
University of Illinois
College of Education
Urbana, IL 61801
(217) 333-1386

ERIC Clearinghouse for Social Studies/Social Science Education
Indiana University — Social Studies Development Center
2805 East 10th Street
Bloomington, IN 47405
(812) 335-3838

(See the Indexes section for another reference to ERIC materials.)

In addition, ERIC has developed a program for the Apple II series (48K) called MicroSearch. The program takes the non-trained user through the process of a search. Searching may be done on authors, words in a title, or descriptors (keywords). Each database diskette contains between 200-300 bibliographic records in a particular subject.

Einstein (sm): The Information Access Tool
Addison-Wesley Publishing Company
Information Services Division
2725 Sand Hill Road
Menlo Park, CA 94025-9915
(415) 854-0300

An online database service that allows access to 90 different databases chosen especially for students and teachers. Einstein is menu driven, all in English, and uses just one set of searching procedures, making information retrieval as simple as possible. A purchase option of single-search passwords makes the use of Einstein budgetable and controllable. Full text of major U.S. newspapers and U.S. and foreign newswires is available.

Knowledge Index (Dialog)
Dialog Information Services, Incorporated
3460 Hillview Avenue
Palo Alto, CA 94304
(415) 858-3785

Over thirty-five databases are available for searching through Knowledge Index. They cover the broad areas of medicine/psychology, corporate news/business and legal information, computers/electronics/engineering/chemistry, magazines/books/news, and education and government publications. The system is designed for searching by the layperson. For a low, one-time startup fee, a manual and time are given to enable new users to begin within two hours to use Knowledge Index. Some of the specific databases included are ERIC, Computer Database, Microcomputer Index, National Newspaper Index, and Standard and Poors News. In addition, there are sections on history, the arts, religion, and literature. An electronic mail service is available, menu-driven, called Dialmail with bulletin board and conferencing features. Further information and order forms are available from the address above.

Microcomputer Index (Dialog)
Database Services, Inc.
P.O. Box 50545
Palo Alto, CA 94303
(415) 961-2880

Microcomputer Index appeared on-line one year after the appearance of its print counterpart. It provides access to over seventy popular microcomputer magazines of which thirty to thirty-five are indexed cover to cover. File content numbers over 55,000 items with monthly updates of approximately 1000 rec-

ords. Representative of the topics covered are the broad areas of business, medicine, and education. Of particular use is the capability of searching for reviews of hardware, software, or books. Furthermore, reviews are categorized as unfavorable, favorable, or mixed. Two support-services include:
1. Availability of all original articles for ordering through the document delivery service.
2. Availability of any software covered in the database.

Resources in Computer Education (BRS)

Northwest Regional Education Laboratory
300 S.W. Sixth Avenue
Portland, OR 97204
(503) 248-6800

RICE is funded by the Office of Educational Research and Innovation and operated by Northwest Lab. It contains information on educational computing applications in the following categories: (1) producers of applications packages for computers in education, (2) the software packages themselves. Each record includes contact information, hardware type, system requirements, grade level, evaluations, subject area, and a descriptive abstract of the package. Evaluative data will be included where available.

Social Sciences Citation Index (BRS)

Institute for Scientific Information
3501 Market Street
Philadelphia, PA 19104
(800) 523-1850

Currently SSCI contains more than 1,600,000 items, with about 10,000 items drawn monthly from over 4700 journals. The majority of retrievable literature is journal articles; letters, meetings and literature reviews are also included. ISI's computer-based operation permits database input within two weeks of item receipt. SSCI is available in printed form or on-line under the name Social SciSearch.

The Source

1616 Anderson Road
McLean, VA 22102
(800) 336-3366
(703) 734-7500 (Corporate Communications)

The Source is a menu-driven multifaceted system of more than 800 databases. Areas fall broadly into the categories of news and information (UPI, Associated Press, Stock Market, etc.), business services, consumer services, entertainment, publishing, travel (including airline schedules), and career information. The Source is applicable to classroom use as it relates to computer literacy. The system permits storage, transfer, and retrieval of information as well as communication. Rates differ for prime and nonprime time use. (For a similar database, see CompuServe.)

Software

The Software section is divided into four parts. For the convenience of the reader, the software is divided by general grade level. The categories are Elementary (K–6), Middle (4–8), Secondary (9–12), and General, which are for use by all. Since many programs overlap in terms of their usage by different ages, and since many times the effectiveness of a program depends on the ability levels of the students, this flexibility should be taken into consideration and a program should be previewed if the reader is considering it for use.

Some of the abstracts in this section are paraphrased either from ERIC or from the catalogs of the publishing companies.

It should be noted that prices are omitted deliberately from this and all other sections because of their constant changes.

Elementary

Cave Girl Clair
Addison-Wesley
Rhiannon Software
One Jacob Way
Reading, MA 01867
(617) 944-3700
Hardware: Apple
Subject: History

The goal of this software is to involve girls in an active role in the computer simulation. Cave Girl Clair spends her days wading through the tall grasses to watch the gigantic wooly mammoth. The adventure game involves her insuring her survival by skillful fire-tending and seasonal gathering of food and medicinal plants.

Holt Social Studies K–6 Classroom II Management System
Holt, Rinehart and Winston
Product Manager-Electronic Publishing
383 Madison Avenue
New York, NY 10017
(212) 882-2000
Hardware: Apple, TRS-80, Commodore 64
Subject: All

This software is meant for use with the *Holt Social Studies Book Series*. The system is known as <u>CLASS</u> (stands for Computerized Learning and Scoring System). It automatically scores and records diagnostic tests from the units, tracks and measures student progress, and prints out plans for further student work.

Jenny of the Prairie
Addison-Wesley
Rhiannon Software
One Jacob Way
Reading, MA 01867
(617) 944-3700
Hardware: Apple
Subject: History

Jenny of the Prairie focuses on involving girls with the computer. The adventure story tells of Jenny who loses the other members of the wagon train and must provide food, clothing, and shelter for herself during the hard winter. The computer commands allow Jenny to move but as she goes, she confronts various obstacles such as animals and creeks. Jenny must find ways of gathering food, keeping warm on the prairie, and watching for dangerous animals.

Social Studies — Volume 3
Minnesota Educational Computing Corporation
2520 Broadway Drive
St. Paul, MN 55113
(612) 481-3500
Hardware: Apple, TRS-80
Subject: Economics

The *Sell* series consists of four programs: (1) *Sell Apples* — grade 3, (2) *Sell Plants* — grade 4 (3) *Sell Lemonade* — grade 5, and (4) *Sell Bicycles* — grade 6. Each program includes factors of production and sales, and each grade builds and expands upon the previous one. Factors include price, advertising, supply and demand, and competition.

In addition, *Civil* simulates fourteen battles of the Civil War. Students simulate the Union and Confederate commanders and make decisions based on the war.

Survey Taker
Scholastic, Incorporated
730 Broadway
New York, NY 10003
(212) 505-3000
Hardware: Apple, Commodore 64
Subject: Sociology

The format in this program allows youngsters to create and take surveys for a variety of assignments and uses in the classroom and community. When all the answers are fed into the computer, Survey Taker analyzes the information and provides bar graphs and survey tables to give the results visual meaning. Features include creating, printing, saving, editing, and erasing surveys.

Unlocking The Map Code
Rand McNally
Box 7600
Chicago, IL 60680

(312) 673-9100
Hardware: Apple
Subject: Geography

This is a program of geography skills for fourth to sixth grade. It is organized to teach and review land and water forms, color and map symbols, direction, location, distance, and time. An instructional management system is also included.

Middle

Agent U.S.A.
Scholastic, Incorporated
730 Broadway
New York, NY 10003
(212) 505-3000
Hardware: Apple, Atari, Commodore 64
Subject: Geography

An action adventure game that sharpens math and geography skills, encourages planning and problem solving, and enhances deductive reasoning skills, awareness of distance, direction, and time. Joystick required.

Black Americans
Medalist Series
Hartley, Incorporated
Hartley Courseware Incorporated
Dimondale, MI 48821
(517) 646-6458
Hardware: Apple
Subject: History

Clues at varying levels of difficulty are included on each person. Students "buy" clues to help them identify the person the computer has chosen randomly. Students who discover the answer by using only the most difficult clues are the winners. There is a large variety of clues which constantly change and point-values that also change, making the program more interesting. The computer keeps track of scores by name and enters top winners automatically in a "Hall of Fame." All other programs in this series operate with the same format.

Choice or Chance
Rand McNally
Box 7600
Chicago, IL 60680
(312) 673-9100
Hardware: Apple
Subject: Geography

This program raises the issue of geographical determination in settling the United States using colonization, westward migration, and industrialization as examples. Students are asked to make decisions on where to settle. No hints as to implications of their decisions are given.

Lincoln's Decisions
Educational Activities, Incorporated
P.O. Box 392
Freeport, NY 11520
(800) 645-3739
Within NY State: (516) 223-4666
Hardware: Apple, TRS-80, Commodore 64
Subject: History

A program that helps develop an understanding of the conflicts and complexities of the Civil War. Students are presented with information and choices and are challenged to duplicate the decisions President Lincoln made in the same situations. The program provides insight into the difficulties facing political leaders past and present. Explanations are carefully presented with maps and time lines.

Map Maker
D.C. Heath Educational Software
125 Spring Street
Lexington, MA 02173
(800) 225-1149
Hardware: Apple
Subject: Geography

Map Maker consists of two programs. With *Map Explorer*, students follow a trail of clues in the explorer's notebook to locate and identify hidden features on a darkened map. Students explore and complete existing maps and practice map reading skills. *Map Creator* allows you to tailor the *Map Maker* program to fit your individual teaching needs by allowing the user to create maps for future explorations. By using *Map Creator*, students learn the importance of giving accurate directions, of writing concise and informative paragraphs, and of creating understandable map features and symbols. Sample maps are included.

Oregon Trail
Minnesota Educational Computing Corporation
3490 Lexington Avenue
St. Paul, MN 55112
(612) 481-3500
Hardware: Apple
Subject: History

This simulation takes the student along the same course followed by the settlers on the Oregon trail. As they move along they are asked to make many decisions about their living and travel conditions. Random life situations are presented. The goal is to complete the journey.

Presidents
Medalist Series
Hartley, Incorporated
Hartley Courseware Incorporated
Dimondale, MI 48821
(517) 646-6458
Hardware: Apple
Subject: History

See description of **Black Americans.**

Road Rally U.S.A.
Bantam Electronic Publishing
666 Fifth Avenue
New York, NY 10103
(212) 765-6500
Hardware: Apple
Subject: Geography

Students select from one of eight road maps, each representing a major region of the country, and from a set of driving modes from Sunday driver to highway hotshot. In competition with the clocks and one another, students negotiate a series of right and left turns to bring them to their destination as they translate the route markings on their maps onto the configurations of unmarked roads on their monitors.

Rocky's Boots
Learning Company
4370 Alpine Road
Portola Valley, CA 94025
(415) 851-3160
Hardware: Apple
Subject: Logic

This program is a sequence of games designed to give students an introduction to how a computer works. Students play with and-gates, or-gates, and not-gates and use them to build small electronic machines. Rocky Raccoon and his "electric boot" take the students in a sequence from easier to harder games. Once they master logic gates they can go on to more complex machines that use other utilities. Students are also given a chance to design their own games using a game editor.

Search Series
McGraw Hill — Webster Division
1221 Avenue of the Americas
New York, NY 10020
(800) 223-4180
Hardware: Apple, TRS-80 Model III
Subject: Geography, geology, archaeology, energy, sociology

There are five sets of programs available in this series. Each set includes software, student workbooks, and a teacher's manual. The sets are as follows: (1) *Geography Search* simulates ships searching for the new world. Students navigate using the sun, stars, ocean depth, climate, and winds. (2) *Geology Search* simulates oil exploration. As the computer "performs" geological tests and keeps track of the budget, students learn about rocks, fossils, and underground structures in order to make decisions about where to drill. (3) *Community Search* simulates an ancient society where students must face choices about migration, occupations, trades, aggression, and building a monument. (4) *Archaeology Search* simulates an excavation of an historical site. Students collect data and formulate theories about the origins of the people who once lived there. (5) *Energy Search* simulates the role of a manager of an energy factory. Students make interdependent decisions as they recreate the steps necessary in the search for new energy sources.

Social Studies Vol. 1
Minnesota Educational Computing Corporation
3490 Lexington Avenue
St. Paul, MN 55112
(612) 481-3500
Hardware: Apple, TRS-80 III
Subject: Current events

Volume 1 includes nine simulations dealing with politics and economics. *Elect 1, 2, and 3* simulate presidential elections. *Policy* models policy making by special interest groups. *Limits* simulates world resource use; *Energy* and *Future*, developed at the Northwest Regional Lab, deal with energy issues; *Crimex* simulates crime control in a large city; and *USPOP* projects U.S. population growth. Manual includes suggestions for use, background information, and references to related materials.

States
Medalist Series
Hartley, Incorporated
Hartley Courseware Incorporated
Dimondale, MI 48821
(517) 646-6458
Hardware: Apple
Subject: Geography

See description of **Black Americans**.

Travels with Za-Zoom: The United States
Focus Media, Incorporated
839 Stewart Avenue
P.O. Box 865
Garden City, NY 11530
(516) 794-8900
(800) 645-8989
Hardware: Apple
Subject: Geography

This graphic program lets students travel on a "magic carpet" with Za-Zoom, the "geography genie." At each location, students take on the role of explorer, observing things like clothing, food, and weather. Za-Zoom provides clues on neighboring countries, bodies of water, longitude, and latitude. Students put clues together as they travel and try to guess where they are. Parts of this program include (1) *East of the Mississippi* and (2) *West of the Mississippi.*

Travels with Za-Zoom: The World
Focus Media, Incorporated
839 Stewart Avenue
Garden City, NY 11530
(516) 794-8900 or
(800) 645-8989
Hardware: Apple
Subject: Geography

See description of *Travels with Za-Zoom: The United States.* The two programs in this package include (1) *The Eastern Hemisphere* and (2) *The Western Hemisphere.*

The Voyage Of The Mimi
Holt, Rinehart and Winston
383 Madison Avenue
New York, NY 10017
(212) 750-1330
Hardware: Apple
Subject: Geography

The Voyage of the Mimi is a curriculum project developed by Bank Street College. The project focuses on a group of young scientists studying humpback whales in the Gulf of Maine. There is a thirteen-segment video that follows the scientists at their work and provides a compelling story line. Video documentaries, computer software, and print materials are also part of the curriculum.

Women In History
Medalist Series
Hartley, Incorporated
Hartley Courseware, Incorporated
Dimondale, MI 48821
(517) 646-6458
Hardware: Apple
Subject: History

See description of **Black Americans**.

Secondary

American History
Silwa Enterprises, Incorporated
2360 George Washington Highway
Yorktown, VA 23690

(804) 898-8386
Hardware: Apple
Subject: History

A drill-and-practice program consisting of four disks, with fifteen topics pertinent to American history on each disk. Each topic contains twenty items. An additional feature is that students can replace existing questions with their own.

Ancient Civilizations
Silwa Enterprises, Incorporated
2360 George Washington Highway
Yorktown, VA 23690
(804) 898-8386
Hardware: Apple
Subject: Sociology

Includes thirteen ancient civilizations — with double emphasis on Egypt, Rome, Greece, and China, for each of which there are forty multiple-choice questions. The nine other civilizations include South America and Asia but not sub-Saharan Africa. The correct answer to each question is provided following each mistake, and a running account is kept of each student's score.

"And If Re-elected..."
Focus Media, Incorporated
839 Stewart Avenue
P.O. Box 865
Garden City, NY 11530
(800) 645-8989
Hardware: Apple
Subject: U.S. Government

Students learn first-hand how it feels to go through the election process. Each time they run for reelection, they are presented with twelve crises such as foreign affairs and domestic violence. Their decisions directly influence twenty-one special-interest groups and will ultimately determine whether they remain in office for another four years.

Appleworks Data Bases
Scholastic, Incorporated
730 Broadway
New York, NY 10003
(212) 505-3000
Hardware: Apple
Subject: History

This template allows students to use *Appleworks* and the data files to simulate the Constitutional Convention. The program makes use of all three functions of *Appleworks* — word processor, database, and spreadsheet.

Balance of Power
Mindscape
Educational Division — Department C
3444 Dundee Road
Northbrook, IL 60062
(800) 221-9884
Hardware: Macintosh, IBM, Tandy 1000, Amiga
Subject: Government

This program gives students the opportunity to engross themselves in world politics. The disk includes a substantial database of information about most of the countries of the world.

Balance
Diversified Educational Enterprises
725 Main Street
Lafayette, IN 47901
(317) 742-2690
Hardware: Apple, IBM, Commodore 64, TRS-80
Subject: Ecology

A simulation designed to show the relationship between predators and their prey.

Basic Principles of Economics
Minnesota Educational Computing Corporation
3490 Lexington Avenue
St. Paul, MN 55112
(612) 481-3500
Hardware: Interactive Videodisc, Apple
Subject: Economics

This is a two-sided interactive videodisc on economics for senior high school. The program provides individualized student instruction for schools which cannot offer full course work in economics. The videodisc comes with ten computer diskettes plus an interface card plus student and teacher manuals.

Biznes
Conduit
P.O. Box 388
Iowa City, IA 52244
(319) 353-5789
Hardware: Apple
Subject: Economics

Biznes is a simulation based on running a firm. It is roughly based on the following theory: In order to survive, a firm must successfully cope with three constraints — (1) the demand curve, which depends on the wants of the consumers and on how well other firms meet those wants, (2) the production function, which describes existing technology, and (3) the supply curve of resources. The user's job is to manipulate the budget and keep the business solvent.

Cartels and Cutthroats
Strategic Simulations
883 Stierlin Road
Building A-200
Mountain View, CA 94043-1983
(415) 964-1353
Hardware: Apple
Subject: Economics

In this simulation students are in charge of a multi-million dollar manufacturing plant. By making decisions about purchasing, production, and pricing, they aim to surpass competition in total income. The complex model is meant for advanced students, grades 10 and up. The game-in-progress can be saved on a separate disk for future play.

Congressional Bill Simulator
Focus Media, Incorporated
839 Steward Avenue
P.O. Box 865
Garden City, NY 11530
(800) 645-8989
Hardware: Apple
Subject: U.S. Government

Students introduce bills into the House of Representatives (bills they create or from a given list). Students then follow the route that the bill travels until it eventually is signed or vetoed by the President. The program exposes students to the U.S. Congress, the legislative process, and the internal and external variables affecting the success or failure of proposed legislation.

Data Plot
The Muse Company
374 North Charles Street
Baltimore, MD 21201
(301) 659-7212
Hardware: Apple
Subject: All

Data Plot is designed to serve as a tool for graphing data in bar, line, scatter, and pie graphs. Terminology is geared to middle and high school students. The program has several special features including the option of a background grid which can help students read the graph. Graphs and tables can be printed out provided the user has the designated printer and interface card.

Decisions Decisions
Tom Snyder Productions
123 Mount Auburn Street
Cambridge, MA 02138

(617) 876-4433
Hardware: Apple, IBM
Subject: History, economics, current events

This series of programs attempts to put the students in a "you-are-there" situation based on both historical and contemporary issues. They discuss options, make choices, and see the results of their decisions. More than just learning history, they learn how to use history to make informed choices. There are seven titles in the series:
1. *Colonization: Exploring The New World*
2. *Urbanization: The Growth of Cities*
3. *Immigration: Maintaining The Open Door*
4. *Revolutionary Wars: Choosing Sides*
5. *Budget Process: A Question of Balance*
6. *Television: A Study of Media Ethics*
7. *Foreign Policy: The Burdens of World Power*

Demo-Graphics
Conduit
P.O. Box 388
Iowa City, IA 52244
(319) 353-5789
Hardware: Apple
Subject: Sociology

Demo-Graphics has five parts. Part 1 is an introduction which includes a lesson in Demographics as well as a demonstration. Part 2 is *Age Pyramids;* this section graphs the age composition of a country in five-year age groups. Part 3 is called *Population vs. Time Plots;* this is a program to project the total population of any subgroup for a given number of years. Part 4 is called *General Program;* this section projects the growth of any item that is related to the total population or a population subgroup. Part 5 is a country editing program allowing the user to change the data. The program is most versatile, allowing the user to project, make conjectures, and estimate changes in population through the use of graphing.

The Economics Computer Package
Focus Media, Incorporated
839 Stewart Avenue
P.O. Box 865
Garden City, NY 11530
(800) 645-8989
Hardware: Apple
Subject: Economics

This is a package of three programs that promote the field of economics. The programs include:
1. *Economics: What, How, And For Whom?* — This program contains five subprograms: (1) *What Is Economics?* — An easy-to-follow introduction to the economic concepts of needs, wants, and factors of production. It includes role-playing simulations. (2) *Economics: Definitions and Laws* — Beginning with the law of scarcity, students learn about fundamental questions for every economic

system: production possibilities, opportunity costs, and supply and demand. (3) *Economic Systems: Traditional, Command, and Market* — Interactive models and exercises allow students to see how the three basic economic systems deal with fundamental questions of economics. (4) *Capitalism, Communism, and Socialism* — Students examine basic concepts of each of these politico-economic systems.

2. *Economics Keyword* — Students learn concepts and terms by trying to identify a word through a series of related clues. Covers many aspects of the field.

3. *Measuring Economic Activity* — Students conduct a research project on measures of economic activity. They collect statistical data, enter their findings, and view graphical representations of their data.

Electoral College
Krell Software
1320 Stony Brook Road
Stony Brook, NY 11790
(516) 751-5139
Hardware: Apple, Commodore 64, TRS-80
Subject: Government

This simulation projects the outcomes of presidential elections by comparing current and past data. Users simulate political elections based on actual numbers and percentages taken from the last three national elections. Graphics are appealing. If a state is carried in an election, the state is plotted on a map of the United States.

Geo World
Tom Snyder Productions
123 Mount Auburn Street
Cambridge, MA 02138
(617) 876-4433
Hardware: Apple
Subject: Geology, geography

In this program students explore the world searching for minerals while travelling over a computer-graphics map accurate to one degree of longitude. They will learn where our most important resources are located and why these minerals are crucial to an interdependent world. A special feature of this program is that information gathered can be transferred to the *Appleworks* program.

Globe Master II
Versa Computing Incorporated
3541 Old Conejo Road, Suite 104
Newbury Park, CA 91320
(805) 498-1956
Hardware: Apple
Subject: Geography

Globe Master II is a set of educational programs utilizing nine high resolution color maps for the study of geography. The student learns *States and Capitals, European Countries, Continents and Oceans,* and *African and Asian Countries.*

Historian

Harcourt, Brace and Jovanovich Inc. — School Department
Orlando, FL 32887
(305) 345-2000
Hardware: Apple
Subject: History

Students explore problems, invent solutions, and search for supporting data relative to events in American history. The nine units in the program are each built around a major historical problem related to United States history. Students pass through four stages: (1) problem presentation, (2) hypothesis generation, (3) hypothesis testing, and (4) hypothesis publication.

Marketplace

Joint Council of Economic Education
2 Park Avenue
New York, NY 10016
(212) 685-5499
Hardware: Apple
Subject: Economics

This program teaches students the concepts behind the supply-and-demand curve and how changes in demand and supply affect prices.

Meet The Presidents

Versa Computing, Incorporated
3541 Old Conejo Road, Suite 104
Newbury Park, CA 91320
(805) 498-1956
Hardware: Apple
Subject: History

A new twist on a drill-and-practice program. While a computer portrait of a president is forming before their eyes, students must try answering questions about him. They are given their score as well as the correct answers. There is space for students and teachers to add questions.

Micro-DYNAMO

Pugh-Roberts Associates, Incorporated
Five Lee Street
Cambridge, MA 02139
(617) 864-8880
Hardware: Apple, IBM
Subject: All

Micro-DYNAMO is a simulation language developed for solving real-world problems. It allows the user to simulate the problems over time, asking a variety of "what if" questions. *Micro-DYNAMO* is a tool that allows individuals, groups, or classes to apply mathematics.(Note: Two disk drives required.) A supplemental text — *Introduction to Computer Simulation: The System Dynamics Approach* — is also available from the publisher. (See Publications above.)

Nationalism: Past and Present
Focus Media, Incorporated
839 Stewart Avenue
P.O. Box 865
Garden City, NY 11530
(516) 794-8900 or
(800) 645-8989
Hardware: Apple
Subject: History

This program begins with a general introduction to the concept of nationalism. It continues by presenting the works of Herder, Hegel, and Rousseau to explore the economic, political, and social/intellectual roots of nationalism. At each step, students are asked to explain, identify, or classify information. This is followed by two case studies: one on the nationalist movements that succeeded in unifying Germany, the other on the events that unified Italy. Students are then asked to assign point-values to the events indicating how close the nationalists came to achieving their goals. Students are then given a chance to do their own research and, with the help of the computer, they take their data and form graphs of the nation-building process. The unit continues with an exercise on destructive nationalism using the Austro-Hungarian Empire as a case study. The concluding unit is on the nationalistic forces in the Soviet Union.

Niche
Diversified Educational Enterprises
725 Main Street
Lafayette, IN 47901
(317) 742-2690
Hardware: Apple; IBM; Commodore 64; TRS-80
Subject: Sociology

A set of three graphing programs to allow students to study the population characteristics of any population based on fertility rate, life expectancy, and infant mortality rate.

Non-Western Cultures
Focus Media, Incorporated
839 Stewart Avenue
P.O. Box 865
Garden City, NY 11530
(516) 794-8900 or
(800) 645-8989
Hardware: Apple, TRS-80, Commodore 64
Subject: Global

This series of three programs covers the traditional curriculum material on Africa and the Middle East, China, Japan, India, and Latin America. A lesson planner is included.

The Other Side
Tom Snyder Productions, Incorporated
123 Mount Auburn Street
Cambridge, MA 02138
(617) 876-4433
Hardware: Apple
Subject: Sociology

The Other Side is a simulation growing out of the concern over nuclear conflict. The "players" consist of two countries (one side and "the other side"), separated and surrounded by an unclaimed frontier in the midle of their world. Between the two sides is a huge chasm. The object of the game is to construct a bridge across the chasm, each team adding to the bridge, brick by brick. To pay for the bricks, each team must generate money by mixing orange, green, and blue fuels. Blue fuel is abundant, found almost everywhere in the world, but the orange and green fuels are scarce, one found only on one side and one only on the other. The simulation encourages cooperation and communication between groups.

PFS Curriculum Data Bases
Scholastic, Incorporated
730 Broadway
New York, NY 10003
(212) 505-3000
Hardware: Apple, IBM or equivalents
Subject: History, government

This program includes electronic files, geared at the college level in the fields of United States government, United States history, life science, and physical science. The social-studies files are as follows:

United States History has three content-oriented data files: (1) *20th Century;* (2) *Inventions;* (3) *Expanding American Frontier. United States Government* includes three content-oriented data files: (1) *Election Results and Voting Patterns;* (2) *Federal Government: Size and Spending;* (3) *Constitutional Convention.* Each data file is accompanied by a set of learning activities that explains step-by-step how to use the files to solve problems and analyze and interpret the data. Most of the activities utilize *PFS File;* some use *PFS Report.* Components include three copies of three data files on two disks with a back-up disk of each plus a user's handbook in a three-ring binder.

Presidency Series
Focus Media, Incorporated
839 Stewart Avenue
P.O. Box 865
Garden City, NY 11530
(800) 645-8989
Hardware: Apple
Subject: U.S. Government

A series of five programs which illustrate the nature of the presidency, this package contains the following:

(1) *The Nature of the Office* — Students analyze and react to the actual suggestions made by delegates to the Constitutional Convention regarding the type of chief executive needed for the new government.

(2) *Presidential Roles and Uses of Power* helps students understand the powers and limitations of the president in various roles.

(3) *Organization of the Presidency* — Interactive exercises help students examine the growth of the office under various presidents and understand the functions of the various agencies and councils to the president.

(4) *Who Can Be President* — Students determine their chances to become president. After gaining insight into real presidents' qualifications, they assess their own backgrounds; the computer compares these qualifications to those of real presidents and provides analyses.

(5) *Evaluating Presidential Leadership* — Students conduct research on the successes and failures of presidential administrations. Results are analyzed visually.

President Elect
Strategic Simulations, Incorporated
883 Stierlin Road
Building A
Mountain View, CA 94043-1983
(415) 964-1353
Hardware: Apple
Subject: Government

A simulation of a presidential campaign, the game allows for the recreation of any campaign from 1960 to 1984. The students can play against each other, against the computer, or have the computer play a third-party candidate.

Revolutions: Past, Present and Future
Focus Media, Incorporated
839 Stewart Avenue
P.O. Box 865
Garden City, NY 11530
(516) 794-8900 or
(800) 645-8989
Hardware: Apple, TRS-80
Subject: History

The program is divided into five parts. Part I is called "What is a Revolution?"; part II, "Historical Models of Revolutions"; part III, "How to Analyze a Revolution"; part IV, "Graphing Revolutions of the Past"; and part V, "Graphing Revolutions of the Present and Future." The program moves from background information to simulations of situations to tool format.

The Right Job
Sunburst
39 Washington Avenue
Pleasantville, NY 10570
1-800-431-1934
Hardware: Apple
Subject: Career

The Right Job is a career development program written for special education students and other non-college bound students. Students are prepared for the job search and selection process while improving their computer literacy.

This four-disk package allows students to explore their interests and skills. A special simulation familiarizes students with the interview process. Students work with a database of job information to search for jobs that meet their interests. Students can save or add information.

Run for the Money
Scarborough Systems, Incorporated
25 North Broadway
Tarrytown, NY 10591
(914) 332-4545
Hardware: Apple
Subject: Economics

This program, although designed primarily to be fun, is based on sophisticated principles of economics. The game gives students (and adults) practical insights into the laws of supply and demand, aspects of competitive markets, game-theory concepts, production processes, market structures, bidding, pricing, collusion, investment, and such business tools as bar charts and spreadsheets.

Simplicon (Simulation Of Political and Economic Development)
Cross Culture Software
5385 Elrose Avenue
San Jose, CA 95124
(408) 267-1044
Hardware: Apple
Subject: Economics

This program involves students in a complex simulation that asks them to make a series of practical decisions to help an undeveloped country become an industrial nation. In the early stages of the game, students must be most concerned with producing food and obtaining medicine for survival. As they are able to accumulate surpluses for their countries, students can invest in education, resource development, and production of machines. In later stages, players must worry about foreign trade, military preparedness, and pollution. The game includes two hundred different production possibilities. Students decide the end they hope to achieve in a series of rounds representing years of development. They then reason backwards to figure out what they must first produce to achieve their goals and how to continue from there. The goals and plans must be revised as their own errors and natural as well as human disasters interfere with their development program.

Social Studies, Volume 2
Minnesota Educational Computing Corporation
3490 Lexington Avenue
St. Paul, MN 55112
(612) 481-3500
Hardware: Apple
Subject: Varied

Volume 2 contains eight programs. The following are simulations: *Bargain* presents negotiations in a collective bargaining setting; *Failsafe* includes roles of the president and advisors in confronting a nuclear emergency; and *Minnag* enables students to explore factors in Minnesota agriculture. Four drill programs provide practice on countries and continents, capitals of countries, U.S. states and their capitals, and the states' shapes and locations. Support material includes role-playing cards, student worksheets, and background information.

South Dakota
Electric Activities, Incorporated
P.O. Box 392
Freeport, NY 11520
(516) 223-4666
Hardware: Apple
Subject: Economics, agriculture

This program was designed to simulate the daily struggle for survival of midwestern farmers. Based on the projection of prices, students must allocate limited resources in hiring farm hands, buying seed, and deciding what crops to plant. In addition to showing students the hazards of farming, this program should help students understand the law of supply and demand.

Standing Room Only?
Sunburst
39 Washington Avenue
Pleasantville, NY 10570
1-800-431-1934
Hardware: Apple
Subject: Sociology

This program provides an interactive model that can be used to study population dynamics. Students are able to model population statistics under different conditions by altering migration, family composition, and life expectancy for seven countries with different population growth rates. The program can be used as a tool to generate data, compare different population scenarios, and test hypotheses about population growth.

STELLA
High Performance Systems, Incorporated
P.O. Box B1167
Hanover, NH 03755
(603) 795-4122

Hardware: Macintosh
Subject: All

Iconic-based continuous simulation language. Bears similarity to DYNAMO.

Telofacts II
Dilithium Press .
8285 Southwest Nimbus
Beaverton, OR 97075
(503) 243-3313
Hardware: Apple, IBM
Subject: All

A tool designed to help administrators, Telofacts allows the user to create a survey instrument to manipulate data on a survey that has already been administered. In addition, the user can do elementary statistics using the program.

Think Tank
Living Videotext Incorporated
2432 Charleston Road
Mountain View, CA 94043
(415) 964-6300
Hardware: Apple, Macintosh
Subject: All

Think Tank is a tool that allows the user to create a flexible outline. Once it has been created, the outline can be expanded or contracted allowing the user at any one time to look at the whole of the project or zoom in on any one segment in more detail. *Think Tank* has also been suggested as a useful tool in the teaching of timelines.

Three Mile Island
Muse
347 North Charles Street
Baltimore, MD 21201
(301) 659-7212
Hardware: Apple
Subject: Nuclear power, current events

This program is a simulation of a nuclear reactor. The students control the reactor, which involves exercising management skills. Their goal is to make a profit, but also to avoid a meltdown.

The Time Tunnel: American History Series
Focus Media, Incorporated
839 Stewart Avenue
Garden City, NY 11530
(516) 794-8900 or
(800) 645-8989
Hardware: Apple, TRS-80, Commodore 64, IBM-PC/PCJR
Subject: History

The program is in game format and takes students through three important parts of American history. Students are given clues to the identity of famous Americans and must try to guess them. Historical periods covered are: (1) 1760–1860; (2) 1860–1917; (3) 1917–1970.

The Time Tunnel: Series 3, The Presidents
Focus Media, Incorporated
839 Stewart Avenue
P.O. Box 865
Garden City, NY 11530
(800) 645-8989
Hardware: Apple, Commodore 64, TRS-80, IBM
Subject: History

Students are asked to identify presidents. Eight different clues are provided for each of America's forty chief executives. These include facts of early childhood, names of political opponents and running mates, as well as major contributions. Other Focus Media software in this series provide a similar format for historical figures, male and female, from the age of exploration to the twentieth century.

The U.S. Constitution: Nationalism and Federalism
Focus Media, Incorporated
839 Stewart Avenue
P.O. Box 865
Garden City, NY 11530
(516) 794-8900 or
(800) 645-8989
Hardware: Apple
Subject: Government

This program is made up of three parts, each one demonstrating the development of the Constitution and its function as the basic instrument of the United States government. Topics covered include government in colonial America, eighteenth century British government, the Articles of Confederation, the framers of the Constitution, Federalists versus Anti-Federalists, and the structure of the new Federal government. Program parts are: (1) *Development of the Constitution*, (2) *The Creation of the Constitution*, (3) *Testing Your Knowledge of the U.S. Constitution*.

U.S. Constitution Tutor
Opportunities for Learning, Incorporated
20417 Nordhoff Street
Department 90
Chatsworth, CA 91311
(818) 341-2535
Hardware: Apple, IBM PCJR, Commodore 64
Subject: Government

This program is designed to prepare students for high school or college exams on the United States constitution. Each response to 175 questions is followed by an explanation of why the answer is correct or incorrect. Questions are divided into levels of difficulty.

Western Civilization
Focus Media, Incorporated
839 Stewart Avenue
P.O. Box 865
Garden City, NY 11530
(516) 794-8900 or
(800) 645-8989
Hardware: Apple, TRS-80, Commodore 64

This program is a standard drill-and-practice, testing the students on various aspects of Western civilization. If, for instance, students can locate the Aegean Sea they may select one of four instruments to help climb Focus Mountain. An incorrect response causes a loss of 200 meters. Much attention is given to the climb, and therefore only fifteen multiple-choice questions appear, covering history from ancient Greece to early Europe.

The Whatsit Corporation
Sunburst
39 Washington Avenue
Pleasantville, NY 10570
1-800-431-1934
Hardware: Apple, Commodore 64, IBM, TRS-80
Subject: Business education

Students put on entrepreneurial hats and use their math skills in this realistic simulation of starting and running a one-product business.

Where in the U.S. is Carmen Sandiego
Broderbund
17 Paul Drive
San Rafael, CA 94903
(415) 479-1170
Hardware: Apple
Subject: Geography

Students travel around the United States attempting to catch the thief, Carmen Sandiego. Geographic information is given to the students as an aid to catching the criminal.

Where in the World is Carmen Sandiego
Broderbund
17 Paul Drive
San Rafael, CA 94903
(415) 479-1170
Hardware: Apple
Subject: Geography

The same format as *Where in the U.S. is Carmen Sandiego* but pertaining to the world.

General

Bank Street Beginner's Filer
Sunburst
39 Washington Avenue
Pleasantville, NY 10570
1-800-431-1934
Hardware: Apple
Subject: Tool

This is a database written for younger students to introduce them to fundamental database concepts. A content data disk on Colonial America will be available in late 1987.

Bank Street School Filer
Sunburst
39 Washington Avenue
Pleasantville, NY 10570
1-800-431-1934
Hardware: Apple
Subject: Tool

An easy-to-use database package specially designed for the classroom. One of the features of this software is the templates which can be purchased to be used with it. Examples include:
1. North America databases
2. Animal life databases
3. United States databases

Bank Street Speller
Broderbund Software
17 Paul Drive
San Rafael, CA 94903
(415) 479-1170
Hardware: Apple
Subject: Spelling

Bank Street Speller is a tool intended to be used with *Bank Street Writer*. It is an electronic dictionary and performs various functions, such as eliminating typographical errors, suggesting spelling for words the user might be unsure of, and inserting corrections throughout a manuscript. One major feature is the ability to create one's own dictionary of specialized words. *Bank Street Speller* uses the *Random House Dictionary* (concise edition) as its database.

Colorfile
Radio Shack/Tandy Corporation
400 Atrium
One Tandy Center
Fort Worth, TX 76102
(800) 722-8538

Hardware: TRS-80
Subject: All

A database program intended for home use.

Exploring Tables and Graphs

Weekly Reader Family Software
245 Long Hill Road
Middletown, CT 06457
Hardware: Apple, Atari
Subject: All

Exploring Tables and Graphs has two levels. Level 1 is meant for ages 7–10; level 2 is for ages 10 and above. Each level includes a double-sided disk, a user's guide, and twelve support blackline masters. Side one of each disk is designed to teach students how to use tables and picture, bar, area, and (in level 2 only) line graphs. Activities provide interaction and experimentation and utilize games and real-life applications. The other side of the disk at both levels is designed as a tool to let students create, print, and save their own tables and make graphs using their own data or data provided by the program.

Friendly Filer

Grolier Educational Corporation
Department 336
Sherman Turnpike
Danbury, CT 06816
(800) 858-8858
Hardware: Apple; IBM PC; IBM PCJR
Subject: All

A database meant to introduce the user to the world of database management. Included are sections on learning the program, practicing, and using the program. Features include sort, select, display, and print functions.

Grolier's Electronic Encyclopedia

Grolier Electronic Publishing, Incorporated
95 Madison Avenue
New York, NY 10016
(212) 696-9750
Hardware: Apple, IBM, Atari plus a CD-ROM drive.

A CD-ROM containing the complete text from the *Academic American Encyclopedia*. The companion software and hardware allows searching the disk using any word or phrase. Information retrieved from the CD-ROM may then be saved on a computer disk and incorporated into a word processor document.

Home Filing Manager

Atari Corporation
1265 Borregas
Sunnyvale, CA 94088

(408) 745-2000
Hardware: Atari
Subject: All

A database program intended for the home market.

Mastertype Filer
Scarborough Systems
25 North Broadway
Tarrytown, NY 10591
(800) 882-8222
Hardware: Apple, IBM PC/PCJR, Commodore 64
Subject: All

An easy-to-use database geared towards home and family use. Functions include selecting a file, creating, editing, sorting, printing, copying, and deleting.

Notebook Filer
D.C. Heath Software
125 Spring Street
Lexington, MA 02173
(800) 428-8071
Hardware: Apple
Subject: All

A database program primarily aimed at the schools. Features include entering data, manipulating data, looking and editing, removing, searching, saving, and printing. Directions are easy to follow.

PFS File
Scholastic, Incorporated
730 Broadway
New York, NY 10003
(212) 505-3000
Hardware: Apple, IBM PC/PCJR, Radio Shack
Subject: All

PFS File is a database program designed for home and school use. Features include designing a form, creating, editing, erasing, saving, copying, adding, searching, printing, and changing the design of the form.

PFS Graph
Software Publishing Corporation
1901 Landing Drive
Mountain View, CA 94043
(415) 962-8910
Hardware: Apple
Subject: All

PFS Graph allows the user to create a graph either using information directly from the keyboard or accepting data from either VisiCalc or PFS files. The types of graphs that may be displayed are: bar, line, or pie.

PFS Report
Scholastic, Incorporated
730 Broadway
New York, NY 10003
(212) 505-3000
Hardware: Apple
Subject: General

PFS Report is a program to be used in conjunction with *PFS File*. The purpose of the program is to produce tabular reports on the database created in *PFS File*. A report is a table consisting of up to nine vertical columns, each of which corresponds to an item in the file. Each row of the report contains information from a single PFS form. Information can be sorted alphabetically or numerically, and calculations can be performed on the numerical information stored in the PFS files. The program includes a program disk, a learning activities disk, back-up disks for each, and a teacher's handbook.

The program is also put out by:
Software Publishing Company
Mountain View, CA
(See *PFS Graph* for a more detailed address.) Software Publishers puts out only the single program disk: the company also publishes *PFS Graph* and *PFS File*.

PFS Write
Scholastic, Incorporated
730 Broadway
New York, NY 10003
(212) 505-3000
Hardware: Apple
Subject: All

Components of this sophisticated word processor include a program disk, a learning activities disk, a back-up disk for each, and a user's handbook in a three-ring binder.

Secret Filer
Scholastic Software
730 Broadway
New York, NY 10003
(212) 505-3000
Hardware: Apple, IBM PC/PCJR, Commodore 64
Subject: All

A database written specifically for the young beginner, *Secret Filer* allows students to create databases on specific topics. Students learn about filing systems as they easily store facts based on whatever they are currently doing in the classroom. Screens are easy to read and directions are clear.

Timeliner
Tom Snyder Productions
123 Mount Auburn Street
Cambridge, MA 02138

(617) 876-4433
Hardware: Apple
Subject: History

Timeliner is a practical, easy-to-use tool. It lets teachers and students at all levels create their own personal and historical timelines and gives a visual sense of the patterns of history. Students can build and print out timelines of any length on any topic.

Resource Centers

The following centers either are known nationally for their work in educational technology, extensive resources, and research excellence or have become known regionally in the field of computers in education. All of the centers are more than willing to share their resources with the public.

Bank Street College of Education
Center for Children and Technology
Dr. Karen Sheingold, Director
610 West 112th Street
New York, NY 10025
(212) 663-7200

Bank Street College is a teaching and research institution made up of the following divisions: a graduate school that prepares students for careers in schools, museums, hospitals, social agencies, and educational settings using microcomputers; a school for children (an on-site laboratory and school for 450 children); a research division that focuses on the development of children and adults in school and family settings and which is conducting research on the effects of microcomputer technology; a center for children and technology, a part of the research division exploring the contribution of new technology to learning, development and education; and a media group, which develops books, software, and television productions (the *Voyage of the Mimi* series was produced here) that support the college's goal of improving the quality of life for children and families.

Center for Learning Technologies
Cultural Education Center, 9A47
NYS Department of Education
Empire State Plaza
Albany, NY 12230
(518) 474-5823

The CLT promotes and supports the installation of instructional-technology systems in the educational and cultural institutions in New York state. Initiatives relating to computer literacy, equity and access, research and development, and demonstration, distribution, and duplication of hardware and software have been designed for elementary and secondary school, continuing education, cultural education (including museums and libraries), vocational rehabilitation, and higher education. The center also manages instructional-television production and teleconferences. In addition, it operates computer training programs and distributes instructional videotapes and technology guidebooks. A major priority has become coordinating state-education-department initiatives to explore and install distance-learning capacities to serve learners of all ages.

ECCO (The Educational Computer Consortium of Ohio)
Teacher Center 271
1123 S.O.M. Center Road
Cleveland, Ohio 44124
(216) 461-0800

ECCO is a group of individuals, families, and school district members interested in instructional computing. Membership in ECCO includes use of its educational software library, which contains public domain software that members can copy and commercial software to preview and borrow. Members also have access to the organization's library of computer books, journals and related audio-visual materials, a subscription to the newsletter, *The Output,* and (for school districts) consulting services. ECCO runs a series of workshops for novice and experienced computer users, an annual educational computer fair, and a statewide spring meeting.

Educational Products Information Exchange Institute (EPIE)
P.O. Box 839
Watermill, NY 11976
(516) 283-4922

The EPIE Institute is education's only non-profit, consumer supported product evaluation agency. It is funded primarily by subscriptions from schools and contracts with state and regional education agencies. The *Epiegram: Materials* is a monthly newsletter covering textbooks and issues concerning their publication and use.

EPIE publishes *Microcourseware Pro/Files,* an in-depth evaluation of microcomputer courseware. It is updated six times a year. *The Educational Software Selector* (TESS) is a source of information on the availability of all types of educational software. In addition, EPIE publishes *The Microgram,* a monthly consumer newsletter on educational computing products. EPIE has an on-line electronic information service available through CompuServe. EPIE also deals with audio visual/video products and publishes *Epiegram: Equipment.*

Educational Technology Center
Harvard Graduate School of Education
Dr. Judah Schwartz, Director
337 Gutman Library
Appian Way
Cambridge, MA 02138
(617) 495-9373

The center, operated by a consortium of research, school, and production organizations, was founded at Harvard in the fall of 1983. It is the newest in the system of seventeen research and development laboratories and centers funded by the Office of Educational Research and Improvement. The center's mission is to examine the present and potential roles of technology in education. It concentrates its efforts on the roles computers can play in the learning and teaching of mathematics and science, and the ways students learn about computers.

Educational Technology Center
University of California, Irvine
Alfred Bork, Director
Irvine, CA 92717
(714) 856-6665

The Educational Technology Center maintains research and development projects on computer-based modules specifically for junior high school students; the project on scientific literacy in public libraries is designed to improve public understanding of science. A new project concerns weak students in beginning science classes. The center has also developed college-level science and math units. Information on these projects is provided in their literature and books.

The Homewood Computing Facility
Johns Hopkins University
34th and Charles Street
Garland Hall
Baltimore, MD 21218
(301) 338-8673

The academic computing center can be used by students, professors, and general public as long as it is for non-profit use. Many word processors, statistical packages, languages, compilers, and other types of tool software are available.

Houston Independent School District (HISD)
Department of Technology
5300 San Felipe
Houston, TX 77056
(713) 960-8888

The HISD is considered a leader in education in an urban environment. It was one of the first school districts to address the growing opportunities of technology.

The Department of Technology is unique and the only one of its kind in the country. Six divisions in the department address seven major areas: needs assessment and planning; technology training for teachers, parents, and administrators; technical applications; centralized procurement; maintenance and telecommunications; systems design; and special projects support. A software lending library currently exists; several magnet schools offer specialized training. Future plans include business connections that will provide experts and/or financial assistance.

Lesley College
Center for Mathematics, Science, and Technology in Education
Dr. Susan Friel, Director
29 Everett Street
Cambridge, MA 02138-2790

Focusing on research in the areas of mathematics, science, and technology in education, this center's goal is to involve teachers and business people in its work so that implementation of research results will be as timely as possible. The center sponsors special courses, conferences, and informal meetings to disseminate information and support educational change. The center works closely with the academic areas at Lesley College.

Lesley College
Computers in Education Department
Dr. Nancy Roberts, Director
29 Everett Street
Cambridge, MA 02138-2790
(617) 868-9600

Lesley College created one of the first graduate programs and development centers for computers in education. The department offers a masters in education, a certificate of advanced graduate study, and doctorate degrees; it conducts ongoing degree programs at outreach sites around the United States and internationally, and sponsors an annual, nationally attended computer conference on campus.

Microcomputer Resource Center
Teachers College
Columbia University
New York, NY 10027
(212) 678-3038

The Microcomputer Resource Center at Teachers College, Columbia University, conducts seminars and workshops on curriculum materials as well as field based training for the use of computers in the classroom. It is also a clearinghouse for hardware and software information.

Minnesota Educational Computing Corporation (MECC)
3490 North Lexington Avenue
St. Paul, MN 55126
(612) 481-3500

MECC, the nation's preeminent statewide instructional computing network, provides services for students, teachers, and administrators in schools and colleges. MECC offers in-service training and curriculum guides as well as developing and distributing educational software. MECC is an excellent source of software and written materials for use with the Apple II, Atari, IBM, Radio Shack, and Commodore 64 microcomputers. MECC has also directed a project to develop computer learning packages for use in social studies, science, and mathematics. The MECC newsletter and courseware catalog are free of charge to members.

National Education Association (NEA)
Educational Computer Service
P.O. Box 70267
Washington, DC 20088-0267
(301) 951-9244
or (301) 652-0872

This teacher's organization provides a comprehensive source of information about computers. In addition to assessing, endorsing, and selling software, the educational computing services provide consultation and offer seminars and courses. Their publication is entitled *The Yellow Book of Computer Products for Education*. It includes over 300 titles and contains five indexes: subject, level, publisher, hardware, title (e.g., special education, etc.). All inclusions must meet the following criteria: ease of use, technical reliability, instructional soundness, and performance data for students.

San Mateo County Office of Education
Microcomputer Center
Ann Lathrop, Library Coordinator
333 Main Street
Redwood City, CA 94063
(415) 363-5472

The product of a joint project by Computer Using Educators (CUE) and the San Mateo County Office of Education, the center exhibits a variety of computers and commercial software for examination by educators. In addition, the center maintains a software library and clearinghouse for California Tech Centers. The center serves primarily the teachers and administrators of San Mateo County, although educators from outside the county are welcome to use the center's resources by appointment.

Technical Education Research Center (TERC)
Dr. Robert Tinker, Director
1696 Massachusetts Avenue
Cambridge, MA 02138
(617) 547-3890

The Computer Resource Center (CRC) of TERC houses information on microcomputer hardware and software and a library of technical and educational publications. The center also has various microcomputers and educational software available for inspection and sample use. TERC conducts workshops by contract on using microcomputers in education. Teachers are invited to visit the center but must call ahead to arrange their visit. TERC is a non-profit research and development group with on-going projects in social science, math/science, and special education as well as in social science software development.

Index